Tomaž Humar

Bernadette McDonald's biography of Elizabeth Hawley, *I'll Call You in Kathmandu*, was published in 2005. For many years she was Vice-President, Mountain Culture at The Banff Center and Director of The Banff Mountain Film and Book Festivals. Her biography of the renowned American climber Charlie Houston, *Brotherhood of the Rope*, won the Kekoo Naoroji Award for mountaineering literature. In 2008, Bernadette McDonald won the Kekoo Naoroji Award for an unprecedented second time with *Tomaž Humar*.

'Besides breath-taking descriptions of what happens on the mountains, this book most importantly helps us understand the main character as Bernadette McDonald sets him free from the swirls of mist.'

Kurt Diemberger

'Inspirational, whether you're a mountaineer or not.'

Active

'Bernadette McDonald uncovers the extraordinary journey that led Humar from the chaotic collapse of communist Yugoslavia to a mountaineering career that has won him awards, earned him a reputation for matchless commitment and courage, and nearly claimed his life. This moving portrayal brings to life the philosophy of a controversial mountaineering hero in an inspiring story of bravery and determination.'

Good Book Guide

'McDonald has done a fine job of crafting this powerful story about a truly remarkable climber and human being. One of the best books about climbing I have read.'

Royal Robbins

'It's been a long time since I picked up a book I couldn't put down. This is quite a story and quite a telling.'

Tom Hornbein

'This book reveals many fascinating secrets: about what motivates climbers who perform at the very highest levels; about the positioning and competition within the climbing communities; about the fascinating world of Slovenian climbers – the best in the world; and most of all, the complex personality of one of the most intriguing and enigmatic high altitude performers of today – Tomaž Humar.'

Reinhold Messner

'An astonishing account of an extraordinary climber brilliantly portrayed by McDonald. It has breathtaking descriptions of climbs, perceptive insights into the climber's mind and strong narrative. This book stands in an inspirational class of its own, emphatically deserving the win.'

Book Jury, Kekoo Naoroji Award for Mountain Literature, 2008

'It's a great read! In fact, I couldn't put it down.'

John Amatt

'This book is an admirable portrait of a climber – controversial, bold, at times surrounded by chaos self-made or not of his own doing – magnified by the mountains and his passion.'

Jon Popowich, *Gripped Magazine*

'It's the close connection between its style and content that makes the book a real benchmark in contemporary alpine-climbing biography.'

Katie Ives, *Alpinist*

By the same author

Voices from the Summit
Extreme Landscape
Whose Water Is It?
I'll Call You in Kathmandu
Brotherhood of the Rope

Tomaž Humar

Bernadette McDonald

arrow books

Published by Arrow Books 2009

2 4 6 8 10 9 7 5 3 1

First published in Great Britain in 2008 by Hutchinson

Arrow Books
Random House, 20 Vauxhall Bridge Road,
London SW1V 2SA

www.rbooks.co.uk

Addresses for companies within The Random House Group Limited can be found at:
www.randomhouse.co.uk/offices.htm

The Random House Group Limited Reg. No. 954009

A CIP catalogue record for this book
is available from the British Library

ISBN 9780099505099

The Random House Group Limited supports The Forest Stewardship
Council (FSC), the leading international forest certification organisation. All our
titles that are printed on Greenpeace approved FSC certified paper carry the FSC logo.
Our paper procurement policy can be
found at: www.rbooks.co.uk/environment

Mixed Sources
Product group from well-managed
forests and other controlled sources
www.fsc.org Cert no. TT-COC-2139
© 1996 Forest Stewardship Council

Printed in the UK by CPI Bookmarque, Croydon, CR0 4TD

CONTENTS

ILLUSTRATIONS

Section one

Tomaž Humar's parents on their wedding day
Tomaž Humar, 1971
Tomaž's birthday, 1973
Climbing Lover Overhang
Sergeja and Tomaž on their wedding day, 1991
Painting church steeples, 1988
Tomaž and Šrauf enjoying hot springs, 1994
Šrauf at Camp I on Ganesh V
Šrauf on ridge between Camps I & II on Ganesh V
Tomaž on the summit of Annapurna, 1995
Climbing Ama Dablam's Northwest Face, 1996
Vanja Furlan at a bivouac on the Northwest Face of Ama Dablam
Tomaž with newborn son, Tomi
The Humar Family, 2001
Janez Jeglič and Carlos Carsolio
Tomaž on the summit of Nuptse, 1997
Sergeja, 1990
Tomaž after summiting El Capitan's Reticent Wall, 1998
Triumphant return after soloing the South Face of Dhaulagiri, 1999
At the Trento Film Festival, 2000
Tomaž in intensive care, 2000
Training at Jannu Base Camp, 2004
Tomaž abseiling on Jannu East

Section two

Stipe Božić filming below Jannu East
Anda Perdan praying at Jannu Base Camp
Tomaž belaying Aleš on Aconcagua
Tomaž belaying Aleš on Cholatse, 2005
Aleš on the summit of Cholatse
Aleš and Tomaž bivouacking on Nanga Parbat's Rupal Face, 2005
Maja and Tomaž
Tomaž greeting Steve House at the Rupal Face Base Camp
Tomaž kisses the ground after being rescued
Tomaž at Base Camp in obvious pain and distress
Tomaž embracing his Sirdar, Javed
Portrait of Tomaž taken below Lhotse's South Face, 2006
Elizabeth Hawley with Tomaž
Rock island on the South Face of Annapurna
View from Annapurna's East Ridge

All photographs are reproduced courtesy of Tomaž Humar.

Maps

REINHOLD MESSNER

I have had the great fortune to climb all over the world. I have also met many climbers who have accomplished much more difficult things than I. Tomaž Humar is one of these climbers.

Modern mountaineering is a British and central European invention. Further developments were made in the USA, in Japan and, above all, in the countries on the other side of the former Iron Curtain. Finally, it was Slovenian climbers who took alpinism one step further. The extent to which Slovenian mountaineers have dominated big-wall mountaineering over the last decade is illustrated by their impressive routes on the South-West Face of Shishapangma (2,150 metres, 1989), the South-East Face of Api (2,600 metres), the North-West Face of Bobaye (2,500 metres), the South Face of Nampa (1,950 metres, all 1996) and the North Face of Gyachung Khang (1999). The new routes that have been climbed in the last decade would have been unthinkable in the 1980s. Only the very best dare to attempt the 'big problems', and drama, failure and tragedy are, unfortunately, an integral part of the game.

It was the Slovenians Vanja Furlan and Tomaž Humar who made the first ascent of the 1,650-metre-high, extremely difficult West Face of Ama Dablam from 30 April to 4 May, 1996, in alpine style. They dedicated their route to the passionate big-wall climber, Slovenian Stane Belak, who made the first ascents of the South Face of Makalu and the right-hand side of the South Face of Dhaulagiri, and then lost his life in December 1995 in the Julian Alps.

Then, Tomaž Humar and Janez Jeglič made an alpine-style ascent of the extremely difficult 2,500-metre West Face of the North-West Summit of Nuptse. Jeglič had gone on ahead a short way below the top, reached the summit at 1.00 p.m. and waved. A short while later, Humar reached the highest point, but failed to meet up with his partner. He could see his footsteps on the south side of the ridge, caught a very brief glimpse of Jeglič and shouted to him. The wind was blowing in gusts as Humar reached the last of his partner's tracks. He saw only the radio: Jeglič was gone.

Then it was Dhaulagiri. For a long time, Dhaulagiri (8,167 metres), a peak that rises high above the subtropical jungle of Nepal, was considered to be the highest mountain in the world. Now, this elegant summit – visible in clear weather from Pokhara – takes its rightful place as the sixth highest of the fourteen eight-thousanders. Even its normal route, the North-East Ridge – first climbed in 1960 by an international expedition led by the Swiss climber Max Eiselin – is difficult. Its south flank, described by Professor G.O. Dyhrenfurth as 'one of the most terrifying walls in the Himalayas', was the highest unclimbed mountain face in the world.

Incredibly steep, this giant face was the objective of a small expedition that I organised and led in the pre-monsoon season in 1977. I joined forces with Peter Habeler, my tried and trusted partner on Hidden Peak in 1975, and for the extremely difficult and hard enterprise, we invited two additional top climbers of international repute: Michael Covington, one of the top American rock climbers, and Otto Wiedemann, one of the best young German mountaineers.

But the South Face of Dhaulagiri is more than just a Big Wall. It is secretive – and it kept its secrets. Like an oracle of an old Gurkha soldier from Bega: 'Dhaulagiri is like five fingers on a hand. The first and last fingers are deadly; the two others too are dangerous. Only the forefinger points the way to the summit.'

There is no single, correct objective in mountaineering; there are only possibilities. One of them leads beyond the impossible. The more I concerned myself with Dhaula's Face, the closer the relationship became. How hesitantly I began planning for it; yet later I could no longer stop looking at it. When I knew everything; when the Face had me completely under its spell; I discovered the answer and did the only correct thing; I organised the retreat.

The decision to give up was not too hard to make. We congratulated ourselves on having made the only logical choice, given the situation. I now saw the expanses of ice and the loose rocks with fresh eyes, like a relief model of the face rather than a possible route to the summit, as it had been just a few hours previously. Everything seemed to have changed now in some mysterious way; even I had changed. I began to feel that I was immersed in some great lake, not in order to sink to the bottom, but to climb out again. The sun, shining through the mist, soothed my overwrought mind and body and a liberating tiredness washed over me.

How easy it was to live with this final defeat. Perhaps it was only because I had considered this as a possibility from the very start, and had come to terms with it. Not only had I not discounted the possibility of failure, I had also made friends with the idea during our preparations for the climb. From the beginning, as often as I thought about the summit, I was also occupied with the possibility of retreat.

I felt that this retreat was absolutely final, unalterable, like a law. There wasn't the slightest chance of another attempt in the future. We had failed, and yet to fail after all we had been through, had still been worth it. It was worth it just to have been up there, cut off from the rest of the world. It was a powerful feeling just to have survived on this 4,000-metre wall of rock and ice, in the drumfire of stone fall and the thundering rage of avalanches. To carry on climbing would have been suicidal. Right up to the point at which we turned back, we had been totally committed to the climb.

What would have become of this Dhaulagiri expedition if we had listened to the pundits? There were those who spoke of suicide and others who talked about self-sacrifice. One body of opinion considered our enterprise to be one of the craziest ideas of the 20th century, while another group reckoned that it was some last act of heroism.

For humankind it is totally meaningless whether the South Face of Dhaulagiri has been climbed or not. It is also immaterial whether a person has ever stood on the summit of Everest. What counts are merely the experiences one gains along the way.

But my experience was in 1977. Twenty-two years later, another history was written on Dhaulagiri's South Face. Was it by luck, coincidence or instinct that the Slovenian climber Tomaž Humar reached the summit ridge of Dhaulagiri directly above this 'forefinger' in the ancient oracle, the forefinger that pointed the way for him to achieve his objective?

With new routes on Ama Dablam, Bobaye and Nuptse to his credit, Humar had already achieved an entire series of 'crazy things'. On 2 November 1999, he completed his new route on the 4,000-metre-high South Face of Dhaulagiri I – solo and in Alpine style – a climb with difficulties up to Grade VII, ice to 90 degrees, M7+. It marked a new watershed in contemporary extreme mountaineering.

Although, after his fifth bivouac, Humar was no longer able to follow his ideal line, there was no way back, either. Nor did the terrain allow him to camp safely. So he traversed diagonally right for 1,000 metres across a couloir and mixed ground to find himself on the Japanese Ridge where he bivouacked at an altitude of about 7,300 metres – his seventh night on the face. The following day was to be his summit day. Leaving his tent and a large portion of his gear behind, he traversed back into the centre of the face. Unfortunately, things did not go as he had expected, with extremely hard sections of climbing – water ice and dry-tooling – slowing his progress considerably. Imagine it, if you will: M5/M6 climbing in the Death Zone! Humar was forced to bivouac again, at 7,800 metres, without a tent, just a sleeping bag. On day nine he was able to finish his climb, and descended via the normal route without summitting.

Tomaž Humar is credited with finding the best solution so far to the South Face of Dhaulagiri I: he is an absolute star amongst today's Big Wall mountaineers. As he himself has said: 'All of my future climbs will be directed towards the greatest possible challenges: summits that can only be reached by climbing devilishly dangerous big walls.'

What is it that makes up an alpinist such as Humar? Experience shows that, of the most successful mountaineers of any generation, only half die from 'natural causes'. The others fall to their deaths, freeze to death or otherwise perish in the mountains. Alpine history confirms this situation as a brutal reality. Is it pure chance that determines who 'stays up on the mountain' and who 'survives', or is there some connection between survival and a climber's experience and circumspection? Today I am convinced that one of the most decisive factors for enduring a borderline situation is the will to survive. I would even dare to suggest that the climber who is in tune with himself and the world will not normally perish on a mountain. These days I see inner harmony as the prerequisite for any climber who seeks to push the frontiers. Without it, he should give up extreme mountaineering. Humar possesses this inner harmony.

It is thirty years since our first ascent of the Rupal Face of Nanga Parbat, years during which I have climbed other mountains and gained many new experiences. It is said that a man is rejuvenated every seven years – that all his cells are replaced. I wonder, does that also apply to his spirit?

For years I have had to defend myself against all the persecution and accusations that this Nanga Parbat traverse brought in its wake. I know now that I will not get very far by constantly going over the whys and wherefores of the accident. I started to listen more to how I felt inside rather than to other people's accusations or to what other people believed they ought to persuade me to do. For the decision to climb down the Diamir Face, I alone bear the responsibility. Whether it was the right decision, or not, nobody can know. Although many have passed judgment, the truth is, we had no other choice.

At the time, bizarre events like these are really desperate affairs, but in a way, they are good for a young person to experience, for it is such experiences that deepen our sensitivity. I had the good fortune to 'die' young; it created the prerequisites for me to occupy myself with the fundamental questions of existence . . . to prepare for the next disappointment – it is part of the drama of life. Tomaž Humar, too, had this opportunity on Nanga Parbat – a desperate situation with a difficult decision about – ultimately – his survival. Despite those who screamed for self-sacrifice, without question, this experience gave him added wisdom and strength for the next drama of his life – his solo climb of the South Face of Annapurna in October 2007. This was a visionary achievement.

How many of us suffer in one form or another from the fact that our skills and energies are insufficiently challenged? . . . I only know that when physical and emotional reserves remain unchallenged, this feeds the spiritual cancer of a life unfulfilled. There are many antidotes, many possibilities for self-imposed challenge. A failed attempt on a 'virgin' face of an eight-thousander gives me much more than the successful ascent of a known route. These high standards, which ultimately provide greater possibility for failure than success, are what I so admire in Tomaž Humar.

Many people only measure things in terms of success and failure and do not know how close together these values lie. On all my mountaineering excursions, the most important thing was never the summits, nor the successes or the fame. Ultimately, the most important thing was the discoveries I made about myself, discoveries that are always new and that have taught me again and again to view the relationship between myself and my surroundings, my world, in new ways.

'The dragon must not die,' I wrote as a twenty-year-old, in the recognition that it was only 'the impossible' that kept climbing so fascinating. Today I would phrase it differently: 'Only the secrets can be conquered' – most of all, the secrets that lie within ourselves.

This book reveals many fascinating secrets: about what motivates climbers who perform at the very highest levels; about the positioning and competition within the climbing communities; about the fascinating world of Slovenian climbers – the best in the world; and most of all, the complex personality of one of the most intriguing and enigmatic high-altitude performers of today – Tomaž Humar.

CHAPTER ONE

RUPAL FACE

6 August 2005, 15.00, Nanga Parbat, Rupal Face

Elevation: between 6,100 and 6,300 metres
Position: small hole on a near-vertical ice slope, rock cliffs and snow
mushrooms above, ice runnels on either side
Weather conditions: thick fog, heavy snow, -5° Celsius
Visibility: zero
Climbing conditions: impossible, due to avalanches

BASE CAMP: Tomaž, we are trying to do everything to get a helicopter
rescue team. Tell me, how are you and what are the conditions like?
HUMAR: I have been trapped for four days now. There is so much snow;
it is avalanching all the time. I can go nowhere. I can't even move!
BASE CAMP: We know; we are trying to get a team willing to risk the
rescue, you know it is hard. Is there any chance for you to come down
lower?
HUMAR: At the moment I can go nowhere, avalanches on both sides, and
if I move even one metre I will be swept down.
BASE CAMP: I understand. We will try to get a helicopter to you at the
latest by tomorrow. But you know that if the weather gets worse, nobody
will fly.
HUMAR: I know the weather forecast – heavy snow from tomorrow until
Wednesday – so I requested a rescue last night. I am in a trap.
BASE CAMP: We activated everything at home and around the world . . .
I suggest you keep yourself in good shape, and if it looks like you can
descend a bit in the afternoon, try to go down; it would be easier for the
helicopter.
HUMAR: I know I am quite high. The only positive side of this is that I am

on top of the mushroom sticking out of the wall, so there is a possibility of throwing me a rope. I know it is complicated, that they have not done that yet. But if I go down I will be on the side of a tower where an avalanche could hit the helicopter . . . It is not only about the descent, I am in a labyrinth, I can go nowhere . . .

Some called it the boldest rescue in recent memory, others called it a soap opera. For ten days in August 2005, millions around the world watched online as Slovenian climber Tomaž Humar fought for his life, entombed in a coffin of ice over 6,000 metres high on the massive, 4,700-metre Rupal Face of Nanga Parbat, traditionally referred to as the 'killer mountain'.

As each day passed and Tomaž's situation became increasingly desperate, the world watched voyeuristically. The expedition's base camp team posted updated reports on the Humar website, and viewers alone with their computer screens wondered if they were about to witness a man die in the mountains – in real time. Could it end any other way? And then there were private feelings of guilt as the viewer recoiled in a moment of awful comprehension: there were two young children also awaiting the outcome.

The plot thickened. A top-level Pakistani military helicopter pilot, a Croatian filmmaker, a beautiful award-winning journalist and a Slovenian climber joined with presidents and NATO in an international effort to mobilise a rescue. This dangerous, almost suicidal mission, conducted on a direct order from Pakistan's President Musharraf, would become the most controversial mountain rescue in recent history. Debate raged over the unacceptable danger, the value of one climber's life, competition in the mountains and the death of adventure. The American climber Mark Twight, mentor of the Grivel climbing team, commented, 'Now every ill-prepared sad sack whose ability falls short of his Himalayan ambition can get on the radio, call for help, and expect the cavalry to save the day.'

But the debate had begun years earlier when this young Slovenian alpinist, Tomaž Humar, emerged on the world stage. As journalist Maja Roš wrote in Slovenia's national newspaper, *Delo,* Humar's character was never simple:

He is aware of his complicated personality but cannot hide his attraction to it: 'I do not allow anyone to know me completely!' Tomaž Humar, although an invalid with one leg shorter than the other and a partially fused heel bone . . . moves the boundaries of what is possible.

A controversial alpinist, and these days a national hero . . . he is not fooled by peer pressure but is rather searching for his own path. He puts content above form, a man who wants to drink at the source and always values honour the most . . . So in spite of the guides and 'whisperers' who have been accompanying him in his life, he makes his own decisions. 'We were born alone, with a tear in the eye, and we will die alone with our tear.'[1]

Tomaž Humar is a man in a vortex of motion, much of it controversial. His physical appearance is typical of an alpinist: he has a moderately small frame, although powerfully built, and is agile as a cat. The real impact of Tomaž's personality is felt only when he begins to speak, to gesticulate or to explode into action. When he turns his attention towards you the effect is dazzling – like a stage light, blinding in its intensity. The Swiss helicopter rescue pilot Gerold Biner's impression of Tomaž is precise. 'He is like Luis de Funès [an energetic French comedian]. I called him Mister Ten Thousand Volts. What a muscle and energy pack,' Biner says, adding, 'He is phenomenal and very smart.' Tomaž's explosive character was not initially evident, for he grew up a quiet child, obedient, well behaved and a model student. But as he matured, he developed a personality destined to lead. He doesn't conform to existing standards; he creates them. His very existence evokes strong emotions: admiration, love, disdain and often jealousy. As the Italian alpinist Simone Moro says, 'Tomaž is a charismatic person: the more charismatic you are, the more enemies you will have.'

Tomaž is also unpredictable. He can be open and sociable, but at other times he is sullen and withdrawn – in his 'cave', as he calls it. And while many regard him as a clown figure, a lover of publicity, superficial and shallow, a few know him as a thoughtful and spiritual person. He laughs, saying, 'I am just predictable in my unpredictability.'

Despite the controversy surrounding this man, he is widely acknowledged as a superb climber and one who is comfortable with an exceptionally high level of risk. Although he is Slovenian, and experienced in the mountains of his native country, Tomaž's identity as an elite alpinist was shaped in a place where mountains are sacred and where risk and death are constant companions – in the Himalayas.

A great and complex range, the central Himalayan mountains are situated in Nepal, while the eastern peaks extend to the borders of Bhutan and Sikkim. The Nanga Parbat massif is the western corner pillar of the

Himalayas in the Karakorum range, an isolated island of peaks rising up from the plains far below, surrounded by the Indus and Astore rivers. Nanga Parbat, or Nanga Parvata, means 'naked mountain'. Its original name, Diamir, is perhaps more appropriate: 'king of the mountains'.

The main summit of Nanga Parbat, at 8,126 metres/26,660 feet in height, is the ninth highest peak in the world and the second highest in Pakistan after K2. The mountain has three vast faces: the Rakhiot (Ra Kot) Face, the rocky Diamir Face, which transforms itself into massive ice fields near the actual peak, and, on the southern side of the mountain, the mighty Rupal Face. Reinhold Messner, the Italian mountaineering legend, who was the first to climb all fourteen of the 8,000-metre peaks, said, 'Everyone who has ever stood at the foot of this face [4,500 metres] up above the "Tap Alpe", studied it or flown over it cannot help but be amazed by its sheer size; it has become known as the highest rock and ice wall in the world!'

But Nanga Parbat boasts a grim history. It was in 1841 that a rock-slide from the mountain dammed the Indus river, creating a huge lake upstream. The floodwater that was released when the dam broke caused the river to rise 80 feet, sweeping away an entire Sikh army. Europeans first set eyes on Nanga Parbat shortly after this catastrophe, in the middle of the nineteenth century. The Schlagintweit brothers, from Munich, arrived in the Himalayas in 1854 and drew a panoramic view of the mountain, the first known picture of Nanga Parbat. Just three years later, one of the brothers was murdered in Kashgar. The curse of Nanga Parbat had begun.

Still, its allure proved compelling, and the mountain became a coveted climbing objective, especially for the Germans. Soon a relentless series of deaths on the peak led to it being dubbed 'the killer mountain'. The tragedies began with a British expedition in 1895 led by Alfred F. Mummery. The British team reached almost 7,000 metres on the Diamir (West) Face, but Mummery and two Gurkha companions later died reconnoitring the Rakhiot Face. In 1934, a storm on the mountain swallowed four German mountaineers and six Sherpas. Three years later an avalanche buried an entire base camp, killing 9 Sherpas and 7 climbers. In total, six German expeditions attempted the mountain in the 1930s, including the 1939 expedition, of which the famous Austrian climber Heinrich Harrer was a member. No expedition was successful in summitting the mountain, though climbers did reach 7,700 metres on the East Ridge via the Rakhiot Face. By the time the Austrian alpinist Hermann Buhl evenually reached the top in 1953, a total of 31 people had died trying.

Buhl's final summit push was dramatic: he continued ascending alone after his companions had turned back, and after reaching the top, he was ultimately forced to spend the night standing upright, with no shelter from the elements at this high-altitude bivouac. Yet he managed to survive and safely descend the mountain, making climbing history as the first alpinist to climb an 8,000-metre peak without supplementary oxygen.

Following a second successful ascent by the Germans in 1962, Reinhold Messner and his brother Günther climbed the giant 4,600-metre Rupal Face in 1970. Members of a strong German team, the two Italians ascended a route on the left side of the magnificent wall. However, their great achievement ended badly. When they realised they would be unable to return via their ascent route, they instead headed down the Diamir Face, completing the first ever traverse of the mountain. But Günther was lost on the descent, presumably killed in an avalanche. For decades his body lay undiscovered, and the tragedy took on a life of its own. Reinhold Messner eventually became involved in a very public battle over the details of his brother's demise. It wasn't until 2005 that DNA testing of some small remains proved that Günther had indeed perished on the Diamir side of the mountain.

In 1985, an expedition led by Jerzy Kukuczka, the Polish alpinist who was the second to climb all fourteen of the 8,000-metre peaks, many of them in winter, managed another route on the Rupal Face, this time on the right side of the wall, up the South-East Pillar. It became known as the Polish–Mexican route, because the Mexican alpinist Carlos Carsolio was part of the team. When Tomaž Humar began his attempts, neither the Messner nor the Polish–Mexican route had been repeated. As climbers thronged the slopes of Everest, the Rupal Face retained its solitude, remaining a formidable objective.

Tomaž Humar first came to Pakistan in 2002, trekking in the Nanga Valley and the Hunza area. After a number of spectacular Himalayan climbs, and recently recovered from a crippling accident, he was eager for another challenge. The atmosphere in Pakistan was tense, for it was less than a year since the 2001 bombings in the United States, and the perpetrators, allegedly hiding out in the border regions between Pakistan and Afghanistan, were not far away. Not surprisingly, there were very few foreigners in Pakistan at the time. Tomaž went alone to the base of the Rupal Face and waited there for three weeks. Although the weather awarded him only occasional glimpses of the mountain, what he saw excited him immensely.

The weeks at the base of the mountain were profoundly meaningful for Tomaž, and not only from a climbing perspective. This was an intensely spiritual period in his life, and his time spent alone below the massive face only strengthened his connection with the gods. Coming from a deeply religious family, Tomaž had evolved and modified his Catholic Christian beliefs into a universally inclusive form of spirituality that embraced the teachings of Buddhism and Hinduism. He constantly searched for connections with an absolute, transcendent spiritual force, however it was named, striving to raise his consciousness to a level that would subsume all categories of his experiences, including his perception, cognition, intuition, instinct, will and emotion. The mountains were the source of his inspiration, and there was very little that divided his feelings for the mountains and his sense of spirituality.

For Tomaž, the two were one. He would never contemplate a serious climb before consulting his spiritual advisers. The Rupal Face was no exception. In Islamabad he met a holy man who told him: 'We wait for you. You will survive. Are you prepared?' Tomaž believed that 80 per cent of alpinism was mental and spiritual, and that his 'third eye' vision and the openness of his mind to the language of the walls were critical. He credited his survival in the mountains to a variety of influences: his belief in simultaneous giving and receiving, positive thoughts, the existence of the soul of non-living matter, and love. 'There are many paths, but only one essence – love.' And to Tomaž, the essence was worth dying for.

Tomaž felt prepared for the Rupal Face, but his confidence was tempered with reality. He knew what the giant Himalayan faces had to offer: steep walls composed of a questionable mixture of rotten rock, brittle ice and unstable snow. He knew about Himalayan storms: horrendous assaults that arrived with little or no notice, with a force that could pin a climber down for days. He knew about avalanches: those deadly, ever-present companions on the steep Himalayan walls. He had seen it all before: on Ganesh, Bobaye, Ama Dablam, Nuptse, Dhaulagiri and other Himalayan giants. Yet still he was here, contemplating a new route, solo, on one of the greatest faces of them all. He was not naïve enough to assume success – or even survival. In fact, he knew the chances of dying on this route were rather high. If not, someone would surely already have climbed it.

By 2003, nobody had attempted the difficult and extremely dangerous central part of the wall. It was then that Tomaž returned to give it a serious try. His first step was to contact his good friend Nazir Sabir, the best-known

Pakistani alpinist and land agent for foreign climbing expeditions coming to Pakistan. It was Sabir who would manage the internal logistics. The Rupal Face, with its 4,600 metres of climbing, presented very complicated route-finding problems, extremely dangerous conditions and technically demanding climbing. A successful climb would undoubtedly demand a lot of experience, outstanding physical and mental conditioning, enormous courage and a certain amount of luck. 'It can be climbed by one of a thousand' was Messner's assessment when they met to discuss the route.

But the weather conditions in West Pakistan in 2003 were extremely warm and the entire team was also suffering from illness. After four attempts at acclimatising on the Messner route, and in snow conditions that saw him wallowing up to his waist in deep, unconsolidated slush, Tomaž abandoned the climb, but only for the moment.

Tomaž wasn't alone in his fascination with the Rupal Face. An American climber, Steve House, initially visited Nanga Parbat in 1990 with a Slovenian expedition to the Schell route. First climbed in 1976, the Schell route follows a spur that forms the left edge of the Rupal Face, and after its first ascent, the route became quite popular for a time. Shortly after leaving high school, House decided to live and study in Slovenia. While living in Maribor, he quickly became a regular fixture at the local climbing club, and soon made a number of deep friendships with Slovenian climbers. Many climbers thought that his apprenticeship with the hard-core Slovenians helped him become an elite mountaineer.

But in 1990 House didn't feel as though he was a member of any elite. He failed to reach the summit, struck down by altitude sickness at Camp II. The experience humbled him: 'It seemed like science fiction to me.' Still, camped under that face for weeks, he began dreaming about something more ambitious than the Schell route, and by the time he left the mountain, he was completely transfixed: 'Nanga was my first love. And like any first love I was innocent of what she would demand of me in time.'[2] What Nanga demanded was a rigorous training regime of increasingly difficult and committing climbs. This House did, chalking up an impressive list of futuristic, difficult ascents with some of the best alpinists in the world, often at lightning speed. 'I worked to make myself worthy of her. I would travel around the world many times in hopes of gaining her favour. I climbed many mountains for her.'[3] One of his climbing partners during this period was the outspoken and articulate American alpinist Mark Twight, generally regarded as one of the best in the world. While together on an alpine route in Alaska, Twight admitted to House that his career as an extreme alpinist was winding down and that House should be prepared to assume his mantle. Even though he was in fact doing just that, House's personality was not well suited to this kind of responsibility – or notoriety – and he appeared unprepared for the public pressure that would soon be forced upon him. House too became outspoken and blunt, sometimes alienating people with his puritanical criticism of others' climbing styles. Although his performance as an alpinist was undeniably at the highest level, some wondered why he didn't simply allow his actions to speak for themselves.

There probably could have been no greater contrast than that between Steve House and Tomaž Humar, for Tomaž seemed to come alive when in the public eye. He could certainly climb at the highest level, but it sometimes appeared that he could talk about it even better. Some described this as 'creative licence'; others simply called it lying, particularly when it came to claims of difficulty. Climbers and journalists began comparing the two men, blending their 'public' styles with their 'climbing' styles, inadvertently causing confusion by comparing two somewhat unrelated things. Tomaž often emerged the loser, for his public style invariably eroded his reputation as a serious climber. One thing the two climbers did have in common was their position in the public eye. Both faced constant scrutiny and criticism, along with adulation.

House concentrated on climbing, and his dream of the Rupal Face did not fade. He had heard of Tomaž's plans, for his climbing activities were well publicized during this period. House had developed a close climbing and personal friendship with another Slovenian alpinist, Marko Prezelj, and it was Prezelj whom he first invited to join him. Prezelj declined, so instead it was the American climber Bruce Miller who accompanied House to the base of the Rupal Face in 2004.

House waited patiently for good conditions, and by the end of August he and Miller were ready to make an attempt on their chosen line. They climbed well and reached 7,500 metres, but House developed high-altitude sickness and Miller insisted that they descend, which they did via the Messner route. Despite the apparent failure, their attempt was praised worldwide as an exceptional achievement. House later publicly stated that the decision to descend was based more on Miller's fear than his own altitude problems, a statement that many climbers felt unfair and untrue. Miller recalled that House had admitted to him just how serious he was about this objective, saying that he was 'prepared to die' for the route. This was quite possibly true, for after Miller left base camp, and despite obvious signs of altitude illness, House made one last attempt on the face – solo. The dream had become an obsession.

Just as in the anticipation in 1953 to climb Nanga Parbat for the first time, there were now two climbers vying for a new route on the mountain best known for its tendency to kill people.

CHAPTER TWO

BASE CAMP

June 2005, Nanga Parbat, Rupal Face

By June of 2005 Tomaž Humar was back. His goal remained the same – to climb, solo, a new route on the Rupal Face of Nanga Parbat. With him on the expedition was an eclectic group of people, subject of much intrigue to the public. Aleš Koželj was an exceptionally talented 30-year-old Slovenian climber from Tomaž's home town, Kamnik, and they had climbed and trained together for the previous two years. Extremely reserved and almost painfully shy, Aleš already had an impressive climbing résumé, with expeditions to Janak in 2002, Aconcagua in 2003 and Cholatse in 2005, the last two of which he climbed with Tomaž. Although widely regarded as one of Slovenia's most promising Himalayan climbers, Aleš was not sure if he would climb the entire Rupal Face with Tomaž. But they definitely planned to acclimatize together when they would attempt to adjust their bodies to survive the debilitating effects of extremely high altitude.

Also at base camp was Tomaž's frequent expedition companion and friend, the Croatian climber and cameraman Stipe Božić. Stipe was Croatia's most successful Himalayan alpinist, having climbed the three highest mountains in the world: Everest, K2 and Kangchenjunga. He had been Tomaž's co-leader on several previous Himalayan climbs. Their personalities contrasted greatly, and yet the partnership flourished. Stipe readily accepted Tomaž's more volatile and explosive disposition, and Tomaž, in turn, appreciated Stipe's generous spirit, for he never appeared jealous of Tomaž's audacious climbs. 'When he sees me climbing he is happy,' Tomaž said. Stipe described their friendship as close, and said he felt responsible for providing Tomaž with essential organisational support: 'I believe in his ideas and I have found someone who can extend my own dreams.' Stipe was experienced, mature, competent and reliable – exactly what Tomaž needed to balance his own mercurial genius.

Another important member of the team was Anda Perdan, a soft-spoken Slovenian doctor from Kranj, a city near Tomaž's home. With her slender figure, short-cropped hair and conservative demeanour, Anda gave the impression of a modest, cerebral and very self-contained woman. In fact, she was an exceptional doctor with an innate understanding of expedition life and its particular challenges, for she had accompanied Tomaž on five previous Himalayan expeditions. Perhaps more importantly, it was Anda who had nursed Tomaž back to life after a near-fatal injury five years before. She knew his body well.

Possibly the most unusual member of the team was Nataša Pergar, a biotherapist whose speciality was auras. Author of *Vidne in nevidne poti* (*Visible and Invisible Ways*), Nataša was particularly interested in the auras of climbers as they attempted difficult climbs, and she had been monitoring and interpreting Tomaž's energies for four years. In fact, she had become a kind of climbing psychic for him, helping him ask himself the right questions – the equivalent of a personal trainer. A wild-looking creature with a head of unruly auburn hair, she added an element of pizzazz to base camp. Her assignment was to observe Nanga Parbat closely, as well as to advise Tomaž on auspicious dates, hours and signs. As he explained, 'Every mountain has its soul . . . if the mountain doesn't accept you and you don't submit to her will, she will destroy you.' As Nataša scrutinised the mountain, she would note its aura. If it was red, its mood was too aggressive. If it turned blue, this was a sign of improvement. But the optimum moment was when the third eye appeared, a sure sign of oneness between the mountain and Tomaž. She had seen it before while he was attempting a particularly daring solo climb on Rzenik in Slovenia, and this was what she was hoping for here. The more pragmatic Stipe was sceptical of Nataša's value to the expedition and would later say, 'She is a wonderful person, but for me, she was not really a help.'

The final member of the base camp team was Maja Roš, a well-respected journalist with POP TV, one of the climb's media sponsors. Her job was to cover this expedition from start to finish, and to relay regular reports back to Slovenia. It wasn't her first assignment of this kind; as a journalist with the Slovenian newspaper *Delo*, she had accompanied the Ski Everest 2000 expedition, which saw the first complete ski descent of Everest by Slovenian skier Davorin Karničar. Her book *Prvi – na smučeh z Everesta*

(*First Descent of Everest on Skis*) chronicled this 2000 expedition. A long-limbed, dark-haired beauty with a high-voltage smile, Maja was very athletic, although not an alpinist.

Also at base camp was an array of equipment, some of which was to record the climb and some for the ascent itself: cameras, videotape, recorders, satellites, batteries and computers. Tomaž's original plan had been a media-free expedition, but his financial circumstances changed, and now his climb would be covered by internet, television and print media.

Although the extra publicity partially solved some of Tomaž's financial problems, it created even more, because with each additional piece of the media puzzle, expenses spiralled upwards. And so did the complications. Tomaž was aware of the dangers of having the media so intimately involved with the expedition, and he insisted he would have excluded them if he had been able to finance the trip in any other way. 'Television is a compromise,' he said, but added confidently, 'I still control the switch.'

This approach was not unheard of in the big mountains, for many expeditions preferred to document and report their progress on a daily, even hourly basis. These ongoing updates provided the media with the news they needed and, in the process, created publicity for any sponsors. Simone Moro welcomed the media on expeditions, stating, 'This is part of the game of being a professional climber.' But not everyone bought into this philosophy. Most climbers agreed that the incessant presence of media on a climb created its own challenges and distractions, sometimes even changing the dynamics and outcomes of an expedition, though it undoubtedly helped pay the bills. Some felt that the presence of media, particularly the internet, cheapened the entire alpine experience, turning it into a kind of promotional exercise. They considered its presence a sacrilege against the 'purity' of alpinism.

Steve House preferred a simpler approach for his Himalayan climbs and couldn't understand why anyone should subject himself to unnecessary complications in order to finance an expedition. Later that summer he would spend six weeks in Pakistan, climbing on the same face, allegedly with a budget of just under $11,000, an amount that certainly didn't require sponsorship. As he put it: 'To me, the money just gets in the way.' It was likely both expeditions to Pakistan cost more than that amount, but in any case the two expeditions were fundamentally different, and comparing their accounting was like comparing apples and oranges.

Though not at Tomaž's base camp, an important member of his team was the Pakistani organiser Nazir Sabir. Nazir was one of the most powerful civilians in the entire country, President of the Alpine Association of Pakistan, owner of Nazir Sabir Expeditions and the most successful Pakistani climber on 8,000-metre peaks. And as the ex-secretary of tourism, he was also well connected in government circles, an advantage that would prove to be absolutely crucial in the days to come.

Before attempting the face, Tomaž, Stipe and Aleš planned to acclimatise on the Messner route. By climbing and sleeping as high as possible, they would gradually adjust to the decreasing levels of oxygen high on the mountain, preparing Tomaž for his solo climb. Depending on his fitness and the conditions on the mountain, Tomaž hoped to begin climbing the face on the day of a full moon, or a day or two later. During the acclimatisation climb and while at base camp, he would study the face, work out the intricacies of the route, become familiar with the avalanche and rock fall patterns and determine the relatively safe zones.

The face was a giant, deadly puzzle that needed to be solved. It changed constantly with the weather. Although the team could access weather forecasts from a number of different sources, none appeared to be accurate, for Nanga Parbat was an enormous, free-standing massif that created its own weather patterns. And with each storm came precipitation, often in the form of heavy, wet snow. This, in turn, created horrendously dangerous avalanche conditions, through which no climber could safely navigate. But they were the terrain and conditions on which Tomaž thrived; it was surviving these experiences that had made him a celebrated Himalayan alpinist and a national hero in his own country. Although the conditions were almost as bad as in 2003, he was resolved and confident that this year he would do it. And he planned to do it quickly and efficiently, for his entire expedition was not expected to exceed 21 days. This kind of confidence was built upon years of experience in the mountains: the Himalayas, the Andes and the Alps. But more than abroad, his skills were initially honed in his home mountains of Slovenia.

Kamnik, Slovenia, 1987

Tomaž was born into a hard-working, religious family on 18 February 1969. During this period of relative stability in the socialist state of Yugoslavia, their life was frugal, but they did not want for their basic needs. But the life of his father, Max Humar, had not always been so stable. At one point, while still a single man, he had fled the country over the mountains into Austria. Once there, he thought better of this rash decision and turned himself in to the Austrian police, after which he was duly sent home. His life then became one of hard work. But Max was a practical and optimistic man who didn't see his life as unduly difficult. While his formal occupation was that of a shoemaker, like many of his generation he was multi-skilled, and he eventually became a builder, working 14–16 hours per day during his peak years. On 4 May 1968 he married Rosalija Globokar, a young woman from the village of Klečet in the Dolenska region of Yugoslavia. Twenty-one years old when she first met Max, she worked in a department store as a salesperson.

Tomaž, their firstborn, was initially a quiet boy, obedient and well behaved. He performed well in school and appeared to be a model student. But he recalled that he felt different, even at an early age: 'I was already strange as a child . . . I was born on the carnival day.' Nearly three years later a second son was born. Marjan Humar was educated as a structural engineer, and would eventually earn a living building autobahns. The third boy, Matej, was born in 1975. A very artistic person, Matej ultimately became a professional wood designer.

As the eldest child, Tomaž baby-sat for his two younger brothers, and that attitude of protective concern for them remained with him. In addition to her considerable domestic responsibilities, his mother worked full-time in a shop. His father worked nonstop at various jobs: by day he was employed in a factory constructing towers, and at night he toiled at private construction, much of which was black market. The Humars had a strong work ethic, which they passed on to each of their sons, although in different ways. They were also very religious, living a devout Catholic life. They said grace before and after each meal, and as Tomaž remembered, it was a real prayer – a blessing of the food. Religious instruction was an important influence in his youth, and Tomaž recalls his confirmation and first-communion ceremonies with pride.

Some weekends saw them visiting his father's ancestral farm, where various animals were raised, along with grain crops and massive gardens. It was very much a self-sufficient lifestyle. In the evenings they ate cabbage soup with pork, accompanied by loaves of delicious bread, freshly baked in the large ovens. There were apples on sticks for the children and schnapps made of plums and chestnuts for the adults.

Tomaž and his father would enthusiastically help out on the farm. Yet they were so frugal that when Tomaž was assigned pig-sty duty, he wore rubber boots into which he would stuff his feet wrapped in old bed sheets. He wouldn't dare wear proper socks, for they were reserved for school and church. On Saturday nights, men from the nearby farms would come and visit, singing loudly as they became increasingly fortified with the delicious and powerful schnapps. This was a bucolic and secure existence that Tomaž would later reflect upon with sharp nostalgia.

From the age of six, Tomaž worked with his compact, wiry father, helping him with construction jobs, hauling wood and bags of cement, even building an entire house. He was a good worker, and Max was pleased that he never seemed to complain. The neighbours sometimes thought his father was too tough on Tomaž, and that he was destroying his childhood. But Max's work ethic applied to his eldest above all.

Their spartan home life was masterfully managed by their frugal, caring mother. The three brothers slept upstairs in an unheated attic room, sharing a pull-out sofa amongst them. If the outside temperature dipped below 10 degrees, they were allowed downstairs to sleep in the heated living room. It would have been unnecessary and overindulgent to heat the entire house.

Tomaž's first climbing experiments took place at the age of eighteen in the basement of the family home, where he leapt about from beam to beam, hoisting himself up and over his father's various saws and tools. Soon he was venturing out to the local crags, clad in his very first harness: a discarded Fiat seatbelt. He joined the local Kamnik mountain club in 1987, and there he found a second home where he was encouraged to climb and hone his skills. In contrast, his parents considered climbing a completely useless and dangerous activity. At home there was always work to be done, and they expected Tomaž to direct his boundless energy to practical matters.

The club system benefited Tomaž as it had so many other young climbers before him, providing instruction as well as equipment that he could use under an instructor's supervision. Since most climbers could not afford to buy their own equipment, this was a valuable benefit of the mountaineering clubs. Each club belonged to the Mountaineering Association, a highly structured organisation that included individual Commissions for huts, climbing, alpinism, education and walking.

In order to become 'an alpinist', the club expected Tomaž to adhere to a strict programme. He couldn't simply head out on an expedition abroad, or even to the nearby Alps, for an official stamp from the Association was required. And in order to get this stamp, he had to progress through a classification process. He started as a walker; then, after a six-month course became a young assistant; next, on to an old assistant; and finally, to an alpinist. But it didn't end there. Even as an alpinist there were notable distinctions. At first he would be classified as a regional climber, then a national one, and finally as an international alpinist. Once he reached international status, he would be awarded an annual stipend.

In theory. In fact, once a climber reached international status, that climber's club, not the individual, was awarded the annual stipend on his behalf. Each club received money from the Association, based on the number of qualified alpinists in their midst. Then, based on the decisions of a small and very powerful committee within the club, this funding was allocated to climbers requesting support for their international expeditions. It was entirely possible that climbers could progress through years of instruction, advance through several qualification levels, be named international climbers, and then watch helplessly as their stipend was allocated to others within the club.

Since mountaineering is not strictly a competitive sport, this complex system was difficult to administer. It left those in power with room to manoeuvre, and climbers without connections could find it difficult to advance their careers. Competition grew between the various clubs around the country, as well as amongst the climbers within those clubs. One of the most powerful clubs in Yugoslavia was based in Kamnik, the town where Tomaž grew up. Bojan Pollak, one of the instructors and a mentor to Tomaž, defended the system convincingly, pointing out that it was an international climber's duty to give back to the club that had supported him in his youth. This was the socialist way, and it worked.

Tomaž was only partially convinced. Although raised in the socialist or eastern bloc, he lived very near western Europe and had already been influenced by the more liberal climbing traditions of neighbouring Italian and Austrian climbers. Their mountain ranges were contiguous, with meaningless boundaries snaking down the ridge tops or along the rushing rivers. He knew that there were certainly no restrictive international climbing classification systems in the Alps, unless of course you planned to be a mountain guide.

Yet the Yugoslavian club structure produced some of the best Himalayan climbers in the world. It was similar to the structure used in the former Soviet Union, where alpinism was a state-supported sport. The Soviets compiled an extensive list of skill levels, tests and specific objectives that must be met before a climber could be designated an alpinist. Under the vigilant, critical eyes of a climbing coach, each climber had to succeed on dozens of climbs at a certain level before moving on to more difficult objectives. After years of training, a few highly skilled and dedicated climbers could participate in climbing championships where they were again tested. Although it was a painfully slow process, the leader of the Russian Big Wall Project, Alexander Odintsov, asserted that 'Those who passed through this rigorous system would find nothing they encountered in the high mountains frightening.'[1] The Poles too produced a veritable army of alpinists, using a similar approach.

In Yugoslavia, Pollak was one of the strictest and most exacting of instructors, and it was he who taught Tomaž, beginning with a six-month introductory course that paired lectures with practical instruction. Every second weekend they would meet: Pollak would teach and the 18-year-old Tomaž would soak it up, along with other young climbers, including Marko Prezelj, the most skilled climber in the club and someone whom Tomaž admired greatly. Pollak didn't initially notice anything particularly outstanding about Tomaž; he was just another eager young climber, keen to explore the nearby Kamnik Alps.[2]

Each Thursday they would attend a club meeting, discuss what they had learned, describe the climbs they had done and make plans for the following weekend. In addition to providing a crucial meeting point and planning opportunity, the Thursday meetings created a tight and vibrant community, all focused on one thing: climbing. Tomaž called these meetings 'Holy Thursday'. For Prezelj, the Thursday night gathering was a 'kind of church'. The two climbers were good friends and urged each other on.

Tomaž valued Pollak's instruction, stating, 'Bojan taught me to survive – how to walk on easy ground, especially on the descent. He taught me important things that helped me later on the big walls.' Nevertheless, the two occasionally disagreed, usually because of Tomaž's disregard of the club rules.

Pollak was a firm disciplinarian and allowed little leeway in his programme. When he took a group of young climbers on an excursion to Paklenica, a superb rock-climbing area on the coast north of Split, Tomaž asked if he could bring his climbing shoes for the high-angled limestone walls. Pollak said, 'Of course.' They walked up the canyon to the bottom of an appealing cliff. Tomaž undid his pack and took out his shoes. Pollak asked, 'What are you doing?' Tomaž replied, 'I'm putting on my climbing shoes.' Pollak responded, 'You are not allowed to wear those shoes; you need to climb in your mountain boots.' Tomaž protested: 'I asked you before if I could wear my climbing shoes and you said okay.' Pollak replied, 'No, you never asked me if you could *wear* your climbing shoes; you just asked if you could *bring* your climbing shoes. Of course I said yes. There is no problem with that.' Disgusted, the young climber threw the shoes back in his pack and donned his heavy, clunky mountain boots. They climbed 14 routes that day.

CHAPTER THREE

KOSOVO

7 July 2005, Nanga Parbat, Rupal Face

As the team arrives at the base of Nanga Parbat's magnificent Rupal Face, they find the wall draped in an ethereal gossamer veil of fog up to 5,500 metres. Suddenly it shifts, revealing huge ice pinnacles, menacingly suspended on a face draped in a blanket of snow, glistening in the afternoon sun. Aleš and Tomaž are transfixed, staring endlessly at the wall, searching for a weakness. They are almost in a trance, or perhaps it is prayer. Tomaž removes his shoes before the mountain in a devout demonstration of respect. Despite her previous experience at Everest base camp, Maja is completely intimidated. 'The highest wall in the world was terrifying in its grandeur . . . I was trying to imagine a person up there . . . no, this was not built for humans.'

Located at 3,550 metres, base camp lies in a rolling meadow near the Bazin Glacier. Once the porters leave, six members of the expedition, plus Javed, their sirdar, and two cooks, Rahmet and Tarik, remain in camp. Tomaž comments that the seventh day of the month is his lucky day; the previous year he arrived on the 23rd, not an auspicious date for him.

The leader of a Korean team camped nearby arrives for a visit. The Koreans, who are attempting the Messner route, explain that they have equipped the route with camps and have left fixed ropes in place as high as 7,600 metres in order to facilitate load-carrying. Since the two expeditions are in no way competitive, the Koreans agree to the use of the camps and their fixed lines by Aleš and Tomaž, who plan to acclimatise on the Messner route. This welcome arrangement is tempered by their sobering news that the route has been subjected to unrelenting rock fall. Three members of the Korean team have been hit and one has even sustained a broken leg from falling rock. Poor weather has led the Koreans to extend their expedition by

25 days. This is very disturbing. The weather will need to improve substantially for Tomaž's lightning-fast plan to succeed.

During that first night in base camp it is difficult to sleep, not only from excitement, but from the roaring sounds periodically coming from the mountain. At times it seems that the mountain's belly is ripping open, as if releasing a giant lava flow. In reality it is simply shedding excess snow. Avalanches and ice blocks tumble thousands of metres, gathering momentum and volume as they descend the length of the face. Each team member lies sleepless, listening restlessly as the ominous rumbles continue throughout the night.

The next morning dawns slowly. As they stir from their tents, it begins to rain. Nataša soon weighs in with her prediction: 'It will be like this all day. I had a lot of visits during the night. Nothing good.' After a hearty breakfast of chapattis, pancakes and granola, Tomaž announces that, despite the continuing rain, he and Aleš will begin climbing, for they must take every chance to acclimatize. This surprises the other team members, since the weather is atrocious. But Tomaž has a plan; he has a timetable, and he doesn't have the luxury of waiting around for good weather. He appears to be in a hurry. He has been at the bottom of this face three times now. This time he feels completely prepared and he wants to get started. But as he studies through the telescope what little he can see of the Messner route, he is visibly worried.

As Aleš and Tomaž head off towards the face in steady rain, Stipe and Maja fly into action, arranging the office, the solar panels, a generator, two laptops, three satellite phones and all the technical support they will need to run the base camp website and to interact daily with radio, television and newspapers. The generator is not cooperating and the satellite connection is down for at least an hour. Maja is frustrated because her job is to communicate; without well-functioning technology, she can't perform. Meanwhile, Nataša concentrates her efforts on trying to decipher the mountain's energy fields. This is not easy, for the entire wall is engulfed in cloud and she can see absolutely nothing. She becomes distracted when a local shepherd decides to slaughter a goat in the middle of base camp. Horrified, she convinces him that this will bring bad luck, and he reluctantly moves downstream a hundred metres.

By late afternoon, base camp has taken on a semblance of order. The two climbers radio in that they have reached 5,000 metres, are about to begin their descent back to base camp, and are 'hungry for some meat'. They arrive in camp well after dark, prompting a round of jokes about the dangers of going into the mountains with Tomaž. Every single expedition member who has ever travelled with him, even for a walk in the forest, knows that one must go prepared for anything. They all agree that it would be folly to go anywhere with Tomaž without a headlamp, for it's seldom that one returns before dark.

Despite the late hour and the horrible weather, the climbers are invigorated by their day on the mountain. Although he has considerable climbing experience, Aleš has never been on a wall such as this, and he is excited: 'You begin to realise how small you really are.' Stipe, with 20 Himalayan expeditions to his credit, is astonished to hear that it was raining at 5,000 metres; normally it would snow at that height. As the team views the climbers' photos, they begin to comprehend the current conditions on the face: deep, rotten snow and slippery, slimy rock. As the expedition doctor, Anda is encouraged by their performance today, for she believes that by managing to ascend 1,500 metres so quickly, the climbers may have retained the conditioning that they gained on another Himalayan expedition to Cholatse earlier in the spring, giving them an edge for the work ahead. But Nataša says only that 'the mountain obviously has its intentions'.

The morning of 9 July dawns warm and sunny and the team members are forced out of their tents by the heat of the sun's rays. The mountain is draped with a fresh blanket of soft snow, but it doesn't matter, for this is a rest day. Over breakfast Tomaž and Stipe discuss their strategy for the acclimatisation climb. Tomaž prefers to bypass the Korean advance base camp and go directly to Camp I. Stipe thinks this might be rushing things. After some debate, Tomaž wins the argument; they agree to try to reach Camp I the next day, and Camp II on 11 July. In four days they hope to reach 7,200 metres and then descend all the way to base camp. If they can use the Korean camps along the way, as well as their fixed lines, this schedule might be possible. But they know the fixed lines are not completely dependable, for they are likely to be buried under snow. If this is the case, and if the trail-breaking is as tough as it was for the Koreans, their progress will almost certainly be much slower.

The rest day is actually a very busy one, with planning, eating, packing and repacking. Anda repairs some ripped clothing while the rest of the team helps prepare a dinner for the Koreans. Nataša builds a chorten, or prayer altar, and Stipe films the construction process. When the Koreans arrive for dinner they bear presents and laughter and high spirits, despite their efforts on the mountain. They show photos of the wall that they have stored on their laptop, and they tell impressive tales of the depth of the snow, the rock fall and the route. They recount the story of their young teammate whose leg was broken by a falling rock, of how the team gave up their summit attempt on that day and instead used four precious days to carry him off the mountain and down to a hospital to have his leg properly set by a doctor. As Tomaž listens to the story, he mutters to himself, 'We will not have that option. Our team is too small for that.'

After the feast, and a couple of rounds of blueberry liqueur brought all the way from Slovenia, the Koreans depart, leaving the Slovenian team with their thoughts and plans. It will be Aleš, Stipe and Tomaž who head up on to the face the next day. The weather forecast predicts good conditions for three days. Tomaž ends the evening with a typically optimistic and exuberant proclamation: 'Life is beautiful, but only if you live it fully!'

During the night, a gigantic avalanche rips down the face, cutting directly across the route that Tomaž plans to solo after he is sufficiently acclimatised. The next morning, after viewing the disturbing sight, he remarks wryly: 'She was naughty last night . . . right down my route . . . yes, this is a difficult wall.'

After breakfast on 11 July, they assemble at Nataša's improvised chorten for a brief ceremony. Ice axes and crampons – the tools that they will use to climb the hard snow and ice – and a backpack are placed on the chorten, together with three rocks to symbolise the mountain. Small items are added by each team member and everyone sits gazing at the Rupal Face. For thirty minutes the mountain is strangely quiet: no rock fall, no avalanches, no seracs – those dangerously unstable towers of ice – breaking off. Yet Tomaž seems disturbed, describing what he sees as 'a black hole which is not letting me through'. When Maja asks him what feelings these thoughts produce in him, he answers, 'A breath of death. A moment earlier I feel more dead than alive. A moment later I am more alive than dead. When a tear silences a word, even grass stops growing, if only for a moment.'

Stunned by these dark words, Maja reflects on her earlier conversations with Tomaž prior to their departure for Pakistan. He told her then that Nanga Parbat had invited him, called him, directly to this face. But now that they are here, she at last understands the seriousness of the invitation, and feels the terror that the face brings to all who view it. She struggles to understand the value of all this risk. Why does Tomaž need to climb it in order to fulfil himself? Does he expect some kind of blessing on the summit? Is this face the key that will open the door to the next stage of his life? Why is it so important?

Maja recalls an ancient legend that speaks of the curse of Nanga Parbat. According to the legend, the mountain is the home of fairies that live in a castle of crystal-clear ice, guarded by snakes and frogs. The fairies allegedly disapproved of the Nazi-style German expeditions to Nanga Parbat; thus the many accidents and deaths. Tomaž knows the legend, too, and once said to Maja that everything depends on 'the reasons for climbing the mountain'. She wonders, will the fairies lead him through the serac labyrinths and the rock towers? Will they give him advance warning of the avalanches? If it's true that the mountain has invited him to climb her, perhaps they will. She is hopeful, but the more she comes to know this man, the greater is her concern. Her concerns are amplified and in Technicolor because by now it is clear to her, to Tomaž and to everyone on the team that she and Tomaž have fallen deeply in love. But she is also a journalist, hired to report on every aspect of this expedition. She will need to isolate her feelings in order to do her job, as will Tomaž when he is on the mountain. Stipe has observed the two as they spend more and more time together, often alone, and he wonders if Tomaž will be distracted by Maja, or if his decision-making will be influenced by her presence at base camp. Finally he concludes that it's not a problem: Maja is a mature woman and 'Tomaž is a big boy' who will make the right decisions when he is on the mountain.

The chorten ceremony complete, the three climbers, Tomaž, Aleš and Stipe, finish their packing and head towards the mountain. The camp, like the mountain, is eerily muted by their departure.

Kosovo, 1988

The actors in this story, Tomaž, Aleš, Stipe, Anda, Nataša and Maja, come from a turbulent region of eastern Europe which only two decades earlier was comfortably embedded within the state of Yugoslavia and ruled benevolently by its socialist dictator, Tito. They have since lived through the death of their country – Yugoslavia – and the birth of another – Slovenia.

Yugoslavia did not die a natural death. Rather, in Tomaž's view and that of many other citizens of the Balkan region, it was systematically and brutally destroyed by ambitious men who had everything to gain and nothing to lose from preventing a peaceful transition from socialism to democracy. Of these men, it is Slobodan Milošević who is most often blamed, for deliberately harnessing the rise of Serb nationalism in the mid-1980s to prevent that transition. Looking back on the period, Tomaž views the break-up of Yugoslavia as a disaster. 'We were equal; we all worked together,' he reminisces of life in Yugoslavia. But there was one problem, he says: 'There was one person who wanted to be more equal – Milošević.'

Milošević's original goal was to step into Tito's shoes as the leader of all Yugoslavia. He envisaged a plan to create an enlarged Serbian state, swallowing as much of the former Yugoslavia as possible. To a certain extent he succeeded, but in the process his centralised, authoritarian approach and his clever manipulation of the politics of ethnic intolerance drove some Yugoslav nations to a point where they simply could not imagine anything other than independence.

As communism declined around the world in the 1980s, Yugoslavia was better positioned than most communist countries to make the transition to a multi-party state. Its strong overall economy and loosely defined government gave it a solid foundation from which to adapt to the changing times and become an important player in the emerging European power structure.

This is not to ignore the ethnic grievances and intolerances which already existed amongst the various Yugoslav nations and which had not been adequately dealt with by Tito. For the country to have emerged as a fully fledged democracy, these grievances would have needed careful handling. This sensitivity was not apparent, for the presidents of the six republics – Bosnia-Herzegovina, Macedonia, Croatia, Slovenia, Montenegro and Serbia – quarrelled publicly. Although they were careful to conceal their true intentions, some of these leaders had their own very personal ambitions and were secretly plotting the demise of their country.

Of them all, it was Milošević who most carefully positioned himself as an iron leader, willing to take on difficult problems. He expanded his power base by creating a series of crises in Serbia and beyond, then harnessed the power of the Yugoslav People's Army (JNA) and eventually presented each of the other nations with a simple choice: stay in Yugoslavia under his terms or fight a war with a large and powerful army, one of the largest in Europe.

In 1991 Slovenia jumped at the chance, and won a quick and efficient war. Croatia was next, but its victory would be much more costly, taking years to conclude and involving horrific atrocities that stunned the world. The United Nations had to intervene and there was a mass exodus of Serbs from Croatian territory. Bosnia then took the bait, with even more disastrous results.

But it was Kosovo that first felt the force of the JNA. The reasons are complex, but possibly the most important factor was that Yugoslavian Serbs considered Kosovo to be their symbolic ethnic centre. Yet Serbs were a distinct minority in Kosovo, and the much more abundant Albanians had grown increasingly less tolerant of the perceived bullying from the Serbian minority within their own community. It was in Kosovo that Tomaž had his brush with war.

Long before, in 1945, the Soviet Army had liberated many eastern European nations from German occupation and then duly installed communist governments in Czechoslovakia, Hungary, East Germany and Poland. But not in Yugoslavia. Even though he ran a communist state, President Tito was seen by Moscow as dangerously independent, and in 1948 Yugoslavia was expelled from the eastern bloc of communist countries.

After the split, Tito managed to steer a fine line between east and west, attracting significant foreign financial backing for the country in the process. He had to balance the interests of many foreign countries, as well as those of one particularly powerful internal force – the biggest nation within the country, Serbia. There were twice as many Serbs in Yugoslavia as there were Croatians, the next largest nation, and Tito worked hard at balancing power amongst the nationalities to maintain some sense of equal footing. He was ruthless in his efforts to suppress any resurgent nationalism, carrying out purges of various internal groups in the process: Macedonians, Albanians, Croats, Serbs, Slovenes and Muslims. Using the slogan 'Brotherhood and Unity', he either forced nationalists into exile or jailed them.

Despite the purges, most Yugoslavs enjoyed tremendous benefits under Tito's rule. They were not subject to the same stultifying restrictions as in other communist countries; many parts of the country enjoyed enviable economic freedom, and all citizens were free to travel and work abroad, often without visas. Tomaž recalled that although Yugoslavia appeared to outsiders as a communist country behind an iron wall, in fact it operated on a neutral ground, backing neither East nor West. The Yugoslavians threatened no one. There was very little poverty and most people had a relatively good standard of living. Debt was almost nonexistent. Food was cheap. The Yugoslavian passport was then one of the most valued in the world.

By the time of Tito's last constitution in 1974, the country was as decentralised as it had ever been. Tito was its undisputed and beloved leader. But as leader, he failed in one important respect: he never planned for succession and there was no obvious heir apparent. As a result, he created an inefficient and dysfunctional system to succeed him, an eight-member rotating presidency that represented each of the six republics as well as Serbia's two autonomous provinces, Kosovo and Vojbodina. When he died in 1980 there was an overwhelming outpouring of grief amongst Yugoslavians. As the Albanian communist Mahmut Bakalli recalled, 'We all cried, but we did not know we were also burying Yugoslavia.'[1]

A year after Tito's death, the first death knell sounded. In the autumn of 1981 the ethnic Albanians in Kosovo took to the streets, demanding their independence from Serbia. They wanted to become the seventh republic. It was then that the JNA moved in and crushed the first signs of unrest.

Meanwhile, in the north, Slovenia enjoyed a liberalism throughout the 1980s that was unprecedented in a communist country. Ljubljana had emerged as the most cultural capital of all the Yugoslavian republics. Perhaps most importantly, Milan Kučan, the tolerant head of Slovenia's communist party, firmly believed that the country's future lay in reform. He was not averse to the idea that at some point Slovenians would be better served by being separate from Yugoslavia. And the JNA seemed powerless to stop the process of reform in Slovenia.

This was not the case further south in Yugoslavia. By the mid 1980s a group called the Committee of Serbs and Montenegrins was firing up Serb emotions, telling stories of torture, harassment and rape in the Kosovo area. Tens of thousands of signatures were collected, supporting a change of rule in Kosovo. When a memorandum from the highly respected Serbian Academy of Sciences and Arts appeared in 1986, the country was convulsed. A passionate listing of Serbian grievances, it averred that Serbs were discriminated against both politically and economically by their Croatian and Slovenian countrymen. The document alleged that in Kosovo, the Serbs faced potential genocide. The memorandum went on to accuse Slovenia and Croatia of conspiring against Serbs, and concluded that Yugoslavia was in a state of disintegration. Communists around the country lashed out against the document, but Milošević remained strangely silent, allowing others to condemn the memorandum on his behalf. Although the document initially produced shock, it soon began to take root in the general populace, igniting and then fuelling years of grievance. Slowly but surely, Serbia began sliding into a mindset of nationalism.

Since Kosovo was the trigger point, it became clear that someone representing the federal government should visit the region and calm things down. The current president, Ivan Stambolič, probably should have made the trip, but instead he sent in his place Slobodan Milošević. The visit was a turning point in Milošević's career. Elated that Belgrade was responding to their pleas, thousands of Kosovo Serbs turned up, vying for attention. When he finally spoke to them, he galvanised the masses with verbal attacks on the Albanian leaders, condemnation of the idea of an independent Kosovo and strong suggestions of a state of emergency. The event ended with the mob chanting: 'Slobo, Slobo!' Milošević, in turn, was electrified by the crowd. It was immediately clear that they saw him as their saviour, and it was also apparent that whoever led the Kosovo Serbs would lead all of Serbia. Unfortunately for Stambolič, and tragically for thousands of Yugoslavians, Milošević never turned back. He grasped the significance of the event and the impact it could have on his personal career. This warm embrace by Serbian nationalists provided him with the impetus to build and expand his power base. It would take only a few short months before Milošević was firmly ensconced as the Serbian leader. By December of 1987, the relatively moderate Stambolič was out and Milošević was in.

Initially, Slovenia took no notice. Croatia too seemed unconcerned. They did not appear to grasp that for Milošević, Kosovo was just the launching pad. The goal was much bigger: Yugoslavia. Throughout Serbia, millions were showing up at rallies, responding to the fanned flames of nationalism. By October, Milošević had bullied the presidents of Serbia and Macedonia into resigning. Montenegro was next. By the end of the year, he had dismissed the leader of the Kosovo communist party. It took only four months for Kosovo to be absorbed by Serbia. Milošević now had complete control of the Serbian League of Communists and had attained an almost divine status with Serbs. Images of Tito began to disappear from public places, only to be replaced by those of Milošević. Now the politicians in Slovenia and Croatia began to take serious note of Milošević's programme to make Serbia 'whole' again. They recognised it as something different: turning Yugoslavia into Serbo-slavia, and it worried them.

Meanwhile, life in Slovenia remained good. Although its population was only 8 per cent of Yugoslavia's 23.5 million people, it produced nearly one third of the country's hard-currency exports. This was greatly facilitated by access to the cheap labour supply streaming north from the poorer regions of Macedonia, Bosnia and Serbia. Slovenia wanted more control of its finances and its destiny, and so in the spring of 1989 proposed amendments to the constitution that would grant it this freedom. Belgrade was outraged and threatened force, but did nothing.

The situation in Kosovo, however, was threatening to boil over, and an intervention by the JNA was inevitable. When it finally took place, the JNA crackdown on the ethnic Albanians in Kosovo was a covert action, masterminded by Colonel Vasiljevič, a man who a few years later would be sent to Slovenia to see what he could do about the emerging dissatisfaction boiling beneath the surface in that part of the country.

When the Yugoslavian government conscripted Tomaž, along with thousands of other eligible young men, to serve in the army, he was only 20 years old. After joining up, he was out for a run one spring day in 1988 when some of his army friends came searching for him. There was an impending inspection, they told him. He needed to return to base. When he returned, however, there were orders to board a train leaving Zagreb. His platoon had been chosen – but for what? He had no time to call his parents, and even if he had, there would have been nothing conclusive to tell them about this secret mission. At first the soldiers' spirits were high. They joked about sharing rooms with their friends and were excited at the thought of a change. Their excitement soon faded as they were herded into box cars like animals.

The soldiers began to speculate about their destination. The lucky platoons were assigned to Croatia. Maybe that was where they were going? At the last minute they learned they were instead headed for Kosovo, to a place near Podujevo. Tomaž soon learned that he would be working primarily with Serbian soldiers, guarding ethnic Albanians who wanted to escape Serbian rule and create their own republic. Although his job was officially entitled 'guard', and he was never expected to kill anyone, he shuddered at the actual memories: 'I was a guard for a hospital. They said they were giving the patients injections for flu, but I heard later that they were sterilising them.' There were many other war crimes, some much worse, committed while Tomaž was stationed there. Countless people died on both sides, but there were also systematic rapes and other atrocities. 'I discovered the bottom of humanity – of human beings,' he recalled.

The soldiers' living conditions were disgusting. The young men slept in tents with no floors, set up a metre underground and overrun with mice and rats. They were seven to a tent, so if one person moved, all the others were obliged to as well. Tomaž remembered, 'The rats were okay: they eat what they want and they go. But the mice – all night long they are nibbling on you.' If the mice didn't keep him awake, the incessant masturbation by another soldier did. Tomaž dug deeply for the strength to sustain him throughout this nightmare.

Hygiene was almost nonexistent. Once a month a truck would come by to hose down the soldiers. Their uniforms were filthy and they had no underwear. They lived like animals in their trenches, in unbearable heat. They were dehydrated and suffered from heat stroke, for they were limited to a litre and a half of water per day. Even this bit of liquid was sometimes contaminated by the Albanians, who frequently poisoned the wells. Tomaž's brain became addled. Throughout this time the soldiers were brainwashed into believing they were doing the most important job – saving Yugoslavia from certain destruction. Yet the Kosovo Albanians were determined to become independent, and they were willing to kill for that freedom. Naturally the young conscripted soldiers from Serbia and Slovenia were perceived as the enemy, and were confronted with a force they could never have imagined: masked fighters destroying property, raping and killing.

At the same time, Tomaž observed corruption from within: senior officers buying cheap equipment and kitchen appliances on the black market and shipping them north for enormous profits. The war was good business for them. He pointed out that some of these officers later became powerful members of the future Slovenian government. In the depths of his soul he knew that this was wrong. But he was caught, and he could see no escape route.

After months of this hell, Tomaž's conscription period was thankfully drawing to its conclusion, so he approached his officer about returning home. The officer simply laughed in his face, taunted him and told him that he would be there for life. With a loaded Kalashnikov in his hand, Tomaž's immersion in violence was such that his first instinct was to kill the man. But some basic sense of morality took over and he held back, for he came from a religious, upright family that held a high regard for decency and respect for human life.

Despite his self-restraint, the preceding months had changed him, and there was a new, aggressive side to his personality that screamed for justice. The next day, while gathering water for the other soldiers, Tomaž ordered the driver to take him to General Pilič, the most important general in the Kosovo arena. He walked up to the general and, without saluting, demanded to know when he could go home. After listening to his story, the general ascertained the name of Tomaž's regular commander, and then dismissed him. By the time Tomaž returned to camp, the general had met and challenged the commander as to why Tomaž had not been paid a regular soldier's salary, and more importantly, why he was not being sent back to Zagreb now that his time had been served. Tomaž had cleverly gambled on this ploy, because it was clear that the army needed fresh reinforcements in Kosovo; by sending him and his fellow soldiers back to Zagreb, they would be forced to bring in some fresh blood.

Everyone in the battalion knew that their next assignment was an army training camp in the searing Macedonian desert. As they prepared to go, Tomaž boldly refused to participate. But his boldness masked his true feelings: he was like a ghost – invisible. He felt helpless. There was nobody back in Zagreb to contact and he could not call his family. As the soldiers prepared to board the train that would transport them to the desert, Tomaž saw his chance and ran.

It was an impossible situation. As an armed, defecting Slovenian soldier, he was now wanted within the army as well as outside. Either way, he was a dead man. The last person he wanted to face was a masked, trigger-happy Albanian. So instead of fleeing completely, he jumped into a huge rubbish-hole at the edge of the camp and hid there in the heat. Finally, at the end of the day, he was discovered. Covered in reeking, rotten garbage, he climbed out of the hole, marched up to his commander and again demanded to be sent home. The commander yelled at him, threw him into the train, and sent him to a detention camp in Macedonia. There, in the desert, his superiors continued the brainwashing process, and limited his water supply. They certainly didn't want this young soldier to return to Zagreb and report what he had seen and experienced.

Suffering severe sunstroke, Tomaž was in a serious condition. Desperate, he tried to escape by swimming down the Vardar river. By now dangerously dehydrated, he drank the disgusting, contaminated water and became even sicker. Finally the battalion's stint in the desert was done and they were taken by train back to camp. There, Tomaž was instructed to gather his few belongings in a pack and one of the other soldiers was ordered to take him by jeep and dump him in the streets of Podujevo – in other words, dispose of him. This they did. He had neither food nor money and his machine gun was empty.

Tomaž looked like a monster, clad in filthy, rank-smelling, mouldy and tattered combat gear, wild-eyed, and holding a Kalashnikov, albeit an empty one. In a few minutes a small group of local Albanians approached him and asked who he was and what he was doing. Their gentle curiosity was a welcome surprise, for they could justifiably have been much more aggressive with him, considering his armed appearance. But his fair complexion may have saved him. They soon learned that he was from Slovenia – a place far to the north and perhaps not as hostile as nearby Serbia. One of the men could see that he was hungry and he offered him some food. Then, by a miraculous coincidence, one of the Albanians mentioned that his brother worked in a factory near Tomaž's home. In that single moment a very real and human connection was created between the two individuals, despite the cultural chasm.

The Albanian man drove Tomaž to the Kosovo Polje train station, where the ticket-seller took one startled look at him and blurted, 'Where do you come from?' Tomaž answered, 'I am coming from hell – Kosovo. I want to go home. I want to go and I have no money.' She said, 'I don't know what they did with you but you look horrible.' With that, she gave him two train tickets and a small amount of money for food. The express train from Greece soon arrived and he boarded. Stunned, he realised that he was heading north, and home.

In Zagreb, he immediately went to his army base, where he called home. Without giving too many details, he asked his father to come to Zagreb and retrieve him. But he was not yet finished with the army, for he had some things to say to his superiors. He exploded recklessly in anger: 'Nobody cared about us down there. You just left us. I know that civil law cannot touch the army but there is also a law within the army. Everybody is supposed to get a small salary. We had nothing. You will all go to court – I promise.' Their first reaction was horror: 'What are you doing here? What is your position? Why don't you salute us? Why do you look the way you do?' Tomaž swore and left. The following day, his father and brother arrived to collect what remained of him.

Tomaž returned home less a person than an animal. He could relate to no one. 'I came from the Macedonian desert and I went up to the mountains, staying in caves. I came down from time to time to empty the refrigerator and then I went back. I weighed only 63 kilos.' He had left his family a relatively polite young man, raised in a proper home with good manners and all the traditional signs of a religious upbringing. His experiences in Kosovo shattered any belief in the goodness of humanity. He returned aggressive, crude, suspicious, impolite and hungry. He was almost certainly suffering from post-traumatic stress syndrome.

A few months later, an officer in the Territorial Defence Forces returned to Slovenia to assume a position of power. He called Tomaž and offered him a job within the civil protection unit, possibly trying to buy his silence. Tomaž said no. The commander then asked if he could do anything for Tomaž. Tomaž answered that he wanted an assurance that his son would never have to endure what he had. This man, who must remain anonymous because of his current position within the Slovenian government, did the necessary paperwork, and pulled Tomaž's name from the files so that neither he nor his progeny would ever need to serve in the army again.

Meanwhile, the bickering between Belgrade and the regions continued, and by the autumn, Croatia had sidled up a little closer to Slovenia, supporting its plan for independence in anticipation of its own bid. On 27 September, Slovenia declared itself a sovereign state, though still within the federation of Yugoslavia. Kučan immediately changed the name of the communist party to the Democratic Reform Party.

Belgrade responded quickly with a series of economic cuts targeted at Slovenian industries, as well as sanctions on Slovenian goods coming into Serbia. But the final showdown would not take place until January of 1990, when, at a party congress meeting in Belgrade, Slovenia walked out in disgust, the Croats not far behind. It appeared that the Yugoslavian nation was coming apart at the seams.

Free elections in Slovenia soon followed, the first of the six republics to hold them. This sent a clear signal that Slovenia was ready to move bravely ahead towards a positive democratic transformation. Kučan won handily, becoming Slovenia's first president. As Milošević had promised, the army wasted no time in responding. It immediately sent in troops to confiscate the weapons that the Slovene Territorial Defence forces (TO) had been systematically accumulating. The troops were initially quite successful, and the TO was relieved of much of its weaponry, but Kučan soon initiated a clandestine strategy to import arms from outside the country. Soon the TO had grown to a force of 70,000 well-armed men with everything from

simple rifles to sophisticated anti-tank weapons. The nation declared itself
armed and ready to defend its new democratic status.

Although he was obviously irritated, Milošević made it clear that Serbia
would not try to prevent Slovenia's secession from Yugoslavia because
there were virtually no Serbs living within the Slovenian territory. But this
was not the case in Croatia, and by the spring of 1991, blood had been spilt
by both Croats and Serbs in neighbouring Croatia. This only strengthened
Slovenia's determination to move even further towards complete
independence.

On 25 June 1991, Slovenia declared itself independent. It was well
prepared for secession, with a strategy in place to assume responsibility
for control of its borders, its air traffic and its port authorities. The nation
was given 24 hours' notice by Belgrade that the JNA had been ordered
to prevent its secession. The specific origin of the order was vague:
nobody wanted to take responsibility. Nevertheless, by 26 June, a force
of 2,000 JNA troops was deployed to Slovenia. The Slovenians regarded
this an act of invasion, and in a late-night meeting, Kučan and his senior
advisers agreed to retaliate. Yugoslavia had finally plunged into outright
war.

The first casualties occurred on the 27th, when Slovene forces shot down
a JNA helicopter over Ljubljana, killing both the pilot and the mechanic on
board. By the 30th, Serbia had withdrawn its support for the JNA's attempt
to hold Yugoslavia together. Soon afterwards the JNA recalled its troops.
During the ten days of war, 44 JNA soldiers were killed, while casualties
on the Slovene side came to only eighteen. The war was over and Slovenia
was free to create its own destiny, move closer to the European Union and
distance itself from its socialist past.

Not everyone felt this was a good strategy, for most Slovenian citizens
had fond memories of the socialist system under Tito: there had been no
unemployment, for instance; either you were a student, or you worked.
Looking back at this time, Tomaž insisted that in many ways socialism was
better for most citizens: 'We belonged to each other,' he said. He compared
those days to the current high rates of inflation, the growing gap between
the rich and poor and the rampant crime. He acknowledged the benefits of
the new government, but pointed out the difficult challenge for a small
nation with only a limited number of people with the experience to actually
run a country. Many of these individuals, he added, were transported from
the previous regime, simply clothed in different colours. Some even came

from the Kosovo mission. 'Every government cuts bread first of all for themselves,' he added.

'We belonged to each other' was a slogan of the past. 'Each man for himself' was the mantra of the future. This mentality gradually affected the climbing club system, as well as the philosophy of individual climbers.

Eventually, following the war in Kosovo, Tomaž was forced to return to the practicalities of life. He studied electronics at university and, in order to earn money, he painted electrical towers and church steeples; he washed floors; he cleaned gutters. He worked twelve hours a day.

When he wasn't working, he climbed – like someone possessed. He became surrounded by a kind of aura, as if he were singled out to be a climber. During this time he often went to the crags alone, on-sighting routes that were, frankly, death routes. It was a very risky period for him, and yet he somehow managed to survive it. Kosovo had given him a much higher tolerance for suffering, for risk and even death. It was through climbing that he expressed that heightened tolerance. 'I did some crazy things in those times,' he admitted. He began speaking about death with unbearable ease: 'Life takes on real meaning only with [the presence of] death. When I am soloing, when I feel the breath of death, when only a moment separates me from leaving, I feel the most alive. Animalistic and alive.' When he soloed, life welled up in him, filling him with a feeling of happiness, and increasingly with a sense of indestructibility. The more encounters with the breath of death he had, the stronger he felt. His antics at first impressed other young climbers, but after a while his behaviour began to irritate them. He was soloing routes that they couldn't climb. And he was vocal about it. He ignored all the rules. He scoffed at their efforts and disregarded the club rules even more flagrantly. 'If you want rules, go to the office,' he taunted.

In Tomaž's quiet moments, he would fondle two precious possessions, two mementos from Kosovo: the dog tag that had encircled his neck and the train tickets given him by the woman at the station. These were his tickets home – tickets from hell to life.

CHAPTER FOUR

SERGEJA

12 July 2005, 14.00, Nanga Parbat, Rupal Face

'Is anybody alive?' Stipe screams into the radio. The air is saturated with rain and the mountain is choked with a thick layer of fog. It is afternoon and there has been no contact with Tomaž and Aleš since yesterday. Stipe had accompanied them as far as the Koreans' advanced base camp on 11 July, but after a night of steady rain, he had descended to base camp. Even now, every piece of his clothing remains waterlogged. Stipe is worried. He senses that it's too early in the season for this face. He has voiced his concerns, but Tomaž thinks the face might be safer with a lot of snow. Nataša agrees with Stipe that the mountain does not seem friendly.

13 July, 08.00

Finally, on the morning of the 13th, Tomaž radioes in from 5,280 metres: 'It feels like we are in a submarine.' While repairing their tent and squeezing the water from their sleeping bags, a rock avalanche releases above them. Luckily, the volley of boulders somehow misses them. They receive a radio message from the Korean team that two climbers are setting off for the summit. Unfortunately for Aleš and Tomaž, there are two other Korean climbers who will be occupying the next camp at 6,000 metres while they await the summit team's return. Therefore the camp will not be vacant for Tomaž and Aleš to use. Additionally, they learn that the camp is buried under a huge dump of new snow.

Completely blindfolded by the dense fog, they grope their way up the mountain. They finally reach Camp II and, thankfully, discover one tent that is still serviceable. Not only a tent; they also uncover some Korean food, along with spoons and chopsticks. They settle in, chewing happily on dried fish, and are in a surprisingly good mood when they radio in to base camp. Tomaž then proceeds to break his tooth on the dried fish and declares that 'Two things fell out of place in my life: my teeth and my hair!' Base camp is encouraged, for it appears that despite the appalling conditions on the mountain, he remains upbeat.

14 July 08.00

The morning of the 14th dawns with a radiant beauty, a rosy hue slowly dissolving into true golden sunrise. Maja glances up at the mountain and can hardly believe her eyes. The entire mountain is clear except for one spot: the area where Tomaž and Aleš are camped. A tower of cloud hovers over them. Nataša comes out of her tent, scans the mountain, nods, and announces her theory of what is happening on the mountain: 'They have not switched in their heads yet.' Shortly afterwards, the climbers radio in. 'God bless you, the sun is shining on you,' Tomaž says, adding that they are completely soaked and numb from the cold. They have been in the clouds for days now and it is once again raining on them.

They have been digging the tent out for nearly two hours now. As Aleš digs above the tent, snow sloughs slide back in almost immediately. Since they have no shovel, he is forced to use his hands and his ice axe. As a result, his gloves are completely waterlogged. Tomaž, in the meantime, appears to be living a life of leisure, carving toothpicks out of the chopsticks to serve as toothbrushes. Later, lying in their saturated sleeping bags, they wear their soaked clothing directly against their bodies, attempting to dry it.

As afternoon fades into evening, the climbers ask base camp for some motivating music. Anda, Nataša and Maja choose songs to play over the radio, but with only 58 batteries remaining, Anda is concerned that they should conserve them. There is still a lot of climbing to be done, and much of it will be done by Tomaž as he heads up on the wall alone. 'He will really need music then,' Anda cautions her base camp colleagues.

14 July 19.00

Tomorrow is supposed to be the highest elevation of the acclimatisation climb. The weather forecast is predicting a dry spell and their plan is to begin at 3.00 a.m. The Koreans have radioed that they have left Camp III in order to establish one higher camp before their final summit attempt. This change in plan is due to the extraordinarily deep snow and the exhausting trail-breaking that will be required in order to reach the summit. This means that Tomaž and Aleš will need to climb 1,000 vertical metres to reach the next camp. Then, having reached a height of around 7,000 metres, they will descend all the way to base camp over a period of two days. But depending on the snow conditions, they may not be able to progress that far. If not, they will be forced to bivouac below 7,000 metres. If all goes well, this will allow them a few days to rest in base camp before Tomaž's solo climb, which is scheduled to begin on 24 July. Stipe is increasingly concerned about the optimistic schedule. Plans are one thing. Reality is something else.

15 July 08.00

Tomaž and Aleš are buried under two metres of new snow and have slept through their alarm. It takes them two hours to dig themselves out. Tomaž radios in shortly after 8.00 a.m. to report that the entire wall is plastered with new snow. They are in the clouds at 6,380 metres, but the limited visibility awards them glimpses of the rest of the mountain, which is completely bathed in sunshine. Base camp too is basking in the sun.

15 July 09.50

Tomaž radioes that they are climbing again and are now at 6,450 metres. It is snowing lightly, and looming above them is a huge overhanging ice serac, which is constantly shedding small avalanches. Snow surges towards them and then splits, bursting like a wave of seawater. These avalanches are worrisome, but their greatest fear is that the entire serac could cut loose at any time. 'If it releases above us it will take us down with it,' Tomaž warns, with obvious tension in his voice. Base camp hears the news and immediately becomes focused on the radio, monitoring the climbers as well as the weather forecast. They are frustrated because the forecast had predicted only 40 per cent humidity and yet on the mountain it is at least 80 per cent. It seems that a cloud of moisture is following the climbing team up the face. Nataša scrutinises the mountain closely and reports vibrant hues of green and red in the vicinity of the climbers. The others in base camp are curious about her pronouncements, although they don't completely understand them. 'This means anger and danger,' explains Nataša, adding that 'It is obvious that they have not become one with her yet.'

Perhaps not, but the Koreans apparently have, for two of them have radioed a message that they have reached the summit the night before, successfully completing the second ascent of the Messner route, 35 years after the first. But it has not been without a Herculean effort. The climbers have been breaking trail nonstop for 24 hours from their fourth camp to the top. Now they have successfully descended to base camp.

15 July 11.50

The climbers radio in from 6,800 metres. They have progressed beyond the overhanging serac and are in an extremely dense, murky fog. They can see nothing, and are lost. They hope that they are climbing in the general direction of the Koreans' fixed lines but they're not certain, for it is impossible to excavate the lines from under the metre-thick blanket of fresh snow. Avalanches are sliding down around them constantly.

They finally discover Camp III by stumbling upon a broken tent pole protruding from the snow. Their radio report is worrying: 'We cannot go up or down. We cannot see enough to go on and there are no fixed lines.' Because everything, including the tents, is buried, they have no alternative but to dig a hole in the snow for an emergency bivouac. And because they were intending to use the equipment in the Korean tents, they will not have any sleeping bags.

The climbers spend all their time digging, digging, digging. As fast as they dig, new snow fills the vacuum. Tomaž digs for a time, while Aleš stands guard, watching for avalanches. At one point an unseen slide descends upon them and almost sweeps them off the mountain. Tomaž explodes in anger: 'Aleš, why didn't you warn me?' Aleš replies, 'I cannot see a thing, so how can I possibly predict an avalanche?' 'It's not necessary to see an approaching avalanche,' Tomaž explains. 'You must listen for them.' They switch roles, Aleš now doing the digging and Tomaž standing by to warn of avalanches. When the next one comes crashing over them, they both dive head first into their snow hole.

15 July 18.00

It's time for Maja to send in a media report, so she radioes up to the bivouac site: 'How are you?' Tomaž replies in a surprisingly curt manner: 'Not the best . . . we are not good. We can go nowhere, and we are soaking wet. It's avalanching on us and it's cold.' Maja presses for more. 'Is it snowing all the time?' 'All the time. We were avalanched in Camp I, now in Camp III.' He continues with some disparaging comments about the weatherman's lack of accuracy. Maja senses his annoyance and fear. She hesitates, but she desperately needs a statement from Tomaž for the media. The radio station has already called her three times, demanding some news. Finally she asks Tomaž for a few words. He responds angrily: 'We are on the edge, on the edge. Really not a time for joking at all!'

It is difficult to report objectively in a situation such as this. The media is naturally most interested in what's happening on the mountain when things get bad. The situation is now, clearly, bad. Maja's responsibility on this trip is as a journalist, so she puts her feelings of concern aside and asks again for a statement. This time Tomaž is more cooperative, holding his anger in abeyance and providing Maja with what she needs. As he recounts the events of the day and evening, she records every word on her portable Dictaphone: 'We were digging like mad. Now we can hardly move, it is so cramped in here we cannot even change our clothing.' She has what she needs for the radio and television stations. Anda advises the climbers to drink as much as possible as well as to keep moving in order to avoid frostbite. Aleš and Tomaž take her advice, massaging each other to keep their circulation going.

Then an email arrives from the weather forecaster, predicting a clearing pattern. Base camp is momentarily cheered up, but when they check in with the climbers, it is still snowing steadily on the mountain. Now it is dark, and the entire valley is covered with clouds. The temperatures drop. At base camp, the rain continues.

As the evening wears on, Tomaž announces to base camp that in their digging they have discovered something really useful – toilet paper. They are stuffing this valuable item into their clothing in order to absorb some of the moisture. They have also discovered a Thermarest and are apparently comfortably perched upon it inside their bivouac hole. Anda urges them to continue brewing tea, and above all to remain awake. Anda, Nataša and Maja stay up all night talking to the climbers, playing them music and singing. Anda is the DJ: 'Night programme from base camp: any requests?'

That night, the stars are brilliant: millions upon millions of glowing orbs in the black night sky. The mountain is clear except for the Messner route, which is still blanketed in cloud. The scientists are predicting sunshine every day, yet the route remains shrouded. Tomorrow, always tomorrow.

16 July 07.00

Morning dawns slowly, the sun brushing the mountain with its fiery hue. Avalanches rumble ominously as the sun warms the new layer of snow. Aleš and Tomaž make the most of this brief break in the weather, descending as quickly as they safely can. They have 3,300 metres of descent in front of them, all of it in extremely dangerous conditions. Stipe radioes in from advanced base camp at 10.00: 'I can see them. They are approaching Camp I.' By the end of the day, they are safely back at base camp.

Tomaž's first act is to go to the chorten, where he prays for half an hour, while Aleš heads directly to the icy waters of a nearby creek for a much-needed bath. His face is badly burned and his nose is scabbing, so Anda ministers to him, giving him fish grease for the burns and urging him to drink endless cups of tea. Tomaž, having finished his prayers, returns to the group. 'Anda, please can you make me a strong cup of Turkish brew.' Both climbers are offered buckets of hot water to treat themselves after their week on the mountain. Then it's time to eat. 'We need meat!' Tomaž declares, before cracking a few off-colour jokes. The rest of the team look at each other and smile. The climbers have not changed!

As they replenish themselves with food and drink, Tomaž and Aleš eagerly recount their experiences on the mountain. 'We could have died in that snow hole. When one of the avalanches came, the stove stopped working, but it was still leaking gas,' Tomaž explains, gesticulating wildly. Aleš reiterates the seriousness of the situation: 'We only had a few minutes before becoming asphyxiated. We had to react quickly.' They joke about their original plan, in which Tomaž had instructed Aleš to bring three days' worth of food and gear. Aleš had a hunch that this might not be sufficient. He has climbed with Tomaž for the past two years and knows his pattern quite well. 'I prefer to take food for five days,' he responded. Tomaž answered, 'Well, if you think so, then take enough for a week.'

They were on the mountain for eight days.

While Tomaž and Aleš celebrate, the more experienced Stipe frets. He knows that Tomaž acclimatizes quickly, but doesn't think eight days is enough to prepare for his solo attempt. 'The acclimatisation was not good because of the conditions on the mountain. They were too low . . . in very bad conditions.' But Stipe is alone with his worries, and the others continue to celebrate.

Sergeja, 1990

When Tomaž returned home from Kosovo in 1990, he was a changed person. He found it increasingly difficult to relate to his family, for their life experiences pulled them further and further apart. His relationship with his father, Max, was particularly difficult during this time.

Despite their ability to work together, Tomaž and his father soon began to quarrel. Max was stubborn. So was Tomaž. Max desperately wanted his eldest to be a 'normal guy', but Tomaž was becoming a free spirit. Despite the calming efforts of his mother, eventually their conversations deteriorated into arguments, then shouting matches. Father and son began to avoid each other, except when they were working together. It was easier that way.

Tomaž escaped this domestic strife by fleeing to the forests and the mountains as often as he could. Almost always, he climbed. During this time he became increasingly bold, soloing routes that many referred to as 'sick'. He remained a member of the Kamnik club, which would meet each Thursday evening to discuss their climbing activities of the previous week, as well as their intentions for the upcoming weekend.

It was during this time that Tomaž began making waves within the club, climbing in a style that was not condoned by the club elders, and stirring envy and jealousy amongst his fellow climbers. One such incident involved a difficult rock climb that he soloed in front of fellow club member Marko Prezelj. It was rated at 6c+ in the French grading system – considered very difficult at the time. Prezelj was somewhat impressed, but he pointed out that Tomaž's style had not been the best. The seeds of competition were seemingly planted, although both climbers vehemently denied this.

Soon afterwards, Tomaž climbed another controversial solo above Kamnik in an area called Stari Grad. He had never previously succeeded in climbing 'Lover overhang', and now he was determined to solo it. This was an unorthodox and highly dangerous undertaking, for if he could not climb it *with* a rope, what could he be thinking, attempting to climb it *without* one? But he felt confident, experiencing one of those spiritual, connected-to-the-landscape moments when all the gods had lined up just for him. He simply felt 'ready'. And he climbed it – solo. Convinced that nobody would believe him, he brought a friend, Danilo Golob, to accompany him the following day so that he could climb it again while Danilo documented the climb with his camera. That evening was Holy Thursday and all the climbers were there, including Prezelj. Looking back, Tomaž felt that this was possibly the beginning of a shift in his friendship with Prezelj. Aficionados called the route 'sick' for a reason. When his previous teacher, Bojan Pollack, learned about the solo climb, he was disapproving but he simply advised Tomaž: 'Please be careful when these things become too easy for you.' Within the Kamnik club, the bar had been raised.

Danilo Golob was a fellow club member and frequent climbing partner of Tomaž. One winter afternoon, he and Tomaž arrived back at Danilo's car, hungry, cold and ecstatic, having just climbed another dangerous and committing winter ice route. Yet after this glorious day in the mountains, Tomaž suddenly became strangely glum. Danilo asked what the problem was. Tomaž explained that he dreaded going home to certain harassment by his parents, who thoroughly, and vocally, disapproved of his passion for climbing. He was loath to lose the magic of the day. No problem, said Danilo, inviting Tomaž home with him. He was living with his girlfriend, a nineteen-year-old girl named Sergeja Jersin, and there would almost certainly be a hot meal waiting. It was an innocent invitation and an equally innocent acceptance. But that evening was a turning point for all of them. Sergeja saw a young, intelligent man with an enormous amount of energy, and said, 'I felt different from him and yet at the same time very similar in a deeper sense.' Tomaž recalled that first meeting with Sergeja: 'When she served me mashed potatoes, green salad and meat, I fell in love. I didn't fall in love with her, but I fell in love with the situation. You come home and it's warm. Somebody with a warm heart is there, waiting – everything that

I needed in my life.' Despite the overwhelming impression she made on Tomaž, they did not see each other again for several months. Meanwhile, he and Danilo continued climbing together.

The next time Sergeja and Tomaž met was 1 May 1990, a traditional time for Kamnik climbers to head south to the coastal climbing area of Paklenica, an ideal training ground. One of the advantages of Paklenica was its much warmer climate. There they could begin their climbing season a month earlier than in the Kamnik Alps. It was also economical, since there was ample space along the extensive beaches to camp, and food was inexpensive and delicious, particularly the fresh fish caught each day. A poor and neglected area, Paklenica boasted spectacular rock walls. Just a short distance from the coast, a narrow winding road led across sandy fields, through the tiny war-ravaged village of Starigrad, and up into an intriguing canyon. Even at the canyon's mouth, one could sense what lay beyond: mile after mile of perfect grey limestone walls. But it was only after exploring further up the ravine that the full extent of the landscape revealed itself, with vertical and overhanging walls rearing up from 30 to 350 metres. Huge erosional features – pockets and scoops and great sweeps of limestone – had created a climbing paradise.

It was to this paradise that Tomaž and his climbing friends journeyed at the beginning of May. They travelled as a group, crammed into the few cars that existed amongst them. Included were Prezelj and his girlfriend, as well as Danilo and Sergeja. Tomaž didn't have a girlfriend – or a car – so he tagged along with the others. It was a high-spirited and close-knit tribe that enjoyed the warm evenings, splendid food, challenging climbing and easy living. They talked late into the night around their campfires, reliving the individual moves of each of their climbs that day.

On their only day of rain, the normally somewhat shy Sergeja approached Tomaž and recounted her previous night's dream, in which they were together – in China. Very strange, thought Tomaž. He was certainly attracted to Sergeja, but had been unaware that the feeling might possibly be mutual. Sergeja recalled, 'From the moment I first saw him I knew that we had a lot of unfinished business from our previous lives. Something was pulling us together and apart at the same time.' Tomaž knew she was forbidden fruit, yet she had inadvertently become his muse. He began to feel an almost exquisite physical pain whenever he was near her. Their mutual interest was obvious to the others in the group, and some even commented on the magnetic tension, but Danilo was thankfully oblivious.

Back in Kamnik, the tight group of climbers continued meeting frequently in a local tearoom. Sergeja was often among them. A natural raconteur, Tomaž would entertain them with his stories of bold climbs and his disrespect for the club rules and authority in general. Sergeja was increasingly intrigued by this strange young man: angry at times, yet joyful and exuberant and so full of energy. She later recalled, 'He could be very funny at times and always did something stupid, always. I think this is still true today. Although he is slowly, very slowly, becoming softer – calmer.'

It was during this period that Tomaž became more intrigued, not only with the idea of a warm meal and a warm heart waiting for him at the end of the day, but with Sergeja herself. As he recalled, 'You cannot force your heart. It happened.' Later he would always refer to Sergeja as his first love. But it wasn't just Tomaž who was interested; Sergeja was increasingly captivated with him, too. And in the middle was Danilo.

Tomaž was still living with his parents during this time, and there was a great deal of tension, especially with his father. One point of strife between the two concerned a car. While Tomaž was still serving in the army, his parents had sent him a letter promising one if only he would come home and settle down. He had always been such a good student, they recalled, and he had only recently become so difficult and wild. They knew that a car would motivate him, because more than anything Tomaž valued freedom. A car would offer him that.

Imagine his delight when, shortly after his return from that hellish period in Kosovo, he came home from a day of climbing to discover the promised Yugo in the driveway. Initially surprised and elated at the prospect of owning a car, he soon learned that it was for Marjan, his younger brother. But his parents assured him that this would not be a problem, for they could share the vehicle. Tomaž didn't accept this solution and challenged them: how exactly would this work? They reiterated that the two could simply share it. Tomaž knew there was no practical way for that to happen, and he became bitter and angry about what he felt was a broken promise.

Then, in the autumn of 1991, the year of Slovenia's independence, Tomaž was invited to join a Serbian expedition heading to the Caucasus Mountains in Russia. His parents were firmly against it: the expedition was too dangerous; it was a useless thing to do; he would die. Tomaž was desperate to go, partially because he wanted to climb a 7,000-metre peak, but even more because he wanted to escape the stultifying atmosphere at home. He wanted out. Unfortunately he had neither the requisite equipment nor money. He solved the equipment problem by borrowing an ice axe from one friend and a set of crampons from another. But he needed 1,500 Deutschmarks to do the trip, and no matter how hard he worked and saved, he could not reach that magical number.

Saturday was his deadline for amassing the required amount, and when the day arrived, he didn't have it. Disappointed, he decided that he needed to see two people: his climbing friend Tomo Drolec, and his forbidden muse Sergeja. He stomped downstairs at his parents' house and phoned Tomo to go climbing. Tomo had already left, so Tomaž decided to drive towards his home and meet him halfway. After informing his brother, he took the car that they jointly owned and drove off. It was a blustery, rainy day and the roads were slick. Still frustrated and angry from his huge disappointment, Tomaž paid no attention to the conditions. Driving at full speed on bald tyres, he quickly gained on a bus as it approached a tight curve. The bus slowed down; Tomaž slammed on his brakes and immediately became airborne. After flipping over a couple of times, he ended up in a ditch, on his roof, suspended between two huge iron tubes abandoned from an old irrigation project. He managed to squeeze out through his open window and escape with just a few bruises and scrapes on one leg. Tomo, who had been coming to meet him, had seen the entire accident take place. Without calling the police, for he knew that Tomaž had no insurance, he bundled him up and took him home. Now Tomaž would have to face the wrath of his family.

Tomaž remembers the scene in the family kitchen with clarity. 'I came home and said, "It's done. It can't be fixed. You can kill me – or whatever."' It's true that he would not have been able to repair the car, for it was completely destroyed. The Yugo was worth 7,000 Deutschmarks and the only solution was to replace it. But Tomaž could not even find the 1,500 DM that he needed for the Caucasus expedition, so he certainly wouldn't be able to come up with an additional 5,500. His parents were strangely silent. Tomaž looked down at the kitchen table. There sat an envelope addressed to him. He opened it and inside found 1,500 DM. His parents had changed their minds the night before and had offered him his ticket to freedom, but in his rage and impatience that morning he had not bothered to look. He had stormed out of the house and missed his chance.

Aghast, Tomaž left the room and once again fled, this time as much in regret as in rage. He escaped to the only place he could – the mountains. He and Tomo spent the day climbing, and that evening when he returned home he knew he would finally have to face up to his actions. He was right. He entered the house and there, waiting for him, were his parents and his brother, co-owner of the Yugo. Nobody said a word. Tomaž began with a promise to earn the money to replace the car. He didn't know how he would do it, but he swore he would try. His parents' response was disheartening. They demanded to know why he had done this to them. They accused him of destroying their hard work. They told him that he was essentially worthless – all he was capable of doing was getting into trouble. He finally exploded: 'What did I do? Okay, I crashed a car, but I am alive. Is that not more important?' Their stony-faced reaction provided the answer. He shook his head and once again stormed out.

Tomaž knew that he was now really trapped. Not only would he not be going to the Caucasus; he would need to remain at home in order to save money and would have to work nonstop in order to try and pay his family back for the car. There would be no time for romantic fantasies about Sergeja, and very little time for climbing.

He went to the electronics factory where he worked as an apprentice and begged to work extended hours. This was not exactly legal, for as an apprentice he needed to be accompanied at all times by a more senior person – a mentor. But they reluctantly agreed to an arrangement allowing him to work 16-hour days at the factory. By working double shifts, he could accumulate enough hours to take every second week off. But not for climbing. By combining that second work week with weekends at either end, he could piece together a nine-day block of time for his other job – painting towers. He was actually earning quite a lot of money now, but his problem was inflation. The Slovenian economy was crashing, and inflation was rampant at around 20 per cent. As fast as he could make the money, it became devalued. He was in a nightmarish spiral from which, at times, he was convinced he would never escape. Nevertheless, all that hard work did pay off, for by the end of the autumn he had saved enough to pay his family back and purchase his own second-hand Yugo. During these months of enforced labour, he did not see Sergeja once.

By early winter, the tower-painting jobs were no longer available, since this type of work was too dangerous in the cold, icy conditions. Once again he had some time to climb, and occasionally began seeing his friend Danilo – and, of course, Sergeja. That winter, Tomaž began paragliding.

On 19 January, Danilo, Tomo, Sergeja and Tomaž made a plan. Three of them would go paragliding, while Danilo would do a back-country ski tour where he would attach climbing skins to his skis to ascend the slopes and then remove them for the run down. After his tour near Grintovec, at 2,558 metres, the highest peak in the Kamnik Alps, Danilo would join up with the others to have a go at paragliding, a sport he had not yet tried. They agreed to meet at 2.00 p.m.

The three finished paragliding and waited for Danilo. 2.00 p.m. arrived and he did not appear. 3.00 p.m. came and went, and still there was no Danilo. This seemed strange, because he was usually very punctual. At 5.00 p.m. he had still not appeared, so Tomaž went home and had a shower. At 7.00 he received a concerned call from Sergeja and Tomo: Danilo had still not arrived. Now they began to worry seriously, so they hopped in Tomaž's Yugo and headed off on the icy winter roads to find Danilo. They drove to where they thought he would have parked for his ski tour, and sure enough, there was his car – another Yugo. Tomaž peered into the car with his headlamp, and to his surprise, Danilo's skis were inside. He deduced that Danilo must have finished the tour earlier than expected and then gone off to do something else – probably climb one of the many ice falls in the area. But which one? Next, they called Tomaž's former climbing instructor, Bojan Pollack, who was also leader of the mountain rescue team in which they all participated. By now the group of friends was distraught and wanted to initiate an immediate search for Danilo. Pollack tried to calm them down, pointing out that a night rescue was out of the question. They would search for him first thing in the morning. The friends wanted action now, so they drove back to Pollack's house and told him what they had seen, begging him to join them in order to at least locate the ice fall. Danilo might have fallen and could be injured. The temperature was plummeting and Tomaž was concerned that his friend might not survive the night. They returned to Danilo's car, parked, donned their winter clothes and head-lamps and headed up in the dark while Sergeja waited below. At 11.00 p.m. they found the ice fall – and Danilo. He had obviously been climbing solo and had fallen about 25 or 30 metres. As the ice was very thin and brittle, they surmised that he had broken through and fallen tragically to his death.

In a state of shock, Tomaž and Pollack stayed with Danilo's broken body while Tomo returned to Sergeja. They summoned the rescue team, which arrived an hour later to help carry Danilo down to the road. Tomo had obviously not been completely truthful with Sergeja, because when they came back to the car, she was under the impression that Danilo was only hurt, not dead. Finally, in grief and shock, she was forced to face the truth that her partner had died in the mountains he had so dearly loved. It was an emotional moment for each member of the rescue team. Danilo was not just another body recovered from the mountains; he was one of their tribe.

Sergeja was soon forced to leave the apartment that she had shared with Danilo, since it had not been hers. During this time of sorrow and anguish, she received little support from her family, for her father had long since left them and she seldom spoke to her mother. As a result of her isolation, she counted on Danilo's climbing friends for support, and the person on whom she relied most heavily was Tomaž. 'We were together like salt and butter,' Tomaž explained. The simmering attraction, which had been suppressed for months, now flourished in their mutual grief over Danilo's death.

After an intense few months as lovers, Tomaž and Sergeja were married on 7 December; Tomaž was twenty-two years old and Sergeja only twenty-one. Since she had not been raised in a religious home, she was baptised and received all sacraments just prior to their marriage so that they could be wed in church, something that was very important to Tomaž and his family. From the beginning, they both believed that their marriage was sacrosanct, immune to external pressures or difficulties. They had no money; they were in debt; but they had each other. They felt that together they could do anything. As Tomaž recalled, 'My concept of marriage was for life.'

After a difficult pregnancy, and an even more difficult birth, their daughter Urša was born shortly afterwards, on 13 February 1992. Immediately after giving birth, Sergeja began bleeding uncontrollably. Urša also appeared quite ill, for she soon turned a deep shade of yellow. The doctor gave them encouraging words, but despite his confidence Urša was not a healthy infant and spent the next two weeks in intensive care. Sergeja's bleeding was eventually brought under control and Urša gradually improved, but in the process Sergeja's milk dried up. The only solution was to buy a formula to feed their delicate child, an unexpected expense that severely impacted on Tomaž's meagre salary. Nevertheless, Urša was fed the best German formula mix that money could buy. Tomaž stopped climbing for a year and a half during this period, for his main priority was working to support his little family. Any dreams that he might have harboured about expeditions to distant mountain ranges were set aside – forever, he thought. 'The Himalayas were out of the question. I had responsibilities. I had to fill the car with gas – feed the family.'

Their life was focused on each other, on Urša and on survival. 'Bills, bills, bills. It was a survival story because I was too proud to ask or to beg from my parents.' The young family lived upstairs in Tomaž's parents' home, but Max and Rosalija were never aware of just how strained their finances were. The topic was strictly off limits. Despite the financial strain, Tomaž and Sergeja's relationship was strong and full of joy – impenetrable. Looking back at this time, Tomaž's memories are painfully poignant: 'What we had between us, no atomic bomb could destroy. We loved each other. We were a cell.' He is convinced that it was during these early years of suffering that they were at their best. Later, when things improved economically, they let their guard down. 'When we allowed the worms to come in, like mushrooms we were finished.'

Tomaž excelled at his electronics job and was eventually offered the position of security systems project manager for a large area. This would oblige him to travel around the country, installing and checking security systems within various businesses. He was given a bigger salary and regular hours. But by now he had started climbing again, and his alpine dreams were beginning to resurface. His work occupied much of his time, and the prospect of supervising a group of staff did not attract him. In fact he had become miserable with this work. Finally, after discussing it with Sergeja and gaining her support, he decided to quit.

His father was aghast, asking him, 'Do you have a fever? Are you sick?' His parents were perfectly aware that Tomaž had family responsibilities, and yet most of his money seemed to flow directly into his climbing. As Max described it, 'He had a cash flow – straight through.' Even Tomaž's boss implored him to reconsider. Tomaž tried to explain that he couldn't be chained in this way; he needed freedom to climb. His boss pointed out that this freedom could all be his, but later in his life, perhaps when he was fifty. Tomaž exploded: 'No, at fifty your life is over! At fifty there is nothing more to do – just go to a better spa or something.'

He did indeed quit, but the bills continued to arrive and food still needed to be put on the table. Eventually he found another security systems job that paid him three times the salary. But there was a personal cost. He was forced to travel even more and was on call 24 hours a day. Every museum and factory in the country had his phone number. However, with the increased salary, the family's lifestyle improved. Tomaž was now climbing more, and at a higher level than ever. With all these external distractions, he and Sergeja saw each other less frequently. Tomaž had the mountains, but Sergeja was stuck at home. Strangely, the more money they had, the less happy they became.

It was at this time that he received an invitation to go to the Himalayas – to Ganesh V. This was his dream, but in order to go, he would need to quit his job once more. Ultimately he did, for he was willing to do whatever it took to climb in the Himalayas.

CHAPTER FIVE

GANESH V

19–31 July 2005, Nanga Parbat, Rupal Face

Tomaž and Aleš are recovering from their eight days on the Messner route. Now that they are back down in base camp, they enjoy, but are somewhat frustrated by, day after day of sunshine. Sleeping in is not an option because the sun heats their tents unbearably by seven in the morning. 'This cannot be happening,' Tomaž rants good-naturedly. 'We were rained on, snowed on, nearly avalanched off, but down here it is so lovely!' It appears to be some kind of cruel joke. But they remain in camp, for Tomaž needs to rest in order to have the energy to launch himself up on to the face. Nothing can replace rest.

For hours each day, Tomaž organises and reorganises his equipment, examining each piece, evaluating its usefulness on the wall and determining if it is absolutely required. He seems obsessed with his equipment, caressing his axes, leaning them against his mouth and breathing onto them with his eyes closed. He even sleeps with his crampons on his chest. With each passing day he becomes more isolated from the team, more focused on the wall, more self-contained. After a few more days, he feels rested and ready to begin his climb. On the 26th he announces that tomorrow is the day. Then the weather worsens, forcing a delay. By the end of July his patience has worn thin. He has a schedule, and the clock is ticking. Then he receives a message from the weather forecaster: 'Mr Humar, we think next week is your week.'

1 August

Throughout the day, Tomaž checks various weather forecasts – American,

Slovenian, Pakistani – trying to get the one that he wants. The forecasts are not bad, but they are inconsistent. The only consistent thread is a possibility of three consecutive days of good weather. The question is, when? On this particular point the forecasters do not agree. Tomaž finally decides that the good weather will probably not begin for another day. The next question is whether to start climbing on the first good day, or go immediately, saving every possible good-weather day for his time on the wall. This might be the best option. On the other hand, if the forecast is wrong and storms move in, he could be lured up on to the wall with no line of retreat. He is obsessed by this deliberation throughout the day, weighing the pros and cons of each option. While he agonises over this dilemma, he sorts his equipment once again, choosing the essential items, and not one more: a 50-metre Kevlar rope, a few short slings, a few flexible camming devices, pitons and carabiners, three ice screws, two ice axes, his crampons, a bivouac sack, an 800-gram sleeping bag, his climbing harness, camera, walkie-talkie, eight batteries, extra glasses, his helmet and his pack. For sustenance, it's very simple: a titanium stove, a cooking pot, some pasta, rice, tuna, garlic, onion, cheese, oil and sports energy bars, and a plastic bottle for the fluids that he will make by melting snow. Every ounce counts.

Early in the afternoon, having decided to leave later that day, Tomaž decides to take a nap. But rather than sleeping, he ruminates on this mountain and the feeling he has that he has been called – almost in a spiritual sense – to climb it. 'How long have this pyramid of ice and these overhanging walls been standing above the heavenly green valley? In reality, for ever. We could call it a sign on the path. It has been written to me a while ago that signs are for the chosen ones – miracles are for all the others – so that they can believe. Believe what? Themselves, the path, illusions, or just expectations of others? Who knows?'

As he considers the challenge that faces him, he reflects somewhat sceptically about his friends, as well as the public who follow his climbs. 'Great stories demand a lot. After a while one realises that to follow the philosophy of 'success at all cost', the biggest, noisiest fans and the 'friends' who are friends only until their ego is not in danger soon step aside, as well as everybody else watching from the sidelines.'

Inevitably his thoughts turn inward, to his unique and sometimes difficult relationship with the rest of the world. 'There are those who are unable to accept some who are different, or the reality that they are not what they and others have believed them to be. Who am I then – someone who is just a little more crazy, someone who dares more, or just someone who is beyond all the rules of the game in the valley, who believes in his own path of the chosen one? Time will show, will it not? Although [you are] with a group of similar souls, deep down you know you are alone, very alone. I know that the time of departure is near, but I am not in a hurry. As the anticipation and melancholy grow in the others, I become insensitive, unreadable, absent.'

While Tomaž rests, others in base camp notice some approaching backpackers. Emerging from their backpacks are tall red umbrellas. As they come nearer, Aleš recognises the American climber Steve House, together with his climbing partner Vince Anderson. The two are somewhat reluctant visitors, for House is concerned about the 'media circus' that he might encounter at Tomaž's camp and he doesn't want his head space to be cluttered. Both House and Anderson are aware of their need to concentrate on their own objective and to avoid anything that might distract them.

They soon arrive in camp and Aleš rouses Tomaž. A photo of this encounter shows House looking young, fresh, like a cowboy – ready for anything. At five foot ten and 165 pounds, he is a powerful package. His demeanour is taciturn and there is a quiet intensity in his eyes. Although he endures the nickname of 'Farm Boy' because, in the words of a climbing friend, 'he looks like he should be chewing on a stalk of straw', this man is clearly focused on the challenge at hand. Tomaž, on the other hand, looks tired, a little dishevelled, and somewhat frustrated by the many delays. The Humar team worries about Tomaž's reaction to House's arrival in camp. Tomaž seems a little surprised, for House had told him in Grenoble that he was finished with Nanga Parbat. House's chosen route is further to the left than Tomaž's but he is as passionate about this face as Tomaž, and he too is a superb climber. Only one of them can reach the top first.

Still, as Tomaž emerges from his tent, he greets the two climbers warmly, shaking their hands in his inimitable, hand-crushing fashion, then inviting them into the mess tent. House's first question is about money, when he asks Tomaž why he paid so much to the local porters. This is obviously a sore point with House, for the precedent has impacted on his extremely tight budget. They drink tea and chat for about half an hour, much of the conversation in Slovenian. House later claims to have felt a certain amount of 'testosterone and aggression' from Tomaž, despite the cordial reception. In contrast, he enjoys speaking to the more reserved Aleš, even more so with Stipe, for they have a number of mutual climbing friends about whom they exchange stories.

While in the mess tent, the climbers study the large photograph of the Rupal Face on the wall. Since House has already been quite high on the face the previous year, Tomaž asks him about details of the wall. House replies only, 'You will see.' Tomaž is genuinely surprised at his evasiveness. When questioned about his response, House later recalls that the question was about something for which he didn't know the answer. House, in turn, feels that Tomaž is vague when asked about his time frame, although Tomaž informs him that he is leaving that day. The tension is palpable.

The route that House will attempt has more exposed rock than Tomaž's – a good strategy, since House is climbing with a partner. They will undoubtedly climb more slowly than Tomaž because the pair will belay each other at times, a method used to secure a climbing partner to the wall. Belaying on solid rock is much safer and more secure than trying to belay on the questionable ice and snow conditions that they all expect to encounter on the face. Tomaž's strategy is different. Although the terrain and conditions are likely to be unstable, his plan is to move with lightning speed. This approach has worked before and he believes it will work here.

Before House leaves, Tomaž offers him three phone numbers for base camp, just to stay in touch, saying, 'Others may see us as competitors, but we don't have to be; here are my numbers.' House thanks him. As the American is leaving, Tomaž asks him for his phone number in case his team needs to contact them. House simply answers, 'I have yours.' The comment offends Tomaž, who naturally assumes that House doesn't want to be reachable by phone. Anderson later explains that they had only recently purchased their SAT phone and did not yet know the number.

House and Anderson leave for their own base camp. They have no computers, no reporters and no video cameras. The contrast in style is considerable. Months later, House will claim, 'I wanted to be as far away from that circus as possible.' Still, in a couple of weeks, an *Outside* magazine reporter will arrive in House's base camp to report on his expedition – with his permission and full cooperation.

Not long after the House team leaves, Tomaž prepares to go. He feels completely acclimatised, despite the relatively short time he has spent on the mountain. The face has dominated his sleepless nights and he is tired of being a victim to its hidden terrors. He has waited patiently for reasonable conditions since early July and the delay is eating at his nerves. It's true that the weather is not ideal at the moment, but there is a three-day window of good weather predicted. He needs just four.

A dense cloud hovers over the mountain and a light wind blows as Tomaž adjusts his pack for the last time. It is the afternoon of 1 August. Stipe and Aleš will accompany him up to the plateau at 4,000 metres and will sleep with him there one more night. Aleš wonders privately what it would feel like if he were to continue with Tomaž up that enormous wall of rock, snow and ice. He knows it's not an option, for they have discussed it and Tomaž has convinced him that even though he is a superb climber – one of the very best – his first experience on an 8,000-metre peak should not be on the Rupal Face, but rather on a normal route. Aleš agrees. Besides, he does not like the look of the mountain. It's not just the weather that worries him; it's also the conditions of the face. It has been snowing for days – no, weeks – and the mountain is buried in snow. Even if Tomaž were to change his mind and invite him on the climb, Aleš is sure he would say no. In different conditions – yes, definitely. In fact, he has already picked out a line he would like to try in the future. What Tomaž has not told Aleš is that in his spiritual consultations about this climb, he had already considered climbing together on the wall. What he learned was not promising: if Aleš went up on the wall, he would not return. For Tomaž, this was enough.

Now that the decision has been made, nobody is talking. The atmosphere is tense. It feels like a funeral. The mood is, as always, dictated by Tomaž. Extremely serious and almost morose, he seems to have bad premonitions. But if that is so, why does he insist on going? Do the atrocious conditions on the mountain not worry him? What is the rush?

Tomaž's behaviour to this point, given the overall situation on the mountain and his previous retreat in appalling weather, has shown extraordinary forebearance. With House's arrival, it would be natural to feel pressure and even be forced into a premature start on the climb. Although Tomaž firmly denies this, Stipe himself later concedes this as a possibility.

But perhaps his decision-making is not being influenced by the American climber. His life has recently been complicated and tortured. Even Nazir Sabir has noticed that although Tomaž is focused and determined, he is also 'somewhat distracted with family problems'. The last months at home have been the hardest of his life and he has never felt so alone and off balance. But now, quite suddenly, he has found love again, with its flush of newly discovered passion. What are the chances that he has slept a full night in the past weeks, let alone the past twelve months? Can it be that he is simply sleep-deprived?

An hour before he leaves for the high plateau with Stipe and Aleš, Tomaž gives Maja his daily statement for the public. It is somewhat ambiguous but the words are the same he uses for all his expeditions: 'Let it happen, what must happen.' Maja must now somehow present this disturbing statement to the public as something positive. Some time later, they walk slowly together to the departure point. Maja chews on an alpine flower, still filming Tomaž who has picked an edelweiss. They exchange flowers and then he leaves. Maja is unable to hold back her tears. At this point everyone is weeping. She can't ignore the overwhelming feeling that this is a tragedy in the making. Finally Javed turns back to her and says simply, 'Go.'

Returning to camp, each person is alone with their thoughts, struggling to understand Tomaž's motivation. As his departure has grown near, his behaviour has become increasingly distracted. He has not let go of his ice axes, carrying them around like a cat would her kittens, holding them in his lap, unconsciously caressing them, explaining that it is so they 'will cut the ice without breaking it'.

Later that evening, those left in base camp hear an enormous roar and stumble out from their tents. Falling seracs have caused an avalanche like none before released on the upper wall. The debris has covered half of the central part of the wall, precisely over the path of Tomaž's route for the following day. Up to this point, the avalanches have been running down the steep narrow gulleys known as couloirs, but this one explodes over the sides, like a tsunami. The mountain seems to respect no boundaries. Anda and Maja stand, overcome by the power of nature with its tons of roiling snow. Maja, although speechless, silently screams.

Ganesh V, 1994

By 1994 Tomaž had settled into a routine, although one which stretched him to the limit. With the financial responsibility of supporting Sergeja and his young daughter, combined with his growing commitment to climbing, there was very little time left for anything else. He went to the mountains at every opportunity, climbing in the evenings and on the days he wasn't working. Sometimes he climbed with partners, other times alone. He pushed himself harder and harder, searching for more difficult routes, new routes, winter conditions and faster ascents. Sergeja seemed to accept his growing passion for climbing. Although she saw little of Tomaž, she could see the contentment in his eyes when he returned home each night from the mountains, exhausted and full of joy and excitement. She still enjoyed the small gatherings of local climbers as they relived their climbs and adventures. But where all this training would lead, she couldn't begin to guess.

Tomaž was only twenty-five years old when he was invited to Ganesh V. He could hardly believe his good fortune. Although he had certainly distinguished himself within the Kamnik climbing club as a bold and ambitious young climber, he wasn't well known throughout the rest of Slovenia. He still had very little equipment of his own, instead relying on the club cache and that of his climbing partners. But he was hungry to learn more and he desperately wanted to experience the big mountains. The Slovenian climbing legend Stane Belak recognised this in Tomaž, and it was he who helped make Ganesh possible. This first Himalayan expedition remained the most precious in Tomaž's memory. As he recalled in his memoir, *No Impossible Ways*: 'I never again experienced the Himalayas in quite the same way. I miss those days when – all of us dressed in brand new Nunar pants with countless sewn-on pockets – we looked at everything with starry-eyed idealism.'[1] Hardship didn't bother the enthusiastic climbers; it simply added spice.

Stane Belak, known by all as Šrauf, was the leader of the expedition. Born in 1940, he was a veteran of big expeditions to the highest peaks: Makalu, Dhaulagiri, Everest, Gangapurna, Aconcagua and K2. Within the Slovenian climbing community, he was one of the most respected climbers of all, and he had a personality to go along with his hard-ass reputation: gruff, outrageous and a fighter, yet kind. Tomaž had admired him for years, although from afar: 'For me it was like climbing with a god.'

At this time, a group of Himalayan climbers originating in eastern Europe completely dominated the sport, and Šrauf was one of the best. 'A huge chunk of the sickest climbers in the Himalayas are Polish, Russian, Czech or Slovenian . . . They're hard core,' said American big-wall climber Mark Synnott. 'Everyone knows that. You can tell when you meet them.' Messner went one step further, stating that the Slovenians were the best climbers in the world. 'They are young, and they are hungry for difficult things.' In addition to being tough and bold, Šrauf was also colourful.

Undoubtedly his style in front of the camera greatly influenced Tomaž, who later embraced this role for himself. Highly entertaining for the public, it would eventually alienate him from many of his contemporaries in the climbing world.

Because Ganesh V would be his first opportunity to climb with the legendary Šrauf, Tomaž was determined to prove himself. Šrauf had originally planned to be on a much more ambitious Slovenian expedition to Dhaulagiri's South Face but he had fallen and injured himself, eliminating that possibility. In fact, many top Slovenian climbers had summarily dismissed him because of his injury and no longer took him seriously as an alpinist. Ganesh V was the consolation prize for Šrauf: a climb that he referred to as a 'ski hill', and the collection of climbers that he assembled for the expedition as the 'forgotten ones'. Tomaž was not yet in Šrauf's league, so he was surprised and thrilled to be invited on this trip. In fact it was Tone Škarja who had actually orchestrated the invitation. Škarja was the single most powerful man in the Slovenian climbing community, head of the Expeditions Commission of the Mountaineering Association since 1979, and responsible for raising money for the Association as well as deciding all aspects of the expeditions, including who went where, and who would receive funding. Škarja had been watching Tomaž, and was considering including him on the Slovenian Annapurna expedition the following year. Curious about how he would perform at altitude, he offered him Ganesh V as a test.

The rest of the team comprised a rather odd collection of climbers, some perhaps a bit beyond their prime, together with a few very young, unproven ones. Tomaž and Grega Kresal (Tomaž's partner for Ganesh V) were the novices. Šrauf, Dare Alič, Vinko 'Cenko' Berčič, Cene Grilc, and Franci 'Štancar' Vetorazzi were the veterans. A largely compatible group, they headed for the south-east face of Ganesh V, planning to do the first repeat of the 2,800-metre Japanese route, hopefully, with a variation of their own. Šrauf dubbed the group 'the underdog expedition', referring to the unlikely combination of 'old ones' and 'pups'.

When they arrived in Kathmandu, Tomaž saw for the first time the city that would so dominate the rest of his life. After a few days of purchasing food supplies and wandering the streets of the Himalayan capital, they piled on to a bus to Syabar Benzi. Everything went well until they encountered a landslide that had destroyed part of the road, forcing them on to another bus – one which, unfortunately, was already fully occupied. Tomaž considered the situation: 'These forty-seat buses must be very sturdy, as there are over a hundred passengers on board and nobody seems to object.' Of course they couldn't all fit inside, so the new arrivals, including Šrauf's team, climbed on the roof. As they swayed precariously along the tortuous road throughout the night, Tomaž was shocked at one point to see a tiny light appear to crawl out of the bus, through an open window and onto the roof. What could it be? He illuminated his own torch and saw the ticket collector clinging to a small ridge of metal at the edge of the roof, his torch clamped between his teeth, dutifully demanding: 'Ticket, please, ticket, please.'

They disembarked at the village of Chilime to begin their trek to base camp. Chilime was the first desperately poor community that Tomaž had set eyes upon in Nepal, and it left an indelible impression. He thought he knew something about poverty, but the spectrum had just expanded. The trek in was another new experience for him, as the team, together with their porters, marched through the lush bamboo forests alive with screaming monkeys. At last they arrived at Ganesh – a name replete with spiritual meaning, Sanskrit for the first son of Shiva and Parvati, one of the holiest unions in the Hindu faith.

Their equipment was pitifully poor. Tomaž later laughingly recollected, 'Today I have more equipment in my car than we had on that trip.' In the process of setting up base camp, he was overcome with an excruciating pain in his head, causing him to wonder if he was seriously ill, or perhaps even dying. Šrauf calmly pointed out that it was just a bit of altitude sickness. This was the first time Tomaž had felt the effect of high altitude, and so began the process of learning how to survive above 4,000 metres. At times, he wondered if Šrauf's heart was really in this trip, for all he seemed to talk about was Dhaulagiri. To be fair, Šrauf wanted another shot at Dhaulagiri: Ganesh was clearly second choice.

Despite a bad turn in the weather, Šrauf, Kresal and Tomaž headed up in the howling wind and heavy snowfall to establish Camp I at 5,900 metres. Šrauf, the undisputed leader, with his uniquely rambunctious style, ranted and railed at the atrocious weather, claiming that he was 'being screwed', but that he wouldn't let that stop him. The 'pups' obediently followed. Šrauf's lessons continued in Camp I, where he patiently explained the value of eating prunes at altitude; prunes were full of iron – his secret weapon on high mountains. They listened attentively and were fully prepared to adjust their diet to be prune-exclusive when Šrauf unexpectedly broke his tooth on one, initiating yet another explosive verbal tirade, but one enjoyed by the younger climbers.

The bad weather continued, but the threesome forged on, establishing Camp II and then attempting a summit climb. Though they reached an altitude of 6,800 metres, they were forced to climb at night and their headlamps died a short distance from the summit. Severely disappointed, they retreated to Camp II. The second-rope team of Cene, Cenko and Dare moved up next to try the summit, but they too failed to reach the top.

Their turn again, Šrauf, Kresal and Tomaž started up from Camp II in the middle of the following night. Almost immediately, Šrauf fell into a crevasse, forcing them to return to their tent. Shortly afterwards, Kresal hurt his ribs, and with this new development Šrauf decided they should all descend. Even though he was terribly disappointed, it seemed the prudent thing to do. But Tomaž objected, declaring that he had no intention of retreating. Šrauf ordered Tomaž to obey him and descend. Tomaž again said no, that he wanted to continue. Šrauf screamed, 'I cannot leave you here!' 'You can scream all fucking day. I want just one chance,' replied Tomaž. Privately he was sure that Šrauf did not take him seriously, despite his strong performance thus far on the mountain. It took them all day to come to an agreement, but in the end, Šrauf reluctantly agreed to give it one more try.

The next morning at dawn the two started out. Although the temperatures were extremely cold when they began, by the time they reached the summit plateau the sun was baking down on them, sapping what little strength remained. After a few more verbal confrontations they continued, exchanging leads until they reached a final rock barrier. Tomaž took the lead, but not without ample direction from Šrauf, much of which he ignored. When Tomaž reached the top of a particularly difficult 50-metre stretch, he was unable to get a piton into the rock. Had he been able to hammer in the metal peg, he could have attached a carabiner to its head and threaded the climbing rope through the carabiner, thereby securing Šrauf at the other end of the rope – standard procedure. Unfortunately, Šrauf could not see Tomaž's predicament and assumed he had followed protocol. Instead of climbing the section, he calmly began Jumaring up the rope towards Tomaž, using the mechanical ascenders attached directly to the rope to reach the next belay. In the process, all his weight was immediately placed on the rope – and on Tomaž. He had no idea that the belay was completely dependent upon Tomaž's ability to hold him since there was virtually no anchor to the wall. Amazingly, it worked. After another verbal explosion from Šrauf about risk, and a quick lesson on how to build a safe belay, the two continued on to the next obstacle, an icy overhang. Surmounting that, they finally emerged on to a steep, snowy slope leading to the sharp, narrow summit. As they reached the top, the sun slowly dipped behind the Himalayan giants surrounding them.

It was 13 November 1994 when 54-year-old Stane Belak and his protégé, the 25-year-old Tomaž Humar, stood together atop their peak. A feeling of pure bliss washed over Tomaž. It was as if the mountain had absorbed him. He was no longer just a climber: he had become a part of the very fabric of this mountain. The moment was triumphant for both of them: the injured Šrauf had wanted a summit badly that year, and for Tomaž it proved that he could climb in the Himalayas – absolutely essential for his future dreams.

The sky was completely dark when they began their descent. First they had to down-climb to a narrow overhanging gulley, commonly referred to as a chimney. Next they needed to abseil – slowly lower themselves down the securely attached rope – until they could again reach the more moderate slope. Everything went wrong: the ropes were iced up; their hands were freezing so badly they couldn't tie proper knots; pulling the abseil ropes was a problem in the dark. It was one thing after another. Finally, Tomaž collapsed on the snow.

This was the real crux of the climb, that moment when the mountain concedes nothing to the climber, not even hope. Šrauf implored him to get up. When that produced no result, he ordered him to rise. Nothing would rouse Tomaž. It was as if the life had drained from his body. All his adrenaline had been left on the summit. He was not experienced enough to understand the importance of saving some energy for the descent. Šrauf became incensed, possibly feeling a certain amount of responsibility for this young climber, probably wishing that he had overruled him earlier. But it was too late for that now. He tried another approach: 'Tomi, you've got a child at home, get up now!' Tomaž, in his half-dead state, vaguely recalled that yes indeed, he did have a beautiful daughter named Urša, and yes, he really should stir himself. But he couldn't. The compassionate Šrauf meanwhile protected Tomaž as best he could from the wind. It was a desperate situation for them both. While Šrauf could undoubtedly have made it down to the tent alone, it was inconceivable that he would leave Tomaž: he had promised Tomaž's father he would bring him back alive.

Finally Tomaž roused himself and began moving. In his exhausted and confused condition he left his pack behind. Again Šrauf took control, rummaging through Tomaž's pack, throwing out those things that were not absolutely necessary and then slinging the second pack over his own. With both packs on his back, he descended beside Tomaž, offering words of encouragement and barking out orders as required. By 4.00 a.m. they were back in the tent, where Šrauf heated water and did his best to force some liquid into Tomaž's severely dehydrated body. It didn't work. Anything that he drank or ate came up immediately as green bile. His body was slowly, systematically shutting down.

Somehow they both survived the night; and the next day, soaking up the life-giving warmth of the sun, they descended to Camp I, where they were met by two of their expedition staff. Then it was down to base camp, where Tomaž first realised that his toes were frost-bitten. It was only then that he began to understand how close he had come to remaining on that mountain; how far he had extended himself; and what he needed to learn from the experience. He realised he had pushed too far, given his limited experience. He had got away with it, but not without the help of Šrauf. He knew there might not be a Šrauf on his next climb to help him down. He would have to remember the lesson well.

Back home, Sergeja and little Urša coped with Tomaž's absence by writing a cross on each calendar day that passed, waiting patiently for his return. Sergeja recalled, "Luckily, Urša and I were very independent, intuitive and positive thinkers. When I look back at the times spent alone with the children, I value them in gold and would repeat those times in a thousand future lives." Her confidence proved correct and everything ended well. The first experience was good, assuring her that each future one would also end well.

On the trek out, Šrauf confided how horrified he'd been high on the mountain: 'Don't you know I was worried sick, I thought . . . You know I promised your father . . .' Tomaž's admiration for the veteran climber turned to affection. For Šrauf, tolerance of his young novice had grown into guarded admiration, and he now began calling Tomaž 'a pup with a good bite'. Tomaž was elated, dreaming of future climbs together.

But before there could be any more dreams of climbing, he first had to deal with reality. Upon his return home, he plunged back into work, trying to make some headway in an endless river of bills. While he was relieved to be back with his little family, a part of his heart remained up high – in the Himalayas, to which he was certain he would return.

CHAPTER SIX

ANNAPURNA 1995

2 August 2005, 07.00, Nanga Parbat, Rupal Face

Early on the morning of 2 August, Stipe and Aleš take their leave of Tomaž at 4,500 metres, just before he crosses a huge snowfield that is threatened by a small serac. After he is safely across the snowfield, Stipe and Aleš finish filming him and then return to base camp, continuing to monitor him with the spotting scope as best they can. At one point, Tomaž calls down to ask if they can determine the origin of the spindrift washing over him. But they can no longer see him. Instead, Aleš focuses the spotting scope on some hanging seracs, hoping to warn Tomaž if any of them shifts. For countless, bone-numbing hours, Aleš leans up against a rock in base camp, patiently scanning the face – a sea of white, subtle gradations of white, moving, shimmering, pulsating, shifting in and out of cloud.

Meanwhile, Nataša has ominous feelings about the wall and its apparent aggression towards Tomaž. She wonders if he should wait for a more auspicious time. Now that he is back in camp, Stipe turns his attention to a Croatian tourism film project that he is obliged to complete as well as a book that he's writing. Maja is a little surprised that he is able to shift his focus so quickly, but she puts these thoughts aside and attends to her own media commitments.

2 August, 14.00

Seven hours pass. Tomaž radioes that he is now approaching a diagonal ice crack which he must climb. Stipe, concerned about the quality of the ice, describes to Maja and Anda what Tomaž is probably facing: 'Conditions are unbelievably bad. Due to high temperatures, everything is melting; water is pouring over the walls; things are collapsing all the time.'

2 August, 15.30

Tomaž calls again, this time to report that he has climbed a total of 1,600 metres. Aleš is worried about the scale of this effort and urges him to stop and eat and drink. Tomaž has not rested for more than five minutes all day and is clearly exhausted after ten hours of climbing. His voice, as he converses with Stipe on the radio, betrays his desperate situation.

'Hey. Old man, this is crazy.'

'You have done a good job, better than I thought. You should think about a break.'

'I can't. I am hanging on the axes. Old man, the rocks are falling from all sides. I have to get out of here, I have to get over, there is no other [way]!'

'Tomaž, hold on. Good luck!'

2 August, 19.00

It is now completely dark. Tomaž is still in motion, digging a hole in the snow, two metres by half a metre. He will try to sleep under a rock in this snow hole so that any avalanches will slide harmlessly over him. He worries about the absence of solid ice in which to place an ice screw for a safe belay, and Aleš is concerned about air circulation in the hole, particularly if he is buried by an avalanche.

For the first few hours, base camp plays music. Tomaž is silent, cooking and resting. They have arranged a protocol that in order to save batteries, base camp will call only if there is an emergency. All other communication will be initiated by Tomaž. And so they wait.

2 August, 20.00

They have still not heard from Tomaž. Finally Aleš can bear it no longer, so he picks up the radio: ' Tomaž, do you read me, base camp to Tomaž . . .' Tomaž answers, 'What is the time?' The effort of climbing and digging the hole has been too much, and fatigue has finally overtaken him. While base camp were waiting with bated breath for some word from him, he had fallen into an immediate and exhausted sleep. Anda becomes anxious, for he has clearly not taken the time to melt some snow for liquids, and she knows that dehydration comes quickly at this altitude, particularly after such an effort. From that point on, in order to keep him awake and hydrating, they read him email messages coming in from Slovenia, some in the dialect of his home town, Kamnik.

Then Maja asks for some details for her media report. Despite his exhaustion and the severity of his position, Tomaž agrees. Maja moves out to the middle of the camp, sits down on a rock, snuggles up in her down jacket and props the Dictaphone against the radio as Tomaž describes his experience.

It was intense all day. The serac released first thing in the morning, like a warning for D-Day, down the whole wall . . . A few critical spots followed. I climbed overhanging rock with bare hands, and stuff was falling over the top of me from the upper snowfields and walls. Soon afterwards I was on an avalanche slope, between the balconies. It took me about an hour to get out of the seracs. Luckily I found an exit. It was close at one point; an avalanche just missed me. I jumped away . . . A few times falling rocks barely missed me. My feet cut loose three times, and twice I felt completely trapped in the middle of ice seracs. But I still had 200 metres of black ice [a mixture of rock, ice and water] to climb to the bivouac spot. I dug for an hour, all soaked. Now I am in my sleeping bag and hope that the mountain will be as forgiving tomorrow as she was today.

That night, the team at base camp do not sleep soundly. Their insomnia is not only due to concerns for Tomaž on the face: there is an emerging situation in base camp too. Although Stipe has known for several days that he must leave the expedition, the team has just learned that he will depart the following day. They have seen his other film commitments distracting him at base camp, but they did not expect this work to actually lure him away. Surely he must have known that the expedition could take longer than originally scheduled. It was an over-optimistic plan and he should have known that. With his departure will also go one of the SAT phones and the best video camera – the one with the long lens so crucial for panning the mountain while Tomaž climbs. Stipe is also the most mechanically minded team member, so with him goes their base camp 'fixer'. He is the only one who has a full understanding of the situation in which Tomaž finds himself, for he has an enormous amount of high-mountain experience and he alone knows how to deal with Tomaž. He always finds the right words for him. Most importantly, Tomaž listens to Stipe. As the team contemplates his departure, they are frankly scared.

Annapurna, 1995

Following the Ganesh V expedition, Tomaž climbed with even greater frequency and he worked long hours in the canals, towers and ditches. After Ganesh V, he was no longer anonymous. Word had filtered back to Tone Škarja, and Tomaž's performance on Ganesh V was sufficiently impressive to earn him a spot on the Mountaineering Association of Slovenia's official expedition to Annapurna I in 1995.

In Škarja's estimation, Slovenia had entered the Himalayan arena rather late: 'If you are late, you must go faster than the train.' When he became head of the Commission for Expeditions, he inherited a vision that had originated under his predecessor, Aleš Kunavar, which was to place Slovenian climbers on the top of all fourteen 8,000-metre peaks. But Škarja wanted to take this vision a step further: to climb the peaks by new routes as often as possible. His record was impressive. Slovenian expeditions had already climbed new routes on Everest, Kangchenjunga, Dhaulagiri, Lhotse, Gasherbrum I and K2.

Now he needed Annapurna. This was his sixth attempt, and the expedition's goals were twofold: get the Karničar brothers, Davorin and Andrej, to the top and down – on skis – as well as add the last 8,000-metre peak to the crown of Slovenian 8,000ers. Along with seven Slovenian climbers, the team included the Croatian Stipe Božić who would be the climbing partner of Viki Grošelj, one of Slovenia's top Himalayan climbers. Viki was attempting to climb all of the 8,000ers and this would be his second-last Nepalese peak, if he succeeded. Also joining the team was Mexico's top high-altitude alpinist, Carlos Carsolio.

At over 8,000 metres in height, Annapurna would be a big jump from the 6,986-metre Ganesh V for Tomaž. He badly wanted to know if he could perform at 8,000 metres, and now he was being given a chance. Annapurna, a Sanskrit word meaning 'goddess of the harvests', is actually not a single mountain, but rather a massif running 55 kilometres with six of its peaks reaching over 7,000 metres. The highest of these peaks, Annapurna I, reaches the magical 8,091 metres, catapulting it into the elite group of the fourteen 8,000-metre peaks. Tenth highest in the world, it is located across from another 8,000er, Dhaulagiri, separated by a deep gorge carved by the Kali Gandaki river.

Annapurna has enjoyed a long and colourful climbing history, with many 'firsts'. It was the first 8,000er to be climbed when Maurice Herzog led his French team to climbing history in 1950. Its South Face was also the first big Himalayan face to be successfully climbed in 1970 under Chris Bonington's leadership. The first all-female Himalayan expedition chose Annapurna in 1978 when American climber Arlene Blum led an international group of women to the mountain, and succeeded. And it was the first 8,000er to be climbed, in the winter of 1987, when the legendary Polish climber Jerzy Kukuczka and his partner, Artur Hajzer, reached the summit on 3 February.

With such a collection of firsts for Annapurna, it would be natural to assume that it is one of the easier 8,000-metre peaks. In fact, it is one of the most dangerous. Particularly prone to avalanches, the mountain had already claimed many lives by the time the Slovenians appeared in 1995. For every two climbers who reach the top of Annapurna, one dies trying. Compared to a three-to-one ratio for K2, and seven-to-one for Everest, this is not a mountain to take lightly. When Šrauf, an old hand in the Himalayas, heard about the invitation, he first congratulated Tomaž, and then added protectively, 'We need to talk.' Tomaž was so pleased with the invitation that the dangers did not dampen his spirits. But he wasn't happy with the financial arrangements. Since this was a national expedition, it was supported financially by the Mountaineering Association, headed up by Škarja. Still, Škarja expected Tomaž to bring some personal money to the expedition. Tomaž had secured some private support from Volkswagen to pay his travel, but he was shocked when he learned that he was expected to funnel this private funding through the Mountaineering Association to be combined with all the other Association money. The total amount would then be allocated to the climbers as Škarja saw fit. Tomaž refused and simply brought his own financing to supplement the Association support.

Although he had been invited on the expedition, it was clear from the beginning that Tomaž was not regarded as a likely summiter. He was there to work: to carry loads, to break trail and to help set up the route for the main event – the first ski descent from the top. Tomaž bit his tongue, put his head down, worked the route and bided his time. He and Janko 'Zumba' Oprešnik, another young and relatively inexperienced Himalayan climber, had their own plans.

On the long trek to base camp, the climbers began to get to know each other better. It was while walking though the Kali Gandaki gorge that Tomaž and Zumba, both full of youthful enthusiasm and energy, hatched their ambitious plan. They had often climbed together in Slovenia and had succeeded on some fiercely technical and dangerous routes. They felt ideally suited for the 3,800-metre north-west ridge of Annapurna. Tomaž also took advantage of Carlos Carsolio's presence. Like a sponge, he soaked up Carsolio's stories of climbing with the Himalayan legends, especially the Poles, and he gleaned precious nuggets of experience from him. They sensed an immediate rapport, and Tomaž would later call the Mexican 'one of my best friends – soul to soul'.

Viki noticed that Tomaž was initially rather quiet, particularly with the older climbers. Soon, though, he began to open up, gaining confidence, talking a bit more, and communicating wildly with his hands. Viki learned to keep a safe distance, for Tomaž's colourful gesticulations could be downright dangerous. He was amused by Tomaž's joyful enthusiasm and bizarre sense of humour. Along the way, they played a number of games requiring little or no equipment, among them a simple one called 'stones'. Viki was the undisputed expert, having even beaten the legendary Šrauf on past expeditions. But now he was challenged by the young upstart Tomaž, and to his surprise, the underdog won.

Although it was the first time that he had met Tomaž, since he lived 500 kilometres away from him, on the Croatian coast, Stipe Božić quickly became friendly with him: 'I found him to be a very open person.' At first, he wondered if Tomaž was a bit deranged: 'I thought that since he was born near the Kamnik Alps he was a little crazy from all of the wind . . . that he had a kind of madness.' Eventually Stipe wryly concluded that although there was an element of truth in his initial assessment, 'nobody moves things ahead without a bit of madness'.

The team finally arrived at base camp, which they established at 4,200 metres. Soon afterwards, Tomaž had his first narrow escape. He was climbing with Carsolio when a strangely flat stretch of snow-covered glacier appeared in front of them. The experienced Carsolio immediately became suspicious and suggested skirting around the edge of it. The less experienced Tomaž insisted on taking the short cut. Part of the way across, the ice gave way and Tomaž plunged into the icy waters of a glacial lake known as a tarn. Weighed down by his heavy pack, he vainly began trying to swim. Thanks to the ski poles offered by Carsolio, he managed to escape an icy, watery death, but not before he promised to follow Carsolio's lead in the future.

A little later, Zumba, Carsolio and Tomaž were working their way further up the mountain through a particularly dangerous area of leaning, precarious seracs when a fierce storm broke over them. Thunder, lightning and snow engulfed them with a fury they had not yet experienced. The Sherpas who were accompanying them with equipment and food dropped their loads and quickly descended. Unfortunately the loads descended, too, rolling uncontrollably down the mountain. Panic-stricken, the three climbers attempted to dig a hole in an ice serac in order to create some kind of shelter from the storm. No bivouac equipment remained from their fallen packs and the situation was desperate. At one point Carsolio looked over at Tomaž, who, despite the severe situation, and with a broad grin plastered across his wind-burned face, quipped, 'Que serac, serac.'

They managed to survive the storm, but while hunkered down in their ice hole, Zumba's stomach began acting up so violently that he knew his time on the mountain was limited. The illness was a bitter blow to Zumba, an exceptionally gifted climber, though in retrospect it may have saved both his and Tomaž's life, for had he not succumbed to it, they probably would have launched themselves on to the north-west ridge in alpine style, a route and style too difficult for them.

With Zumba's descent, it was left to Carsolio and Tomaž to continue up with the Karničar brothers and the Sherpas to establish Camp III at 6,500 metres. There, amply supplied with food and equipment, they were ordered to wait out the next storm. It was up at Camp III that Tomaž learned some lessons about big expeditions: not about conditions and climbing, but about positioning. He learned that for this expedition, and this camp in particular, the important thing was to conserve enough food for the Karničar brothers to complete their goal. It soon became clear that the food was for the brothers, not for Tomaž and Carsolio. Tomaž recalled the situation at Camp III: 'For the first time I realised that not all people welcome the sight of others in the mountains, and that the motto "all for a common goal" sounds like a socialist slogan which does not relate to our situation.' Radio messages went back and forth to base camp, many of them not friendly. Carsolio, who did not understand the Slovenian language, was completely baffled. Why were they going hungry when the adjoining tent was overflowing with food? It became evident that Tomaž would have to go down. He had been useful up to this point, but above

Camp III he was regarded as a liability, for he would only consume food needed for the brothers. Carsolio was given the okay to continue going up, since he was carrying the camera. In the middle of that night, he and the Karničar brothers started up towards the summit. A very bitter Tomaž headed down.

By the middle of the next afternoon he had reached base camp, where he was greeted by Škarja with an offer of tea. Škarja heaped Tomaž with congratulations and thanked him for his efforts in establishing the route and setting up camps. He had done what he had been brought to Annapurna to do, and he had done a great job. From Škarja's perspective, everything was going as planned. In a large expedition of this kind, it was expected that some climbers were there to prepare the route and others were there to summit. As the leader, it was Škarja's job to ensure that the appropriate people did the appropriate jobs. Therefore he was justifiably shocked when Tomaž not only refused the tea, but exploded in rage, threw his pack to the ground, and challenged him to a serious confrontation about the previous day's order to descend. Škarja felt that he was behaving like a spoiled brat. If this continued, he would soon gain a reputation that would severely limit his future opportunities.

The two men moved away from the rest of the climbers at base camp and continued arguing loudly. Tomaž railed at Škarja that he had earned his keep on the mountain, but now that the weather had improved, it was the others who were up high, claiming the summit. What about him? Why had he not been allowed to try? Škarja once again explained the objectives of the expedition. The first priority was for the brothers to do their ascent and ski back down. The second objective was for Viki to get to the top, for he was hunting 8,000ers and Annapurna was on his list. The last and most important priority was for everyone to get off the mountain safely. In this list of priorities there was neither room nor time for Tomaž to climb to the summit. Tomaž wouldn't back down. Although he understood Škarja's position and his strategy, he flatly refused to go along with it: 'I'm going anyway, and I don't care if you pack up base camp!' With that announcement, he stomped away.

The next day, 29 April, Andrej and Davorin Karničar reached the summit of Annapurna I, together with Carlos Carsolio. Slovenia had successfully summitted all fourteen of the 8,000-metre peaks and it now only remained for the brothers to ski down. They did so, but not without a price, for Davorin lost his toes to frostbite in the process. Meanwhile, the expedition's second objective was unfolding. Viki and Stipe were at Camp IV, waiting for their chance. But the summit was not to be theirs, so they decided to retreat off the mountain.

Now it was Tomaž's turn. Zumba's stomach problems had abated by now, and he too was ready to go. The two, together with Sherpa Arjun, defiantly headed up, skipping Camp I, which was destroyed anyway, and spending their first night at Camp II. In a blizzard the following day, they forged on to Camp III. But that night Zumba's stomach acted up again, a malaise obviously connected to the altitude. He tried to continue the next morning, but with regret was forced to turn around and finally give up any hope of summiting. Arjun and Tomaž continued up towards Camp IV, and on their way met Stipe and Viki descending towards the valley. The two veteran alpinists both expressed concern about the pair heading up, suggesting that they should descend as well. But neither was ready for defeat, and so they continued on in deteriorating weather. By now, visibility was zero, and they simply could not locate the tents of Camp IV at 7,500 metres. Base camp became increasingly worried each hour they were out in the full force of the elements, but finally, at 5.00 p.m., they radioed in that they had found the life-saving tents and would rest there for a day before attempting the summit. Škarja responded forcefully: either head up this very night for the summit or come down. Tomaž said no, insisting that he needed a day of rest. He had never slept this high before and could sense that his body needed respite, but what he didn't realise was that here in the 'death zone', there was no real recuperation: one more day would only add to his fatigue. Tomaž later accused Škarja of not explaining the folly of his strategy, for Škarja would have known better due to his vast experience in the Himalayas. Perhaps so, but Škarja had just been publicly humiliated by this disobedient upstart and was possibly not feeling terribly benevolent towards Tomaž.

There was not much rest that night. The wind howled, threatening to destroy their meagre tent and catapult them off the mountain. Tomaž and Arjun hung on through the night, but in a terrified state, called to base camp to explain the situation. Again they were ordered to descend at the first opportunity. Clearly this was not a helpful suggestion, at least for the moment, so they turned off the radio and hunkered down for the long night. The next morning they again turned on the radio and were assaulted by increasingly shrill orders from base camp. 'Descend immediately,' demanded Škarja. Of course he and the others were worried about the conditions high on the mountain, and were becoming more and more agitated because this crisis was completely unnecessary: the expedition was already a success and everyone was supposed to be off the mountain by now. Škarja once again ordered: 'You've had your chance, now come down at once – if you still can.'

Little did he know that if there had ever been any chance of convincing Tomaž to cooperate and obey, that opportunity had slipped away with those fateful words, 'You've had your chance'. Tomaž didn't see it that way. He felt that his best chance had been a few days ago when he had been at Camp III in good weather with the Karničar brothers and Carsolio. That had been the optimum time. But he had been sent down in order to make room for the others, and had obediently descended to base camp. Nobody now needed the tents high on the mountain; there was still food available at the high camps; it was his turn. Unfortunately the weather wasn't cooperating, but Tomaž refused to let that stop him. He would at least try. He refused to descend and once again turned off his radio – this time for six long hours.

The mountain magnifies: an unkind word, a dropped glove, an act of rebellion: each is irreversible and has long-lasting reverberations. This single act of defiance would end any possibility of an amicable relationship with Tone Škarja and forever change Tomaž's relationship with the Mountaineering Association of Slovenia. In retrospect, he understood Škarja's motivation for ordering him down: he probably would have done the same thing, he would later admit. Even at the time he felt bad for not keeping base camp apprised of his actions. But not bad enough to dissuade him from his goal – the summit.

Shortly before noon, Tomaž packed up his camera, one ski pole, one ice axe and his radio, and headed up with Arjun. In the approaching storm it didn't take long for Arjun to realise that this situation was spiralling out of control. He turned back, but Tomaž ploughed on through deep snow, sometimes waist-deep. Although his progress was soul-destroyingly slow, his body seemed nearly mechanical, as if it could go on for ever. The storm arrived with enormous force; it assaulted, then engulfed him, as did the cold. Still he plodded on. After five hours of effort, he reached the base of the summit couloir, at which point he once again radioed base camp. When they realised exactly where he was, and that he was alone, their tone changed from anger to concern, for they knew he was still at least two hours from the summit. At 7.00 p.m. he called once more to report that he was very close to the summit and that he was surrounded by an absolutely splendid sunset, for the clouds had momentarily lifted and the view to the west was magnificent. There is no doubt that all who were monitoring his progress must have felt sick at that moment: 7.00 p.m. on the summit ridge of Annapurna and Tomaž was waxing lyrical about the sunset instead of tagging the summit and beginning his descent immediately? They were convinced that he must be hallucinating.

But somehow he held it together to make those last steps to the summit, where he was quickly overtaken by darkness. He stayed there only a short time, taking some photos, catching his breath and trying to assess his situation in a calm and logical way. His summit self-portrait is revealing: a face clearly on the edge, deep red from the cold and swollen with oedema from the altitude. His eyelashes are thickly coated with rime and his anorak hood is pulled tightly around his head to retain what little warmth remained in his body. His headlamp is completely caked with snow and the look emanating from his eyes is one of primal fear.

As the intense cold seeped into his body, Tomaž knew he had to begin moving. His descent was somewhat unorthodox as he ran in brief spurts, only to collapse on the snow, and then ran again until his lungs forced another collapse. After two and a half hours he felt that he must be near the tent, but where exactly was it? He began calling to Arjun, and within a short time he heard him call back. The wave of relief he felt at having a human being close by was overwhelming. His debt to Arjun's call was undoubtedly his life.

Arjun pulled him into the tent, checked him over for frostbite and began feeding him liquids, after which Tomaž again called base camp to report that he was safe. After a surprisingly good sleep at such a high altitude, on 7 May they both began the long descent to the valley below. Sometimes down-climbing together, but often apart, they threaded their way through the seracs, crevasses and avalanche slopes. When they reached Camp III, they found that it had been removed. Their next goal was Camp II, which was visible in the distance, and where they could see people moving about. But when they reached the site of Camp II, it too had been stripped. Tomaž couldn't believe it. How could they remove these life-saving camps before everyone was off the mountain? Viki later clarified that it wasn't Škarja who had ordered the camps to be cleared: the Sherpas had done it themselves. He added that there had been many problems with the Sherpas on that expedition. Finally, late that afternoon, they reached base camp, where the rest of the team was waiting. There were congratulations and heartfelt embraces of relief that they were safely down. Škarja too greeted him warmly, despite the fact that Tomaž had flagrantly disobeyed him. But he gave Tomaž notice that the conversation was not yet over: this kind of behaviour would have consequences, despite the summit success. As before, Tomaž exploded in anger, further widening the rift.

On the walk out, Tomaž reflected on what had happened and why he had reacted so strongly and negatively. The expedition should have been perfect: sanctioned by the Mountaineering Association; reasonably well funded; seasoned climbers balanced by young, ambitious hopefuls; strong leadership; and a stunningly beautiful mountain. What had gone wrong? To all outward appearances, very little. It was an unqualified success. But for Tomaž, it had not been a team effort. He had felt taken advantage of throughout the climb: treated like a worker, and not respected as a climber. He accepted the fact that he was not one of the first-priority climbers, but he did not – and would never – accept the premise that he should not be given a chance for the summit. That was why he had come to Annapurna – to test himself at 8,000 metres. He had big plans for the future and had needed to find out if he could function at that elevation. Now he knew.

The trip summary that was initially penned by Nepal's official Himalayan chronicler, Elizabeth Hawley, did not even mention Tomaž's name as a member of the team, and certainly not as a summiter. As leader of the expedition, it was Škarja who had met with Hawley in Kathmandu to report on the results of his team, and it was Škarja who had given her the names of the summiters. There was no doubt of his having reached the top, for he had photographs to prove it. Years before, in the mountains of Slovenia, he had learned that if you were going to solo climb, there was one important unwritten rule: provide proof. He always made sure to leave something at the summit, remove something from the summit, or take a summit photo that was conclusively from that location, in order to prove that he had been there. In the case of Annapurna, he had taken a photo and a piece of rock from just below the summit snow mushroom. His name was omitted for another reason, as Hawley explained: 'I concentrated on the noteworthy ski descent eight days earlier by the Karničar brothers, rather than on his more routine ascent and descent. He was the eighty-sixth person to summit the mountain, and his route was the normal one.' The ascent was critically important for Tomaž, but less so for Himalayan climbing history, although Hawley hastened to add that she added his name to her official list of that season's climbs.

The strange and emotionally charged conflict between the older, experienced and more powerful Škarja and the young brazen pup was certainly exacerbated by their contrasting personalities, but it may have originated in the changing culture of Slovenia. While the country lurched quickly, and sometimes awkwardly, from a socialist state to a free-market economy, individual attitudes began to change too, often much more quickly and easily with the youth, for they were naturally not as entrenched in the old ways. As the country's leading alpinist from the socialist régime, Škarja had formulated a strategy for his national climbing team that relied upon strong and unchallenged leadership as well as a style of teamwork that resembled a paramilitary exercise. Tomaž applauded him for accepting the leadership of climbing the fourteen 8,000-metre peaks, for this long-term, ambitious project was a goal for all Slovenian climbers and was the pride of the country. For Škarja, it was a commitment that went far beyond his personal ambitions – and one that he accomplished brilliantly. But the younger generation were becoming more skilled and ambitious to achieve their own individual climbing objectives, and didn't necessarily embrace this team concept. Tomaž was one of the most vocal of the group, but he was certainly not alone, and he was also not the first. He might have learned from the experiences of the brilliant Slovenian climber Tomo Česen, a man whose ambitions eventually destroyed his reputation as an alpinist.

Česen's is a complicated story, going back to his claim of soloing the South Face of Lhotse in 1990, a tremendous achievement. After Lhotse, he was praised by Messner and became so famous, even outside Slovenia, that he didn't need Škarja or the support of the Mountaineering Association. As a senior figure within the Association, Škarja represented authority, strict rules, national goals and little room for individualism or creativity. Česen was a superbly gifted climber who had no intention of tagging along on the expeditions envisioned by Škarja, expeditions he referred to as 'snow slogs'. Not only a world-class climber, Česen was tall and handsome, articulate and adept with the media. After Lhotse, when he realised that he could support his climbing through sponsorship, he was free. Years later, Prezelj asserted that Česen was probably the first climber to become a climbing businessman, but added that he was 'a cockerel who cried too early'.

Despite his initial success, Česen eventually made a fatal error that brought him into conflict with Škarja. It didn't start with Škarja, but rather with Viki Grošelj. Viki's dream of climbing all fourteen of the 8,000-metre peaks was well supported by Škarja and the Mountaineering Association. In a press conference at which many of Slovenia's leading climbers were present, the interviewer turned to Česen and asked him what he thought of Viki's project. The camera panned back and forth between Česen and Viki while Česen formulated his answer. Finally, he said that he didn't think this was a project for the future. It was clear from the look on Viki's face that he was insulted and angry.

Some time before, Česen had borrowed a photograph of the summit of Lhotse from Viki. Česen claimed that he had neglected to take his own summit photo, and he needed one for an article about his solo ascent in the French climbing magazine *Vertical*. Rumours had already been bubbling in Europe about this confusing and suspicious photograph, and within a few days of the press conference Viki announced publicly that the photo in question was his, not Česen's.

Škarja seized the tool that Viki had provided, renouncing the climb, discounting Česen's claim of a solo ascent and effectively destroying his career. He didn't limit his criticism to the Lhotse débâcle, adding that Česen's record on other climbs above 8,000 metres was also suspicious. Even though many climbers, including Tomaž, believed that Česen was fully capable of climbing the South Face of Lhotse, there was now considerable doubt about his claims. Tomaž would only say, 'I wasn't there,' adding that 'Česen is something special. He still climbs a lot – and well.'

As the grand leader of Slovenian climbing at the time, there was no doubt that Škarja was humiliated by this blot on an otherwise brilliant Slovenian Himalayan record. It wasn't only *his* humiliation, for he pointed out that it was a black moment for all Slovenian climbers. 'It deeply affected them, more than they think,' he explained. Škarja was still a very powerful force; of that there was no doubt. So it must have taken an enormous amount of self-confidence, naïve stupidity, or both, for the younger and not nearly as accomplished Tomaž Humar to stand up to him in the way he did. It could have been terminal to his career.

These early, heady days of independent spirit may have been the genesis of the climbing revolution in Slovenia, where the younger generation summarily denounced the old ways – and the old power-brokers. After the 1991 Česen affair, the Mountaineering Association split into two parts; the Commission for Expeditions led by Tone Škarja and the Commission for Alpinism led by a group of younger alpinists, including Prezelj, Štremfelj and Pavle Kozjek. But this revolution was not without casualties.

Slovenian climbers, like young climbers everywhere, were always short of money. The one opportunity that remained from Socialist times was a kind of point system, now controlled by the Commission for Alpinism within the Mountaineering Association. For each new route or major climb that an alpinist completed and recorded, he would be awarded a certain number of points. When a particular level was attained, that climber would receive a special classification from the Commission, resulting in a small salary. This was what all eager young alpinists coveted, for with this modest stipend they would have a base on which to live, freeing them to concentrate their efforts on becoming world-class alpinists.

Tomaž worked hard at his climbing, and by 1994 he had already accumulated an impressive number of points – enough for the classification. Then the rules changed and the required number increased. The official reason was that there were too many climbers who had achieved the level that year, so it was obviously too low. He was furious, and remains furious more than a decade later, because he is convinced that the Commission for Alpinism blocked him. 'With this salary they knew I could survive and then I could climb more, and they did not want this to happen.' The Commission vehemently denied the allegation, insisting that they had supported Tomaž, and that under their leadership, the Commission had assisted him financially on five major Himalayan expeditions. Tomaž snorted in disbelief at this assertion.

It is possible that Tomaž's flamboyant personality and already outrageously explosive style were so far outside the Association's culture that they did indeed attempt to control him. It must have been abundantly clear to them that he would not be a willing participant in their grand collective vision. Tomaž's loss of classification had a severe and direct impact on his life, for he was obliged to earn a living, yet he also needed to climb. How could he manage both? The stress was enormous for both him and Sergeja. To add to his misery, he had no credit. And because he worked independently outside of an official company, he had no way of even obtaining a credit rating. There was no international classification stipend to help pay the bills that continued to pile up each month. Instead, in the summer he painted towers, and in the winter he worked from 6.00 p.m. to 6.00 a.m. cleaning canals for 12 Deutschmarks per hour. He would come home, sleep until 10.00 a.m. and then go out and climb as fast as possible until around 3.00 or 4.00 p.m., then rush back home to eat and once again head back to the canals.

Some time later, Tomaž and Škarja met once again. When Škarja asked about his plans, Tomaž replied, 'Now I'll fish for myself.' And so he did. This independent style would now define his approach to climbing in the Himalayas. It would give him freedom to make his own choices about mountains, routes and partners. But it would also bring him untold misery as he tried to function outside the constraints – and support – of the Mountaineering Association. He would need to earn every dollar. However, it wasn't just about the dollars. Ultimately, his words to Škarja would bring him enormous emotional pain, although he was loath to admit it. The Mountaineering Association had raised him, taught him and nurtured him as a climber, and they had become his second family. Now he was leaving them, and the terms were not friendly. Škarja insisted that he never held it against Tomaž for disobeying him on Annapurna. But he knew that the confrontation was the end of their previous relationship.

Despite all the squabbling with the Mountaineering Association, Tomaž had other more important things to think about: Sergeja was pregnant again.

CHAPTER SEVEN

AMA DABLAM

3 August 2005, 07.00, Nanga Parbat, Rupal Face

The atmosphere at base camp is tense. Both Stipe and Nataša are leaving the expedition. Stipe has other film commitments, and Nataša's predictions and cautions have gone unheeded by Tomaž. Stipe and Nataša are both concerned about Tomaž's somewhat ambitious schedule and the unrelentingly bad conditions on the mountain, and Nataša is worried about his emotional entanglement with Maja. Aleš is the only alpinist left in camp, placing enormous pressure on him. Maja must now craft a message about the departures for the public, which are following every detail of the expedition on the internet. As for Tomaž, he is alone on the wall and must try to process this news dispassionately. He will now have to rely completely on his own powers of intuition for each decision on the mountain.

Maja interviews Stipe one last time before his departure. He is cautiously confident: 'Today is perhaps the most dangerous day for him. But I believe he will make it.' Both Stipe and Nataša are emotional as they radio Tomaž to say goodbye and to wish him well. Maja, Anda and Aleš are worried, sensing that this is a psychologically dangerous moment for the expedition. Morale is clearly down in base camp. It is absolutely critical that Tomaž feels none of this gloom or sense of abandonment. He must remain focused and positive and powerful, for he is on the Rupal Face.

3 August, 08.00

The radio crackles with life. It's Tomaž, calling Aleš. 'Do you see me?' he asks. Aleš replies, 'I don't see you now. It's foggy.' The next transmission stuns everyone as Tomaž screams, 'Fuck, Ali. It was sunny for an hour.'

Their worst fears are realised. Tomaž appears to be losing control. Stipe's departure must be affecting him terribly and he is venting his frustration on Aleš, who is helpless at base camp. Maja is appalled at the screaming and swearing on the radio and Aleš is devastated. 'I will not respond any more. I really won't,' he says. Tomaž later recalls that moment, but rather than pointing to Stipe's departure, he blames his stress on his inability to find a safe bivouac – a place to escape the constantly falling snow, ice and rock.

Tomaž instructs base camp on his communications protocol: he will climb with his radio continuously on. This will allow him at any time to ask base camp to focus the spotting scope on the route and give him details about a threatening serac or a potential dead end. The strategy means that base camp must be watching – and listening – at all times. His expectation places a terrible strain on all of them, particularly Aleš, the one most able to give him accurate and relevant information.

3 August, 09.00

Tomaž crosses an exceptionally dangerous spot on the wall where a number of avalanche paths intersect. He calls it Point Zero, and he is forced to do the crossing in the fog. It is perhaps just as well, for he is unable to see what is looming above him. After five more intense hours of climbing he reaches 6,100 metres. What's left of the base camp team is forced to listen to every agonising moment. They hear the wall release avalanches all around Tomaž. They hear falling ice and rocks crashing down. They can even hear the wind as it howls around him. At one point they hear Tomaž exclaiming, 'It is damned hard!'

3 August, 13.00

Tomaž continues, but the conditions are dangerously unstable, even more so the higher he climbs: snow mushrooms, wet rock, melting ice. In one hour he advances only 20 metres. After swimming through mushroom-like formations of snow, he arrives beside a rock tower. He tries to describe his position to Aleš: 'Desperation . . . I came under the tower, I am climbing it now. I am trying to find a bivouac. I have been on my fingertips all day. It is black ice, detached.' Despite his decision earlier in the day to stay off the radio, Aleš reassures Tomaž that they are monitoring his every movement with the spotting scope as best they can. But at the moment their efforts are futile for he is once again immersed in the fog.

For three agonising hours, Tomaž struggles with the next 100 vertical metres. He has been climbing for nine hours straight, much of the time on the front points of his crampons and hanging off his ice axes. The wall is steep and the strain is palpable. Finally he radioes Aleš that he needs help to locate a suitable bivouac spot because he is physically and mentally spent. Aleš can do very little because Tomaž is still in the fog. Nevertheless, he tries to help.

'A bit above you, you might find a ledge; there is a ledge 200 metres above you.'

'To the left, ah . . . can you hear me . . . ALI! Do you see a rock arête covered with ice 100 metres above me?'

'I can see it!'

'How does it look? . . . Hello!'

'Copy, I am watching, Tomaž! I can see a mushroom above you, but it is hard to decide from here if a bivouac is possible there.'

'To the left, not above me, left, left, arête to the left! . . . There are couloirs above me to the left and right, right above me a rock with a cornice . . .'

'Would you want to bivouac on this arête?'

'Give it to me straight, 50 metres right above me is a rock arête, I am asking if it is flat on top! Give me Maja!'

'Copy.'

Shocked once again at Tomaž's orders, Aleš hands the radio over to Maja. They both know that this demand is a mistake, for not only is Maja's eyesight poor, she has no real idea of what to search for on the face. It is only Aleš who can help Tomaž in this situation, and Aleš has once again been summarily dismissed. Tomaž screams his demand:

'C'mon, Maja, you look.'

'Tomaž, I see nothing, absolutely nothing. I cannot even look through the scope because of my glasses, it's true! And even if I could see, I am not an alpinist, how would I know the best place to climb?'

Maja and Aleš are beside themselves. Tomaž is obviously exhausted, almost certainly dehydrated, and is struggling to maintain control of his nerves. He has been on his front points for 12 hours now.

3 August, 20.00

An hour later, the radio comes alive.

'I found a hole!'

'Bravo, congratulations!'

'But I do not know where I am in this murk!'

'We lost you in the fog. If you know, tell us where you went.'

'To the end of the arête, to the top of the serac, I am to the left somewhere on top of the arête.'

'You went up and left?'

'Yes, but not much left, directly up on the arête . . .'

Aleš immediately moves to the scope to try and locate him. Anda takes over the radio to reassure Tomaž that Aleš is searching for his position. Tomaž responds: 'He cannot find me, I am inside, everything is hollow, but I dug deep, I will clip into ice screws.' Anda asks if it is a safe bivouac spot. Tomaž replies: 'I think it is. I was completely disoriented before, everything is vertical, no place to rest, I sunk in on the arête, I fell down into the hole and I started digging – like a cat.'

Maja has been recording all this radio chatter, and now she must calm her rattled nerves and set her frayed emotions aside in order to respond professionally and accurately to the radio station, which has already called base camp twice that day.

3 August, 22.00

Later that night, after he has settled in to his bivouac, Tomaž calls again. He is soaking wet because it has been snowing all afternoon and water has been spraying on him from the rocks above. He explains that he is attempting to dry his clothing inside his bivouac bag, which he has secured to the wall by clipping it to his ice screws. But it's his socks that are particularly problematic: all three pairs are completely soaked and he is worried about frostbite on his feet. He has been melting snow for rehydration and has managed to eat a one-pot meal, his first food of the day. He relays his thoughts on the day that has passed, expressing surprise that the tower was so difficult. He knew that crossing Point Zero would be dangerous but he thought that the terrain would ease off after that. He was mistaken. In fact, he fell several times in the process of attempting to dig his way through the overhanging seracs. The last fall was a lucky one, for he fell through the ceiling of a hole, directly into a minuscule snow cave. It is this cave that he has enlarged into a bivouac. He estimates that he is at about 6,400 metres. After a long day of bashing, his ice axes and crampon points are dull. Finally he admits, 'Today was one of the hardest days of my life. I was on the edge a few times. Or over it.'

They talk about the following day and what lies ahead. Tomaž believes he will first have to do a steep traverse to the left. But he's not sure. Orientation in this fog is almost hopeless, and with the overhangs that loom above him, it's impossible to see far ahead. 'I can recognise the main features of the wall, but when I am in the couloirs I can see practically nothing,' he relates. How far will he attempt to go tomorrow? It is impossible to say. If the weather is good he will continue up, but if not, he must consider traversing to the Messner route. 'I hope it will work out' are his parting words before signing off for the night.

After their radio conversation, Maja thinks about Tomaž, about why he is here, and about this game of alpinism. She wonders just how far he will go, how much he will risk for this mountain. Is it worth his life? Above all, she thinks about the power of nature. It's clear to her that it makes no difference to the mountain if there is a climber on its face: avalanches will continue to release, seracs will continue to break off, rocks will continue to fall. Unlike others, who see the mountain as a living, feeling entity, Maja is sure that it doesn't care if there is someone who is afraid, who is bold, who is in love, or who loves life. The mountain just *is*. It has no emotions. She wonders if Tomaž will be in touch with the mountain and be in the right place at the right time tomorrow. Or not.

Ama Dablam, 1996

Throughout the autumn and winter of 1995, Tomaž spent little time at home, for he was either working or climbing. This left Sergeja ample time to reflect on their relationship and to proceed through her second pregnancy with only her young daughter as company. Her memories of Urša's difficult birth left her fearful. But she was also excited about another child: 'I wanted to have many children. I knew that I was born for them and that they would be the biggest joy of my life.' Tomaž was spending increasing amounts of time with Šrauf, who was by now a very close friend.

Sometimes they climbed together, and at other times Tomaž helped him build his new house. Their conversations inevitably turned to climbing. Šrauf shared his vast knowledge of the history of alpinism with Tomaž, giving him countless insights and bits of information that helped Tomaž form his own climbing strategy. Šrauf was a true mentor for him, a fact that Sergeja recognized and approved of. She knew that Tomaž had been fundamentally changed by Šrauf and that he had set himself the goal of, one day, becoming a legend himself.

After a long day of moving furniture in the cold December air, just two days before Christmas, Šrauf and Tomaž finally decided to finish up. Šrauf offered Tomaž a lift home. Their conversation felt strangely stilted, possibly due to Šrauf's increasingly complex and troubled personal life. During the drive, Šrauf asked what Tomaž was doing the next day. Tomaž replied that he would be spending the Christmas holidays with his family. Šrauf told Tomaž that he intended to go climbing with his girlfriend. As he prepared to leave, he shook hands with Tomaž, said goodbye and drove off.

The next day, 24 December, Šrauf was killed in an avalanche on the north face of Mala Mojstrovka in the Julian Alps. He and his climbing partner, Jasna Boratanič, would not be discovered until months later, when the warm spring sun melted the avalanche debris that was piled at the base of the face. Šrauf's death was a deeply personal loss for Tomaž. He, along with every other Slovenian climber, was stunned, saddened and grief-stricken. None of them could believe it. Šrauf was indestructible. He had been gruff and harsh, tough and clever, and his climbing abilities were legendary. They all knew that if it could happen to Šrauf, it could happen to any of them.

Shadowing Tomaž's grief was the ever-present burden of how to make a decent living for his family. Their four-year-old daughter Urša was almost painfully beautiful, and now, with Sergeja's pregnancy, the pressure only increased. To ease it, Tomaž demonstrated an amazing level of flexibility in his choice of work: cleaning, painting, construction, anything that came his way. Viki, aware that he was desperately short of money, asked if he would paint his house. Tomaž jumped at the offer of work. Years later, after Tomaž had become a national hero, Viki laughingly considered inviting people into his home and charging them a fee to touch the ceiling that he had painted. But that was still years away. For now, it was just another job that brought in a bit of badly needed money. And the relatively repetitive work gave Tomaž time to dream: Himalayan dreams.

Almost a year had passed since he had last been in the Himalayas. Though the expedition dynamics had been tumultuous, reaching the summit of Annapurna had given him confidence and more determination than ever to return to the big peaks. Quietly he had already begun planning his return, this time to the North-West Face of Ama Dablam. Located in the Khumbu region of Nepal, the 6,812-metre peak is one of the most elegant in the Himalayas. Even the name is exquisite, for it means 'Mother and Pearl Necklace'. When Bill Tilman and Charlie Houston explored this area in 1950 in an effort to determine if there was a feasible route up the south side of Everest, they were constantly distracted by the beauty of Ama Dablam. 'It's like the Matterhorn, just as sheer and sharp but ten thousand feet higher and pulls your attention from all else, even the scores of other peaks near and far,' Houston had enthused. They could see no viable route up the savagely steep flanks of Ama Dablam.

Though the first ascent of Ama Dablam would not take place until 1961, by 2005 there had been 1,472 ascents of the mountain, making it the most frequently climbed peak in the Nepal Himalayas. But the North-West Face was special, untouched: this was still a prize to be won. Tomaž and two others felt they were up for the challenge.

Leading the expedition was the well-known Slovenian climber Vanja Furlan. Furlan was not only a great climber, but also an outgoing and personable man who was extremely skilled at developing his public profile, a talent that sometimes created tension amongst other Slovenian climbers. It was a skill that allowed him to secure his own financing, providing him with considerable independence from the Mountaineering Association, as well as the freedom to choose his own climbs. The third member of the expedition was the very experienced Slovenian alpinist Zvonko Požgaj, who had summitted K2 just three years before.

The North-West Face of Ama Dablam would not be Furlan's first new route in the Himalayas, for he had already soloed a new route on Langshisha Ri in 1994. But for Tomaž, this would be his first attempt at something so bold. The North-West Face was widely acknowledged as a difficult objective, since a number of very talented climbing teams had already attempted it and been rebuffed. Furlan was insistent that they do it alpine style, which meant no fixed lines along the way, no Sherpa support and no supplementary oxygen. Tomaž agreed with that approach up to a point, but he admitted that his primary goal was simply to get up the face, declaring: 'I don't care if we climb it alpine, Himalayan or even Mediterranean style, as long as we climb it!'

Leaving Slovenia wasn't easy. By now, Sergeja was very advanced in her pregnancy and they knew that Tomaž was likely to be in Nepal when she gave birth. She remembered the last day before his departure: 'I was standing in the kitchen. Tomaž gave me a hug, like always, and said: "Hold on, you are strong" and he left, just like that. I stood there for a while and I did not know what to do with that experience. Maybe he is only joking, I thought, and he will turn around at the airport. Maybe this is all just a dream. I stood there for a short while and I became very sad. I needed somebody with me even more so because of the bad experience during my first delivery.' She simply couldn't fathom Tomaž's need to climb this mountain at this particular time. Surely he could wait for another season? Was his family not more important? But Sergeja was strong and she recalled what she did next: 'At that very moment I pulled peace from my inner depths and it lasted until the delivery. I completely switched off any thoughts about Tomaž. I was not involved in where he was, what he was doing. I had my own mission and preparations for the delivery.' Nevertheless, his leavetaking created considerable tension between them.

There was also a certain amount of tension with the Mountaineering Association of Slovenia. At first it appeared that they would support the climb financially. Then it became clear that all of their support would be going to the much higher-profile Everest expedition taking place at the same time. Led by Viki Grošelj, this was another attempt at an 8,000-metre ski descent with Davorin Karničar, one of the brothers who had successfully skied down Annapurna the year before.

By now, Tomaž was learning how to work with private companies, and he had secured some funding for his expenses. Even with his very first efforts, he developed relationships with his supporters that more closely resembled patronage arrangements, possibly due to his engaging personality and absolute commitment to his objectives. This too landed him in trouble, when accusations and counteraccusations about 'ownership' of sponsors swirled about the Slovenian climbing community.

Despite the Association turmoil and the pressures at home, the Ama Dablam team was finally off. After a few days in Kathmandu to top up their food supplies, they headed up to the Khumbu valley, where their first stop was a symbolic visit to the Thyangboche monastery. There, the resident lama duly blessed them and sent them on their way. Base camp was at the foot of the face, allowing them a full view of the intimidating scene: so intimidating that Požgaj soon realised that the North-West Face wasn't the route for him. They were now a rope of two.

They assembled base camp, set up their tents and decorated the camp surroundings with prayer flags and a chorten to protect them from danger. Shortly afterwards, they received an unusual note from Škarja, who was nearby on Everest, wishing them luck: 'If you manage to do it, you'll really be big shots. The whole Mountaineering Association of Slovenia is backing you, but do use your heads when you tackle this beautiful face. Cheers – and good luck!'[1]

For acclimatisation, Furlan and Tomaž first ascended the nearby 6,173-metre Imjatse. Then it was time to get serious about Ama Dablam. Back at base camp, they patiently waited out the threatening weather and began to prepare for the climb, organising their ropes, hardware and food, repeatedly trying to pare their loads down to the bare essentials. Their final negotiation concerned the amount of food they would take up the mountain. Tomaž wanted to take two bags; Furlan preferred less, insisting that all he had taken on Jannu in 1991 had been two packets of biscuits and one and a half litres of tea. 'How did that work out?' Tomaž asked. Furlan answered: 'The second day in the bivouac, Bojan [Počkar] was so dehydrated that he said he was having visions of a two-litre bottle of Coke, so we went back.' Tomaž countered with, 'I told you so.'

Tomaž wanted neither dehydration nor hallucinations on Ama Dablam, pointing out that it would be fine to go light if everything went well on the face, but what if they got caught in a storm? If they were stranded in a bivouac for even a couple of days, the extra food that he was insisting upon would be a welcome sight. He won the argument – their packs were heavy.

They rose at 3.00 a.m. After heading over to the wall, their first challenge was to cross the bergschrund – the gap that separates the glacier ice from the wall itself. That accomplished, they headed up unroped through deep snow. Above them hung a number of threatening seracs, motivating them to move as quickly as they safely could. Suddenly, and without warning, the first of the seracs exploded above them, shooting lethal missiles of ice and snow over them. Luckily they escaped injury. Next they were faced with a much steeper headwall, where they roped together and attempted to protect the climb by constructing belays with their ice screws. But in the entire first pitch (one rope length of fifty metres) they managed to place only one screw. Pitch after pitch they continued, belaying each other in turn. At one point Furlan was forced to dismantle the lower belay while Tomaž was still climbing because Tomaž simply ran out of rope before he could locate another suitable belay location in the steep, shattered rock. There was no alternative but to climb together, with no belay to protect a fall.

Now it began to snow, lightly at first, but soon increasing in intensity until it was a full-blown storm. Between the snow-filled air and the avalanches streaming down around them, it became difficult to breathe, for their lungs were filled with snow. In the process of trying to climb through this nightmare, Tomaž managed, not only to bend one of his ice axe picks, but to break the second pick as well. Finally, late that afternoon, they found a small spot underneath a serac which they cleared of snow and flattened into a tiny platform for their tent. Furlan was so exhausted that he was incapable of retaining even a drop of tea in his stomach. The day had been a tough one, but at least they had found a place where they could spend the night and hope for an improvement in the weather by the following morning.

Unfortunately, the weather did not improve. Rather, it snowed all night and throughout the following day. Their challenge now shifted from trying to climb the wall to somehow keeping their tent on its precarious perch. Avalanches streamed down around them, on top of them and behind them, threatening to push them off the wall entirely. They struggled with the tent all the following night, almost willing it to stay in place. The third morning brought an eerie calm, accompanied by an even more ominous sight: nearby Everest wreathed in a lens-shaped cloud. This signalled a major storm. They quickly dismantled the tent and began climbing once again, but almost immediately had to turn back due to the avalanches brought on by all the new snow. An hour later they tried again. Once more they were turned back by avalanches. By now it was clear that the face needed time to rid itself of excess snow, so they decided to retreat to base camp and wait.

After five days on the mountain, they were back in base camp, eating, drinking and repairing their equipment. The twenty-sixth of April was a relaxing day as they readied themselves for the next assault. Tomaž could not know it, but that day, back in Slovenia, Sergeja gave birth to their second child – a son named Tomaž.

Oblivious to the momentous event back home, they waited four more days for the weather to stabilise and for the mountain to stop sloughing snow and ice. On 30 April they were off again, heading up with their packs full of equipment and even more food than before. They reached their previous bivouac site by early afternoon, set up the tent on its precarious perch and began the process of rehydrating, eating and resting. By midnight they were awake, and by 3.30 a.m. on 1 May they were on the face again. When they reached the high point of their previous attempt, they realised that the mountain was now too steep and the climbing too technical and delicate for them to climb with packs, so they began the arduous job of hauling them. After 12 hours of climbing on mostly vertical ice they reached an overhanging, snow-covered rock barrier. Only 25 metres high, the rock section took Tomaž two and a half hours to climb. As he recalled the effort, he said, 'I do not know to this day how I managed to cheat my way over, as I was unable to peg a single piton. My calves burned with pain, and I had lost all feeling in my fingers and toes . . . I would rather not repeat such a pitch in a long time.'

Above this pitch, Furlan took the lead. But not more than 10 feet above the belay, he broke off a large rock and catapulted into space. His only piece of protection on the wall was one piton, which promptly pulled out. Tomaž managed to hold him from the belay and he ended up falling about 15 feet. Luckily, only Furlan's jacket and one of the ropes were damaged. He quickly collected himself and went back up, climbing well into the night. He finally lowered back down to their only secure belay stance to hang, together with Tomaž, suspended throughout the long, cold night.

As the third morning dawned, they slowly began to move their frozen, aching bodies, surveying the damage from the previous days: numb toes and bleeding fingers. Furlan went up first, ascending the fixed lines he had left from his high point the night before. Tomaž had just begun to disassemble the belay when suddenly there was a loud bang, and a huge bag hurtled past him down the face. It was their bag of equipment: ice screws, bolts, deadman and everything they would need for a retreat off the face should it become necessary. Both Tomaž and Furlan screamed out in terror and then, almost immediately, in an automatic response, went back to the task at hand. There was really nothing else to be done. Perhaps they were in shock. The hurtling pack had just sealed their fate; they no longer had the alternative of descending their route. Their only chance was to reach the summit and descend by the easier South-West Ridge. But for this they would need strength.

The wall continued, unforgivingly steep. They spent another miserable night stuck in the open, since there was no spot flat enough to erect their tent. Thankfully there was a small ledge on which to sit through the night, so at least they weren't forced to hang from their axes. The fourth day on the wall was the longest yet. They climbed on and on, forcing themselves to concentrate, concentrate. Each move was precise, for there was no possibility for error on this steep, shattered face of rock and ice. At midnight they finally found a secure spot in the shelter of a crevasse. They set up the tent, unfurled their sleeping bags and sank into an exhausted sleep.

The wan morning light of 4 May revealed an imposing rock barrier looming above them. They attempted to make radio contact with Požgaj in base camp so that he could provide them with some directions. But the radio connection was very bad and they could not decipher his replies, so they were forced to navigate the maze by instinct. At last they arrived at a couloir that led up and up – to the summit. They had done it. Furlan described the moment: 'A few metres below the summit, Tomaž stops, turns around and waits. When I plod up to him, we take each other by the arm, stop for a while, and then slowly, arm in arm, climb onward. On the top, we give each other a clumsy hug and thump each other on the rucksack. And then tears, tears again . . .'[2] The North-West Face was climbed. As if to celebrate, the sky cleared and they were rewarded with spectacular views of the Himalayan giants surrounding them. As they gazed about, and at each other, they agreed that a lifetime of climbs still awaited them.

But first they had to get down. Nobody had been up the ridge that season and it was easy to see why: it was in appallingly poor condition due to the continuous storms. They carefully began their descent and by the seventh day were back at base camp, celebrating and happy to be alive. They agreed that their success, and the name of the route, would be given to their mentor, Stane Belak – Šrauf – who had lost his life in an avalanche on Mala Mojstrovka six months earlier.

Meanwhile, the big Slovenian expedition was nearby on Everest, so the Ama Dablam team headed over to the Everest base camp. Davorin Karničar reached a high point of 8,200 metres on 9 May but then chaos reigned as one climber after another succumbed to the storm that engulfed the peak. In all, eight people died on Everest on 10 May, making it the worst climbing day on record.

While at Everest base camp, Tomaž obtained the use of a satellite phone to call Sergeja. Only then did he learn of the birth of their son. Thankfully everything had gone well and the birth had been much easier than with

Urša. In fact, she was in the hospital only twenty-five minutes before giving birth. Tomaž's parents had been there for her, supporting her. Urša was there too, and as the new big sister, she was proud and almost lady-like in her demeanour. But something was missing. Sergeja recalled, 'I was crying. I was missing Tomaž's first look at our son . . . to share this unique moment, this diamond was meant to be only for me.' Tomaž was ecstatic and could hardly contain himself. He walked from base camp to Thyangboche in record time, fuelled by 'liquid oxygen', otherwise known as schnapps.

Years later he looked back on this moment and recognised it for what it was: a turning point in his relationship with Sergeja. He had succeeded beyond his wildest dreams on Ama Dablam, but at what cost? Sergeja had been left alone to shoulder the responsibility of childbirth. She had felt abandoned by the man she adored: he should have been there. 'My regret is that I left her when she was pregnant. It was a decision. It was a day. I had to make a choice and life changed completely. I went to Ama Dablam and she had Tomi and I wasn't there. Ama Dablam gave me the chance to become a Himalayan climber, but the cost was my family. That was the deal. I didn't know it at the time . . .'

He returned home as quickly as possible to rejoice in the miracle of new birth – and a son! Sergeja predicted that he would one day be a very fine football player and she loved to watch as Tomaž carried Tomi around the apartment, staring at him endlessly. But there was also endless work to do to try and make up for the time lost in Nepal. The bills continued to arrive each month and the mouths – four of them now – all needed to be fed.

Just three months after the expedition, Vanja Furlan fell to his death on Maestrica in the Julian Alps. First Šrauf and now Furlan. Tomaž couldn't help considering his own mortality amidst his grief. And he couldn't ignore the increasingly worried looks that the mother of his two young children cast his way.

Later that autumn, Tomaž learned that he and Furlan had been nominated for the prestigious mountaineering award, the Piolet d'Or – an international prize founded in France by the French magazine *Montagnes* and the French mountaineering association, the Groupe de Haute Montagne (GHM). Since its foundation in 1991, the prize had quickly became the most coveted mountaineering award in the world, even though most serious alpinists doubted that individual and very different climbs could be judged and compared in this way. Nevertheless, the organisers and an invited jury struggled to establish competitive criteria each year, sometimes choosing winners that were hotly contested by the rest of the mountaineering world.

In fact, climbing awards had existed since the eighteenth century in one form or another. When Jacques Balmat and Dr Michel Paccard made the first ascent of Mont Blanc in 1786 they were awarded a sum of money from Horace-Bénédict de Saussure, the Swiss aristocrat often credited as the founder of alpinism, as well as a prize from the King of Sardinia. In 1988 both the Polish climber Jerzy Kukuczka and the Italian Reinhold Messner won silver medals for their ascents of all fourteen 8,000-metre peaks. Some climbers wondered what it would have taken to win gold! The Soviet Union had been pitting their climbers against each other in organised competitions since 1948. The competitions were part of the Soviet training strategy and undoubtedly produced some of the world's toughest climbers. And now it was the Piolet d'Or. Since one of the founders of the prize was a French climbing magazine, some criticised it as a blatant promotion of the magazine itself. But the Piolet d'Or soon became very respected – and coveted by climbers from all over the globe.

The competition attempted to adhere to the strict ethics of the founding values of the GHM, rewarding not only a high technical level of climbing but also 'commitment' to the mountain, a reference to the fact that there might be no easy way of turning back. The GHM also valued both the originality of a climbing objective and the innovative nature of the ascent. Their mandate stated:

> The practice of alpinism is in effect in perpetual evolution, and this dimension should not be forgotten. It is by the crossing of certain stages that were considered impassable that mentalities have evolved, and ascents reputed to be impossible have become commonplace . . . Respect for the mountains that surround us, the beauty of movement, and the spirit in which people climb those mountains are also primary conditions for the awarding of the prize. We cannot in fact pass down to future generations summits mutilated in the name of a destructive climbing style without profoundly altering the spirit itself of this activity.

Given these lofty standards, it was indeed an honour for Furlan and Tomaž to be considered, though it was not the first time a Slovenian climber had been nominated. The very first award, presented in 1991, went to Andrej Štremfelj and Marko Prezelj, for their 3,000-metre, alpine-style ascent of the South Pillar of Kangchenjunga as part of a large Slovenian expedition. Still, being nominated was one thing; winning was another. Tomaž was sceptical. Prezelj, too, thought Ama Dablam unlikely to win.

Nevertheless, on 7 December Tomaž journeyed to the little village of Autrans in France, where the prestigious prize was to be announced at the local mountain film festival. In practical terms, this was an unnecessary, inconvenient and costly trip abroad when he felt he should be at home, looking after business. But the trip provided an opportunity to renew his somewhat strained friendship with Marko Prezelj, for the two climbers travelled together with their wives to France. Tomaž waited impatiently along with the other nominees, and he was absolutely stunned when the winner was announced: Ama Dablam. He accepted on behalf of Vanja Furlan and himself.

Tomaž soon learned that winning the prize meant a great deal more than he had anticipated. The associated media attention thrust him firmly on to the international stage of alpinism in one five-minute ceremony. *American Alpine Journal* editor Christian Beckwith referred to the climb as 'perhaps the most impressive climb of the year' and an achievement that was 'firmly rooted in the heart of significant climbing'.[3] Virtually unknown outside Slovenia before the Piolet d'Or, Tomaž's name was now suddenly on the lips of climbers around the world, with everyone watching to see his next step. He later ruefully observed that Ama Dablam launched his career as a professional climber, but cost him his marriage.

CHAPTER EIGHT

BOBAYE

4 August 2005, 11.00, Nanga Parbat, Rupal Face

Tomaž has been searching for an exit from a labyrinth of overhanging seracs and snow mushrooms for five hours. The soft, unstable snow formations will simply not support his weight. He calls base camp on the radio and describes his meanderings so that Aleš might locate him with the scope and help guide him up the wall: 'I went into the couloir, directly into the vertical area where everything is coming down. I went all the way inside, where the rocks start, then traversed to the left.' Although Aleš systematically scans the face, it is impossible for him to spot Tomaž.

4 August, 12.00

An hour later he calls in again, this time more agitated. 'I can go nowhere. I would have to climb the rock, overhanging mushrooms, powder!' he yells. Aleš searches in vain for some clue to offer him. Tomaž calls back in twenty minutes to enquire about the arête to his left. Aleš replies that it looks marginally better, but as they go back and forth discussing possibilities, it becomes evident that accurate orientation between the two is impossible. The tower above Tomaž seems unclimbable and he is unable to traverse further left to reach what looks like easier ground. He is squatting, trapped on a delicate snow mushroom, soaked and in pain from a rock fall earlier in the morning. He has absolutely no idea how to proceed.

4 August, 18.00

When he next calls base camp late in the afternoon, his concerns are obvious: 'I was avalanched on as soon as the sun came out . . . I was hit by rocks, snow, ice . . . It was looking like the end. I did not know what to do today. I can hardly breathe.' Since he can't move anywhere safely, he decides to sleep on the snow mushroom and try to climb it in the morning. When Maja asks him if he's injured, Tomaž responds, 'I do not feel anything because everything hurts. I feel like I am caught inside a fridge.' Maja doesn't know how to respond to this. She waits in silence. Then Tomaž comes back on the radio with an unusual request: 'Can you read me the text for the Saturday news edition [of *Delo*]?' Maja is taken aback. Is he going mad? She responds that he would be better served by saving his batteries. 'What about authorisation?' he asks, joking about his own approval of the text. Clearly he is not about to let this go. So Maja begins reading her text, something she is loath to do.

> *Tomaž Humar is not a sport climber, a collector of 8,000-metre peaks, or a big-wall specialist. Instead, the world gives him credit for being an alpinist such as the legendary Mummery, Cassin or Terray; great icons who moved the boundaries of the possible and took alpinism to new dimensions . . . His mastery on ice and rock made Reinhold Messner compare him to Kukuczka, Heckmair and Dibon . . . Famous Himalayan chronicler Elizabeth Hawley said about this alpinist, whom the American media named a 'climbing animal': 'He is crazy. But definitely not stupid!'*

Maja stops to say, 'That was an introduction. Is that enough?' Tomaž responds immediately, 'No, no! I will switch to the old set of batteries. Just read on . . .' It is this kind of behaviour that, in the months to come, will elicit criticism. Steve House will observe in an *Outside* magazine article that he finds it 'interesting' that Tomaž appeared to be running out of food and fuel, and yet seemed to have an unlimited supply of radio batteries with which to communicate with his base camp team and, more importantly, with his media sponsors. But Tomaž had his own technique for prolonging his batteries' life: a combination of warming and biting them! And he claimed to know exactly how many batteries he had – old batteries, useless for transmission because of their reduced power – to listen to the

Delos piece. He was saving his good batteries for more important matters.

Maja checks to see if he is still awake. He is, so she continues, giving him a summary of his own climbing career. Some time later she suggests stopping, for his radio batteries must surely be running low. But her voice is like a drug and Tomaž wants more. Both Maja's version of his life and the quotes he knows so well are comforting him, giving him strength for the days ahead. More than anything, her voice is a connection – a vital link to life and survival – something he needs more than anything this night.

Maja reads on, with a description of his personality within the larger climbing community. She wonders what he will think of her analysis.

Alpinism has been described as 'an exploration of the useless world' by those who see nothing in it. However, for Humar, alpinism surely has some higher meaning, as proven by the thousands of email messages he is getting these days. He symbolises inspiration, hope and longing to people all over the world. His story reminds us of Lance Armstrong. 'It is not just about climbing! It is about a game for life!'

'Let it happen!' is written on the yellow canvas of his tent where he is squatting high up on the mountain . . . However, this modern gladiator will not give up easily. 'If you want to kill me, you will have to kill my name first!'

Maja finally stops, worried about his response to her very honest attempt at understanding and communicating his essence. She is quiet for a while, and then breaks the silence: 'So, are you asleep?' Tomaž has been digesting the contents of her article, and responds, 'Hmm, I don't know, it's a bit cruel, but most of what you say is true. Maybe I should add something about my parents. We have become very close again. I have returned to my roots, which is very important for the continuation of my path.'

The batteries are running low. Maja retires to her tent and Tomaž burrows in to his vertiginous tunnel, each deep in their own thoughts.

Bobaye, 1996

Despite Sergeja's urging to stay home and be a proper husband and father, Tomaž had become obsessed with the Himalayas. Each attempted climb in these savagely beautiful mountains had ended in victory, feeding the inner voice that urged: go back; go back; keep climbing; don't stop now. While his self-confidence and his climbing skills grew, the charm of domesticity was fading. He and Sergeja spent very little time together now, but she was content to be with her children. She was gradually drifting away from him, becoming deeply spiritual and developing her own circle of friends, far from the climbing community that had once been her surrogate family. She had stood at the edge of that society, craving its warmth and companionship, for long enough. She was now determined to end her isolation and join the rest of the world. Tomaž barely noticed her edging away, intent as he was on the Himalayas.

And so it was that, less than six months after returning to his newborn son, Tomaž was back in Nepal, this time for a 6,808-metre peak named Bobaye. The idea had originated with Šrauf, who, with a childlike eagerness, had shown Tomaž photos of the unclimbed peak the previous year. Now Šrauf was dead, but the unclimbed peak remained. First Šrauf, then Furlan – in less than a year. Two close friends and climbing companions dead. It was almost too much, too frightening for Tomaž. When would the finger point at him? Undoubtedly these worries consumed Sergeja as well, although she had developed her own coping methods: 'I started reading a lot of books and developed the ability to predict the future. In essence I used every expedition for my own inner peace and development. I always knew how it would finish for him and I was not worried.'

By all counts, the Bobaye plan was ambitious. A team of 10 climbers, led by the well-respected Slovenian alpinist Roman Robas, intended to simultaneously climb Api, Nampa and the as-yet-unclimbed Bobaye, all by new routes and in alpine style. It was a Slovenian dream team, including the likes of Marko Prezelj and Andrej Štremfelj. Despite Tomaž's disobedience on Annapurna the year before, he had been invited on the climb. But even with the presence of several great climbers, he would never feel so alone on an expedition.

The three peaks stand near each other in a triangle, with Bobaye south of Nampa and south-east of Api. Both Api and Nampa had been climbed before, but the Slovenians were after new routes. They would use no Sherpa support, no fixed ropes and no fixed camps, and some would climb solo, including Tomaž. Everything would be done out of supply depots dropped at the foot of each mountain face.

Tomaž was the first to leave the raspberry field that served as their base camp. On 30 October he packed his rucksack, struggling with emotions that he could not completely understand: memories of his partner Furlan, images of his long-suffering wife, their beautiful daughter and newborn son, and the presence of Šrauf, his teacher and guide and visionary for this climb. He packed alone, for each climber was concentrating on his own objective. The climbers had not gelled into a team; they were merely a collection of individuals with individual aspirations. Tomaž's head was eerily full of Šrauf. He missed his mentor, someone to encourage him, speak with him and give him much-needed confidence.

By 31 October he was ready. After a short night's sleep at a supply depot at the 4,300-metre base of Bobaye, he began his climb at 2.00 a.m. The first hurdle was a sinister, crevasse-ridden glacier, each hole obscured by a blanket of deep snow. It was extremely dangerous terrain for a solo climber and there were times when he fell to his hands and knees as he tried to distribute his weight as evenly as possible over the hidden crevasses. After gingerly crossing this minefield, he heaved a sigh of relief and moved on to the west face and into a small diagonal couloir, above which loomed teetering ice seracs and the entire massive triangular face of Bobaye. Unfortunately, the 80-degree angle of the couloir created the perfect chute for chunks of ice hurtling down from the seracs above. Moving quickly and sometimes erratically to dodge the airborne ice, Tomaž managed to avoid all but a couple of chunks, which struck him on his arm and shoulder. Next, he traversed the face towards the North-West Ridge, where he planned to carve out a bivouac for the night. The snow on the ridge was too deep and soft, so he moved back on to the face and dug a hole at 5,500 metres in an ice cave directly under a serac. His plan was to dig a ledge on which to set up his tent, but after several exhausting hours of hacking with his ice axe, the ledge was still pitifully narrow. He assessed his options: continue digging well into the night in order to establish a proper spot for his tent; or stop, conserve his energy, and simply attach the tent and himself to an anchor. He chose the latter. The result was not very comfortable, but at least it was secure.

That night, two dreams battled for control of his partially conscious mind: the unknown challenges he would face in the next 1,300 metres to the summit, juxtaposed with thoughtful words of encouragement from Šrauf.

The next morning he resumed climbing at 5.30 a.m., leaving most of his equipment and food in the suspended tent. He took only enough for an emergency bivouac, plus his camera and radio. When he reached the North-

Max Humar and Rosalija Globokar
on their wedding day, May 4, 1968.

Tomaž Humar, showing early
signs of strong character, 1971.

Birthday smiles
for Tomaž, 1973.

After returning from Kosovo, Tomaž took to solo-climbing with a vengeance. Here he is on Lover Overhang, 6c+.

Tomaž and Sergeja were married on Dec 7, 1991.

Tomaž paid the bills by painting church steeples in 1988.

Tomaž and Stane Belak (Šrauf) enjoying hot springs on their way back from Ganesh V in 1994.

Šrauf at Camp I on Ganesh V after removing his tooth from a prune.

Šrauf on ridge between Camps I and II on Ganesh V.

Self-portrait on
the summit of
Annapurna,
May 6, 1995,
Tomaž's first
8,000-metre peak.

Climbing Ama
Dablam's North-West
Face, April, 1996,
with Vanja Furlan.
This is the second
rock pitch following
a hanging bivouac
and after losing all of
their ice protection.

Vanja Furlan at a
bivouac on the
North-West Face
of Ama Dablam,
April, 1996.

Returning home to a new-
born son, Tomi, after climbing the North-West Face of
Ama Dablam, May, 1996.

The Humar Family
portrait: Tomi, Sergeja,
Urša and Tomaž, 2001.

Janez Jeglič and Carlos Carsolio in their bivouac tent just below the summit of Lobuche East. Carsolio is trying to replace his lost goggles with plastic film containers.

Self-portrait on the summit of Nuptse, minutes after discovering that Johan had disappeared. Oct 31, 1997.

Sergeja, 1990.

Tomaž, elated and relieved after summitting El Capitan's Reticent Wall, 1998.

Triumphant return
to the Ljubljana air-
port after soloing
the South Face of
Dhaulagiri on Oct.
31, 1999. Stipe
Božić, Viki Grozelj,
Tomaž Humar,
Reinhold Messner.

Reinhold Messner,
Riccardo Cassin,
Tomaž Humar
and Sir Edmund
Hillary at the
Trento Film
Festival in 2000.

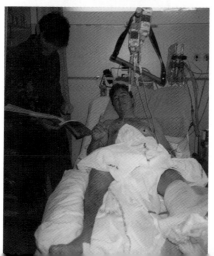

Tomaž, in intensive
care, after falling
into the basement of
his home in 2000.

Tomaž, training on seracs at
Jannu Base Camp, Oct 13, 2004.

Tomaž abseiling from
the first rock-grass pillar
after acclimatising on
the left side of Jannu East,
Oct 11, 2004.

West Ridge for a second time, he radioed base camp in order to gather his bearings on the face, based on the information given him from below. But the sightlines were poor and those at base camp could not provide him with the detail that he needed. He would have to feel his way up, with difficult climbing and complex route-finding ahead. After climbing delicately up the mixed ice and rock of the North-West Face, Tomaž arrived at a vertical granite groove festooned with a thin layer of ice. Completely unstable, it somehow supported his weight.

He moved steadily and carefully towards the col that separated the middle and main summits, each step upwards exposing him more to the freshening wind that buffeted him in a series of balance-destroying gusts. His concentration intensified as he struggled to remain upright. Then, just before the col, he faced yet another hurdle – an exposed traverse on a granite slab covered in light, sugary powder snow. There was nothing he could do to protect himself – only move lightly and delicately across, willing himself not to make one wrong move. Even a small slip would have meant plummeting to the valley below, and certain death. Finally he reached the other side of the slab and topped out on to the ridge, where the full force of the wind slammed up against him. By 1.00 p.m. he was on the top.

After hours of tiptoeing across 60–90-degree ice flakes, rock slabs and unconsolidated snow, all unroped, a surge of relief overcame him. Though the sun shone brightly, the temperature remained brutally cold due to the unrelenting wind. Blowing snow buffeted him, and at one point while walking along the narrow, exposed ridge, he was knocked to his knees by a gust of wind.

He remained on the summit for about 20 minutes, taking photographs of the splendid view and gazing down at base camp, three kilometres below him. When he radioed in to base camp, he informed Robas of his position and then announced his name for the route: 'Golden Heart', in honour of Sergeja. He didn't waste time, for he realised he must begin his descent in order to reach his tent that day.

Tomaž made good progress down a pillar between the north-west and west walls, thereby avoiding the difficult North-West Face up which he had come. Soon he came up against the first obstacle: a vertical rock barrier. He located a chute of ice that broke through the barrier and immediately switched his mind and body back into technical mode, carefully swinging his axes and placing his crampons to descend safely. It was a perfect descent: his concentration was complete; his fitness was outstanding; his technique was flawless. He was back in his bivouac by 4.00 p.m. and immediately began eating and rehydrating. While he was resting, he decided to name the descent route for his recently deceased partner and friend Vanja Furlan.

The next morning, aided by detailed advice coming up from base camp, he was able to avoid his ascent couloir, but rather down-climbed through a series of snow slopes and ice falls that threaded through the maze of black rock bands. By noon he was at the foot of the face, where his team-mates met him and helped carry his pack back to camp. There he was met with jubilation and celebration. In two days he had accomplished the first of the team's three objectives.

The following day, 3 November, Matic Jošt and Peter Mežnar reached the summit of the 6,755-metre Nampa, pioneering a new route via the central couloir of its South-West Face. Number two objective completed. And by the 4th, the 7,132-metre Api was summitted by Dušan Debelak and Janko Meglič. Apart from an accident that injured both Prezelj and Štremfelj, the expedition was an unqualified success: all three peaks had been climbed in the intended style.

But in base camp, joy was tempered with sadness when they learned that two of their compatriots had died on Karbu, a mountain in eastern Nepal. Tomaž wandered away from the rest of the team and began counting: Šrauf, Furlan, Svetičič, Bojan, Jasna, Žiga. He realised with a sickening start that half of the best Slovenian alpinists had been killed within the last year. How could he reconcile his passion for climbing with the blindingly obvious danger? It was clear by now that his family could not. Sergeja wanted him home, wanted him to have a normal job and to be with his family. She wanted more children but was beginning to realize that this might not be possible with Tomaž: 'He was simply away too much and I had to forget these dreams. Sometimes I am sorry for not being braver, I wish I had more of them, three, four . . .' His parents too did not support this hunger for the Himalayas and his finances were a mess. Perhaps he should stop. Go home and stay there. Get a real job. But at some level he knew it was much too late for that. Sergeja knew too: 'He did not have an easy task; sometimes even he did not know why he had to go to the mountains.' Here on Bobaye, once again, he had tasted the sweetness of success, the intensity of adrenalin, the perfection of a Himalayan face. Regardless of the price he might have to pay, his thoughts were already on his next objective.

While the Bobaye solo ascent never caught the attention of the media, like some of Tomaž's other climbs, it certainly caught the eye of Himalayan historian Elizabeth Hawley. 'I first took notice of him when he soloed Bobaye in the autumn of 1996. The 6,808-metre-high Bobaye had never been attempted by anyone before him. He made its first ascent alone in pure alpine style, and he descended by a different line from his ascent route. That seemed to me an outstanding accomplishment,' she said. The climb was also an important confidence-builder. As Tomaž had negotiated his way amongst the complex configurations of that Himalayan wall – alone – he had learned more about his physical, technical and mental capabilities. He found that he could push further than he had ever done before, testing previously untapped reserves. He felt a quiet assurance that somehow the Himalayan peaks welcomed him on to their faces. He had found a home – unlikely as it might seem – on the steepest, coldest, harshest places on earth. It was here that he felt happy, challenged and engaged. Most of all, he felt alive.

But back home, his marriage was in serious trouble. Outwardly their relationship still looked reasonably solid, but Tomaž knew it was not. 'We were a tight drum and then we developed a leak. Drop by drop, it leaked out.' He and Sergeja managed their troubles in different ways. The usually outgoing Tomaž switched off his phone, went into his private space and licked his wounds. For the traditionally quiet and restrained Sergeja, the solution was to reach out.

Much of the tension was due to finance, for all of these expeditions had drained their reserves. And as the arguments with the Mountaineering Association intensified, Tomaž became more agitated, moody and difficult. He and Sergeja fought constantly. Sergeja joined a new group of friends, strangers to Tomaž, who saw only that Sergeja was deeply unhappy at home. With her friends she was much more at peace. As their acrimony intensified, Sergeja and Tomaž began to lose respect for each other; then bitterness crept in. 'When we're good we are an untouchable couple,' Tomaž said. But even he knew that they were no longer untouchable. Strangely, he blamed others, such as Sergeja's new friends, rather than accepting it as their own responsibility: 'They won. They were jealous and they destroyed us. Stone by stone.'

CHAPTER NINE

NUPTSE

5 August 2005, 06.00, Nanga Parbat, Rupal Face

Waking from his snow hole after a bitterly cold night, Tomaž is dismayed to find that avalanches are hissing down to the left and right of his bivouac. The humidity and fog are stifling. He assesses the situation and concludes that conditions are too dangerous at the moment to continue climbing up. Unfortunately, they are also too dangerous to descend. He is stuck. His radio transmission to base camp describing the situation is short and strained. The cloud above him thickens.

5 August, 06.20

Tomaž calls again to camp, explaining that it is now snowing even more heavily and avalanche activity is increasing. He explains that for the moment he will have to wait, but as soon as this storm passes he will try again to climb the overhanging snow mushroom in order to gain an arête that he thinks may provide a safe line out to the left. If he succeeds in finding an escape route, he will climb as high as he can, or at least until he can find a safer spot to bivouac.

Three times he tries to leave his snow hole, and each time he fails. On each attempt he slips and barely catches himself from falling the entire length of the face.

5 August, 08.20

Tomaž calls again. 'The air around me is wet, and there is spindrift from the avalanches . . . I am squatting on the ice and am trying to shiver in order to at least partially dry out my socks and the rest of my clothing. I have damp things next to my body and completely wet clothes on top. I have nothing to change into. Other than shivering, I cannot move much because of all the avalanches around me.'

There is a long period of silence that day, with no radio communication from Tomaž. Base camp worries because they know that 'when Humar quietens down, then it is really bad'. It is during these long periods of silence that he 'switches' his state of consciousness in order to save energy, and possibly to retain his sanity. When he finally breaks the silence he is obviously contemplative. 'I can squat here for another few days,' he says, explaining that he has used only one of his three gas canisters. He assesses his food supplies: two soups, five pieces of cheese, a small packet of ham and some biscuits. He hasn't been eating much but will now reduce his caloric intake even more in order to stretch his food as long as possible. He appears to be retaining some control of his spirits, for he quips, 'With all these biscuits I can survive another week for sure!'

An hour up the valley, House and Anderson have been trying to prepare for their own climb. Although bad weather has prevented them from viewing the entire Rupal Face, they have managed to begin acclimatising on the Schell route. Because of rock fall, they are climbing only very early in the morning or late at night when the temperatures are colder. The weather worries them, for as House explains, 'You don't usually get more than one weather window on a mountain like this in one season . . . it's kind of luck if it comes when you're acclimatised.' He knows that he and Tomaž are on completely different schedules. The good-weather window – if it comes at all – could arrive in time for Tomaž, or it might appear for him. Without any communication devices other than a SAT phone, which they are using primarily to procure weather forecasts, House states that he knows absolutely nothing about Tomaž and his situation, even though it's being broadcast on his internet site and is well known to climbers elsewhere around the world. House is concentrating on his own goal.

In the meantime, Tomaž's base camp has received a curious message from the internet site 24hours.com, which has been closely monitoring the climb. Their message poses a troubling question: has the team considered the possibility of a helicopter rescue for Tomaž? Maja begins her response: 'Rescue from the central part of Rupal Wall is not possible.' Tomaž has emphasised this a number of times in conversation, but to be perfectly clear with her reply, Maja calls on Aleš to help with the wording. He adds, 'That is the essence of alpinism, the reason that many walls are unclimbed. Some of them remain unclimbed – also for this reason . . . All alpinists who venture on to such [a] wall consciously accept the ultimate risk.' Maja continues, 'They know that it is only *they* who can help themselves, and "the One up there", as Tomaž likes to say.' This is a decisive moment, for with this response in writing on the internet for the entire world to see, the Humar expedition has taken a stand: Tomaž is on his own.

But in fact, base camp has been quietly discussing just such a rescue. They know that Tomaž was obliged to pay a $6,000 deposit for helicopter rescue in order to obtain a climbing permit. They are also aware of the Pakistani rescue policy, which states that the MI-17 helicopters can only fly as high as 5,000 metres, and the Lamas – more powerful machines – up to 5,500 metres. The rules also specify that a rescue will be initiated only if the helicopters are able to land at the rescue site. In Tomaž's case, that would mean descending to around 3,700 metres in order to find a reasonable landing site. He has made it clear in his radio transmissions that descending to 3,700 metres is completely out of the question. He can't even move a few metres from his bivouac without risk of being swept down the face by avalanches. So although they consider the possibility, they know that a helicopter rescue is highly unlikely.

As the situation continues to deteriorate with the worsening weather, everyone grapples with their feelings of helplessness and what appears to be bad luck. In fact, there is a logical explanation for the weather that has very little to do with luck. The summer has been extremely hot up to this point, with a high-pressure system that has completely surrounded the mountain. As the warm air from the nearby plains approaches the isolated massif, the rising air mass is continuously fed moisture from the slopes of Nanga Parbat, 'cooking' the South Face, transforming its vast snowfields into a microclimate of high humidity, clouds, rain and snow. The result is a series of storms, a typical meteorological behaviour in hot summers such as 2005. They are not experiencing bad luck with the weather, but rather a logical phenomenon associated with the current weather patterns. But that doesn't make it any easier to accept.

Maja and Anda peruse the thousands of emails arriving on the expedition web page, choosing particularly supportive ones to read to Tomaž when he periodically makes contact with base camp. Then they discover a bizarre message from the Explorets Web team, host of their American weather forecaster. This email has no forecast, only a poem:

> *It's easy to fight when everything's right,*
> *And you are mad with the thrill of the glory;*
> *It's easy to cheer when the victory's near,*
> *And wallow in fields that are gory.*
> *It's a different song when everything is wrong,*
> *When you're feeling internally mortal;*
> *When it's ten against one, and hope there is none,*
> *Back up, little soldier, and chortle:*
> *Carry on! Carry on!*

They shudder as they contemplate what the outlook must be if the forecaster can't bear to send it.

5 August, 14.00

Finally, later that afternoon, they hear from Tomaž. He describes the conditions: it is snowing constantly, with rivers of snow passing on either side. Even as he speaks, they hear the roar of an avalanche passing within a metre of him. He has not moved all day. He is trapped. Somehow he retains a semblance of humour as he describes his sock-drying technique: 'I took a sock from under my armpit; I pulled it over my arm, and am stretching it with all my five fingers. I breathe into it . . . it does dry a bit; just one of the tricks I am using.'

Then his voice changes. There is just a hint of panic: 'It is coming down constantly. It is not giving up . . . I really cannot go anywhere.' As they huddle around the base camp radio, they feel utterly helpless. There is nothing they can do for Tomaž as he clings to his perch on the face. Then, from the radio, they hear what they have all been thinking about but have not dared to articulate. Quietly he says, 'Call Nazir, I need to discuss my options.'

Nuptse, 1997

Why is it that one person survives an accident and another does not? Who decides? Are there small warning signs that are ignored? Is it completely random? What kind of responsibility rests with the one who lives? How does the survivor manage his grief? These are all questions Tomaž would face on Nuptse.

Located in the Khumbu region of Nepal, just two kilometres from Everest, Nuptse (Tibetan for 'west peak') is 7,855 metres high and forms the westernmost part of the Nuptse-Lhotse massif. The main ridge, separated from Lhotse by a 7,556-metre-high saddle, is a complex one, studded with seven distinct peaks. The ridge continues west-north-west until its steep west face plummets more than 2,300 metres to the Khumbu glacier. The steep South Face of Nuptse is 2,500 metres high and five kilometres wide. The north slopes rise up from the Western-Cwm valley, which also gives access to Everest. It was from here that the main peak was first climbed in 1961 by a British expedition. The peak that Tomaž was interested in was Nuptse W2, 7,742-metres high, and his chosen route had never been attempted: straight up the imposing face itself.

The team was small but powerful. Janez Jeglič, known as Johan by his friends, was acknowledged as one of the top three Slovenian alpinists by the time he teamed up with Tomaž on Nuptse. Tomaž referred to him as one of the 'holy trinity': Jeglič, Silvo Karo and Franček Knez. In fact, it was Jeglič who had first espied this face on Nuptse during their descent from Everest the previous year and began thinking of it as a worthy objective. Johan had climbed extensively in the Alps as well as in the United States and Scotland, but his greatest achievements were in Patagonia and the Himalayas. Frequently climbing with fellow Slovenian and friend Silvo Karo, he had climbed impressive new routes on Baghirathi III in India and on Fitz Roy, Torre Egger and Cerro Torre in Patagonia. Tomaž rated him among the best alpinists in all Europe. Though they knew each other by reputation, it was the first time they would actually climb together. That Jeglič would consider Tomaž for such an imposing objective attested to Tomaž's soaring reputation. Marjan Kovač, the third member of the team, was not as well known, but was a strong climber nevertheless. At the last minute the Slovenians were joined by Carlos Carsolio, a good friend of Tomaž from their days together on Annapurna in 1995.

Upon their arrival, they first had to deal with acclimatisation. There was no shortage of choice in the nearby vicinity, for Lobuche and Pumori were both close by. To start, they chose the North-East face of Lobuche East, a so-called trekking peak. At 6,119 metres, the face was as yet unclimbed. Kovač was suffering from a harsh cough and high fever so Tomaž, Carsolio and Johan climbed the 50–85-degree slopes in alpine-style, taking three days. They reached the top of the 900-metre wall on 1 October and named their route Talking About Tsampa.

Now they turned their attention to Pumori, again for acclimatisation purposes. Kovač was feeling a bit better so he too was ready to climb. Their chosen line was a variation of the French Buttress on the South-East Face. Meanwhile, a Czech/Slovak team had also been climbing on Pumori's Normal Route, and at 6,300 metres on the face, the Slovenians were shocked to learn that the other party had fallen. In the end, three climbers died and one, Milos Kijonka, was very badly injured. Tomaž's team descended immediately in order to assist Kijonka down to Gorak Shep, where he could be transported to medical care by helicopter.

Back on Pumori, they adjusted their plans and moved to the normal route. Climbing in extreme cold, they came across the equipment of one of the dead Czech climbers. As they continued up, other pieces of equipment came into view. In fact the entire slope was strewn with debris. Finally they caught a glimpse of two of the deceased climbers on the slope. This cast a distinct pall on the Slovenian team. In groups of two, they separately reached the 7,165-metre summit on 15 October, but not before Marjan came close to committing a fatal error. He had been climbing more slowly than his partner, Johan, and so was still ascending when the others were already on their way down. Upon meeting him, Tomaž suggested that he leave his pack in order to move more quickly, for the weather was beginning to change and there was a cold wind blowing. Marjan chose to continue with his pack, and it wasn't until 5.00 p.m. that he reached the summit. Cold and tired, he lost his concentration on the descent and slipped on the same slope on which the Czech climbers had so recently died, falling about 200 metres. He survived, but it was very late that night when he finally arrived in base camp, exhausted and battered from his ordeal.

All safely down, they celebrated long into the night. Now it was time to concentrate on the main objective: Nuptse. Because of consistently atrocious weather throughout that season, most expeditions in the area were packing up to go home, as did Carsolio. Tomaž, Jeglič and Marjan decided to wait: maybe the weather would improve. After all, they were perfectly acclimatised now, and the face of Nuptse was right in front of them. Burrowed into their base camp, the trio waited out the storms for an entire week. Even Johan, a veteran of the fierce Patagonia winds, was impressed: 'I've seen some bad weather in my day, but a wind like that – not even in Patagonia.' They ate, rested and attempted to stay warm.

The weather finally cleared on 25 October. And with that clearing came more strong, cold winds. By now it was apparent that Marjan's earlier illness had returned, and it was impossible for him to contemplate the Nuptse climb. This unfortunate development changed everything: they were now a climbing team of two. Johan and Tomaž decided to dispense with the rope altogether, reasoning that soloing would be quicker and therefore safer: belaying would take too much time. Consequently, they packed only a five-millimetre Kevlar static line in case of emergency. After two days of fastidious packing, they were ready, and on 27 October they headed towards the foot of the wall.

The static line proved useful almost immediately as the climbers used it to weave through a complex network of crevasses near the bottom of the face. This dangerous section was their first real challenge and would prove even more serious on the descent, still a lifetime away.

Immediately after the crevasse field, they arrived at an ice couloir that varied in steepness between 50 and 80 degrees. The gradient was not the problem: ice seracs, hanging threateningly above them as they climbed up through this section, were the real worry. Anxiously they continued up, climbing as quickly and carefully as they could until they reached a relatively level ledge at 5,900 metres where they settled in for their first bivouac. They dubbed the exposed and dangerous funnel 'the Orient Express'.

The weather deteriorated during the night as the high-pressure system broke down, and 28 October dawned with high winds and suffocating fog. As a result, they delayed their start until late morning and managed only four hours of climbing. Moving slowly and carefully through dense cloud and frequent avalanches, they gained another 400 metres of elevation. That night they set up their second bivouac at 6,300 metres, this time in an overhanging crevasse. The wind intensified, buffeting their small tent mercilessly. Despite the precarious situation and the incessant noise, they managed to both eat and sleep.

On the 29th they dug their way out of the snow drifts but managed to climb only another 400 vertical metres of mixed rock and ice. The terrain was steep, and pieces of rock and ice ricocheted off them constantly. Even with the now-improved visibility, the deadly missiles were almost impossible to predict. When their hands began to freeze, they were finally forced to stop in order to create yet another bivouac, this time by chopping out a narrow ledge on the steep ice slope. They secured their tent to the wall with ice screws and settled in for another night of howling wind and snow. It was during the night that Tomaž became aware of a splitting headache. Although common at that altitude, it was an unusual symptom for him, particularly since he felt completely acclimatised from the two previous climbs. Upon closer examination, he realised that it wasn't the elevation that was bothering him; it was the lack of oxygen in the tent, which had almost completely caved in from the constantly avalanching snow. They were, in effect, suffocating.

After digging themselves out, they spent the rest of the night sitting up, supporting the wall of the tent with their backs. To make matters worse, they discovered a gas leak in the stove, making it almost impossible to melt snow for badly needed fluids. By now the tent was beginning to show the effects of the strain from the continuous wind, as were the climbers, so they took a full day to mend their tent, to eat and drink as much as possible and to plan a strategy for the following day. They decided to attempt to climb the remaining 1,000 metres in one push – an ambitious undertaking to be sure, but better than hacking out yet one more uncomfortable bivouac. This strategy provided the advantage of carrying extremely light packs, with only their clothing and a bit of food and liquid.

As they talked that night, Johan confided: 'If we climb this, Tomaž, we'll be happy the rest of our lives, and if we don't, we'll make half of Slovenia happy!' This statement, from one of the country's top alpinists, summed up the highly competitive state of climbing in Slovenia. They drifted off into a restless sleep.

By 4.00 a.m. on the morning of 31 October they were up and climbing. They made good progress, despite the persistent spindrift, the high winds, and temperatures that hovered around -30 degrees Celsius. At about 7,000 metres the two climbers briefly separated. Johan headed up a difficult section that Tomaž insisted was avoidable; he instead climbed up a partially hidden couloir that was very straightforward. Tomaž was surprised at this route-finding disagreement, because Johan was a more experienced alpinist. But Johan hadn't been to the Himalayas for a few years, and Tomaž later wondered if this short bit of extremely difficult climbing added to Johan's fatigue. He berated himself for not insisting that Johan follow his lead up the easier terrain.

At this point they stopped briefly to refuel their cold bodies with tea and a few pieces of chocolate. They exchanged some words about their tea canteen that illustrated the state they were in. Tomaž pointed out that the canteen had very recently (the previous night) been used as a pee bottle. 'Are you sure it's going to be all right?' asked Johan. Tomaž reassured him. 'We'll rinse it out, Johan. It can't hurt. Besides – as long as it's liquid!'[1]

After the refreshing drink, they radioed their location to Marjan at base camp. The next section of climbing was very difficult and precarious, with an awkward mix of steep rock and loose, powdery snow. Once above this dangerous section, they again radioed Marjan. It was now 11.30 a.m. and they were at 7,500 metres. From his vantage point Marjan could see a lenticular cloud streaming over Everest and a gale-force wind howling over the ridge of Nuptse. This might be the forerunner of a storm. They sensed the urgency but also knew that there were still two hours of climbing to the summit.

Johan and Tomaž discussed what lay ahead of them and came to an agreement: they would climb until 2.00 p.m. and then come down, regardless of whether they had reached the summit. With the thickening haze, they knew they had to discipline themselves to remain within this time limit, or they would be flirting with death.

They continued, climbing solo, waving to each other periodically with their ice axes. Johan was out in front, climbing fast and strongly. Tomaž followed behind, and at 1.00 p.m. he looked up to see Johan waving, apparently on the summit. With a surge of relief, he realised that he was almost there. This interminable slope would finally end. He waved back and kept plodding on, anticipating the summit ridge.

Fifteen minutes later he was there, on the top, and was immediately assaulted by a gale-force wind. And there were Johan's footprints in the snow, leading in the general direction of Peak W1. Tomaž followed them but wondered why Johan was continuing. Was he just taking a look around? Was he not sure if this was the summit? Was he confused? Tomaž desperately wanted to get out of this storm and start heading down. Wandering around this ridge seemed pointless. And then the footsteps ended. There, on the snow, beside the last track, was the radio that Johan had been carrying in the open position. But where was he? He had simply vanished. Tomaž suddenly had the strange sensation that he could see

Johan, but he was being tossed around by the strong winds. 'I can't be sure. I was concentrating on not falling,' he recalled.

Tomaž lost his balance and slipped a bit in the cold, dry snow. At this point the reality of the situation slammed him squarely in his stomach and he collapsed to the ground. He screamed into the wind, calling out Johan's name. There was no reply. Johan had apparently gone beyond their summit, must have been blown off balance by the wind, only to plunge to his death 2,500 metres down the hard ice and overhanging rock of the South Face. The summit of Bobaye flashed through Tomaž's mind as he recalled being knocked off his feet by the wind on the summit ridge. He grabbed the radio left lying on the snow and called in to base camp.

'Base, come in, base . . . Marjan, what's happened? Marjan!'

'What's the matter, Tomi, where are you?'

'Johan! Johan's gone!'

'What do you mean – gone? Where did he go?'

The insanity of the situation smothered Tomaž. Time and understanding took on a fantastic slowness: his location, that he was alone, the time of day. It was 3.00 p.m. before he collected himself sufficiently to contemplate what lay ahead of him. They had soloed the route, with no belays and no fixed ropes. He would need to reverse each step on the 2,500-metre wall below him, and the storm was intensifying. He wondered if he had pushed too far.

Marjan urged him on via the radio. Tomaž forced himself to focus, took a few photographs in all directions and then willed his body to begin the descent. He reasoned that he had two ice axes and that with great care and concentration, it might just be possible. Things went well at first. As soon as he left the ridge, the wind abated considerably and he made good downward progress. Then he lost his goggles. He was at 7,100 metres when night began to fall, but cruelly, the extremely cold temperatures had snuffed the life from his headlamp batteries. Now he had to feel his way down the steep slope, completely devoid of visual aids, clinging only to his courage. This was one of many moments during the nightmarish descent when Tomaž seriously doubted his ability to survive. With no light and no partner, he felt completely alone. Exhausted and emotionally spent, he began falling asleep on his feet. Thankfully, Marjan's voice woke him repeatedly with words of encouragement. He knew that he had to keep moving in order to reach the shelter of the small, battered tent, but he was completely lost.

Determined not to die standing still, Tomaž kept on, forcing his body not to give out on him, drawing on all of his accumulated experience and climber's instincts to pick his way down – always down. One by one he bashed each ice axe into the frozen surface. One by one he kicked his crampons into the slope. Base camp continued calling him, the voices increasing in their intensity. Then they began playing music, hoping to revive and encourage him. They knew as well as Tomaž did that the bivouac tent, as pitiful as it was, remained his only hope. Without protection from the elements, he would die. Finally, around midnight, he sensed that he was nearing the tent. The night was inky dark, with no moon and no headlamp, but at this moment he thought he saw a strange milky light, in the middle of which appeared some kind of dot. At the centre of that dot he was sure he could see a tent. Perhaps this momentary lapse in concentration was what caused him to fall, a slip that almost cost him his life. Miraculously, a mound of ice at the bottom of a steep ice groove caught his crampon and stopped him short. Moments later, he was at the tent.

He unzipped it, threw himself in, utterly exhausted, and fell asleep almost immediately. In a coma-like state, he became delirious. 'I distinctly saw seven people in the tent with me,' he recalled. Shortly afterwards his mouth filled with green bile and he realised he had to contact base camp to let them know where he was. Relieved, they continued playing music – anything to keep him from drifting off. Tomaž knew that he needed fluids, so he first lit a candle to see what he was doing, and then attempted to start the stove. It simply wouldn't work. After an hour's effort he lay back and slipped again into unconsciousness. Unbeknownst to him, the stove was slowly and steadily leaking fuel. After about two hours, the leaking fuel, combined with the burning candle, exploded into a fiery inferno. In a semi-conscious state, he grabbed the burning stove and threw it out of the tent, but not before the nylon structure was badly scorched. He fell back on to his burned sleeping bag inside the tent, now full of holes, and once again lost consciousness.

Snow sifted in through the holes while the hallucinations returned. A white tunnel appeared, inviting him to enter. Then he saw Sergeja, Urša and Tomi – and finally his parents. The tunnel beckoned him again. He had to decide what to do: go further into the tunnel or step out of it. He decided to step out. Beside him in the tent were his seven imaginary companions. Tomaž struggled in this semi-conscious state, trying to waken completely to begin his descent. Then the bearded man on his right said, 'Don't worry, we'll take care of you.' So Tomaž put his head down and slept again. Eight hours later, at 11.00 a.m., he finally awoke completely and responded to the radio calls from base camp asking if he was still alive.

It was noon of 1 November before he emerged from what remained of his tent to continue the hellish descent. But something was seriously wrong. Then he realised – it was his raging thirst. He needed to drink something. He climbed steadily down until he reached the overhanging crevasse where he and Johan had set up their bivouac two days earlier. The ice bridge they had used had now collapsed so Tomaž was forced to hurl himself over the gaping hole. He managed to land safely and then began descending to the ice funnel they had named the Orient Express. Down-climbing the hard, brittle vertical ice was awkward, but his training paid off. Only a few metres from the snow cone at the bottom of the funnel, he heard a deafening roar. A piece of ice had broken off above him and was hurtling down through this slot. In a flash, he realised that although he had made it all this way, he would now be cruelly swatted off the mountain like a tiresome mosquito. Death seemed certain. He could taste it – smell it. Relying on instinct, he slammed both of his ice axes into the slope and pressed his body against the wall. The lethal chunks of ice ricocheted erratically off the sides of the funnel, but only a few actually hit him. The roar stopped.

In the days to come, some would describe this near disaster as a miracle. After all, he had been trapped in a gulley bombarded with an ice avalanche. Tomaž described it differently: 'Signs are for the chosen ones but miracles are for all others to believe.'

With an intense surge of adrenalin and another chance at life, he threw himself on to the snow cone, slid down in a partially controlled glissade, and continued down to the edge of the crevasse field. Now it was twilight. Here he stopped, for he could not risk wandering amongst the gaping deadly holes alone. He would have to wait for help. Again he slipped into unconsciousness, deliriously dreaming of water. It had been three days since he had eaten or drunk anything, with the exception of some of his own urine, which he had finally been forced to swallow in order to survive.

It was midnight before Marjan reached him. By now, Tomaž knew that his feet were in trouble. He could no longer feel his toes, and in fact, four were frostbitten. Marjan helped him through the crevasse field and other climbers came up to the edge of the field to help him to base camp. Just before reaching camp, he sat down and immediately fell asleep. Two hours later, he awoke and dragged himself the last 50 metres.

Tomaž was alive and safely off the mountain. Back in Kathmandu, he visited Elizabeth Hawley to provide her with the post-expedition report. In addition to gleaning details about the climb, she pressed him for reasons: why would he be attracted to a place like this? He tried to explain that he had had an 'obsession about Nuptse's West Face', which he described as 'gorgeous'. He tried to explain to Hawley that Himalayan faces were what roused his mountaineering passion. Simply looking at a photo of an unclimbed Himalayan face made it impossible for him to resist wanting to climb it. There were so many still waiting: the unclimbed centre of Makalu's West Face, or the middle of Dhaulagiri's South Face.

Returning home was painful: physically because of his frostbitten feet; emotionally because of the loss of Johan. He felt responsible, and couldn't fathom why it was he who had survived. Johan was so much more able. Somehow they had gone too far – pushed too hard. Certainly, Johan had been under some pressure from home not to go on this expedition. Could that have affected his performance or judgement on the top? 'We've eaten the forbidden fruit,' Tomaž said.

Tomaž was widely acknowledged and praised for this incredible climbing achievement, but within the Slovenian climbing community something else was brewing – blame. Johan had been a favourite of many. He had enjoyed close friendships within the community, more so than Tomaž. He had been one of the best, most established, most reliable and safest climbers, and now he had been snuffed out. Although they weren't explicit in their blame, a few climbers felt that Tomaž was responsible. Some alleged that there had been acrimony between them and this was what had killed Johan. But the nearby Everest research station had observed the two climbers and reported a friendly and companionable team. The salacious gossip persisted. Many nasty things were said; some were unreasonable and some completely outrageous. Steve House likened the situation to when the much-loved American alpinist Alex Lowe was killed by an avalanche on Shishapangma, and his climbing partner, Conrad Anker, survived. It was undoubtedly difficult for Anker to return to his climbing community without Alex, and House was sure that it had been equally hard for Tomaž. House thought that the blame said more about people's grief for the loss of Johan than their dislike of Tomaž. Whether in the United States or Slovenia, the loss of one climber and the survival of another would always result in grief, regret and ultimately blame. This was not the first time, and it would surely not be the last.

There were additional complications with Johan's widow, Irena, for she needed a death certificate in order to receive a pension. With two small children, and pregnant with a third, she would need this financial support. But because there was no proof of death, it appeared that she would be forced to wait five years for an official death certificate. When Tomaž confirmed the circumstances of his disappearance before a civil court, the certificate was finally issued. At the same time, a group of climbers organised a benefit event in the coastal climbing community of Osp. There, they celebrated the life of Johan. This became an annual party, which Tomaž did not attend. He was criticised for this apparent lack of respect, but he scoffed at the criticism, calling the event an excuse for a bunch of climbers to party together, rather than a real effort to help Irena. He later established a foundation for her, maintaining that his efforts of support went directly to her and her children. And so the feelings of regret and grief seethed and rumbled within the community, occasionally erupting into moments of cruelty, and sometimes kindness.

It took seven months for Tomaž's feet to heal: seven months of idleness, oozing sores and smelly pus. Emotionally and physically crushed, he was suffering from short-term memory loss from his time on the mountain and leaned heavily on his family. Sergeja recalled, 'He was consumed by his pain and didn't know how to deal with it. It was like living with someone in a coma. For the first time in my life, I doubted my ability to endure it.' Tomaž's home life was irrevocably changed. He had developed an absentee lifestyle, away for months each year while he pursued his passion in the Himalayas. Time didn't stop at home. The children were growing up without him and Sergeja had moved steadily away. There was less and less to talk about.

As the blame for Johan's death continued to swirl around Tomaž, fewer climbers came to visit. Added to this were growing financial worries, because Tomaž was unable to work. His 'profession' was painting towers and church steeples; it was impossible to paint towers with oozing toes. Pressure mounted. Rumours floated amongst the climbing clubs that 'Humar's over'. Then his club president Slavko Rajh unexpectedly loaned him $500, a small amount but one which meant a lot to Tomaž and Sergeja. This gesture made it even more difficult when soon after he withdrew from his club, permanently.

Strangely, the official climbing report that was initially sent out from Slovenia implied that both climbers had perished on Nuptse. This report was printed in the well-respected French climbing magazine *Vertical*. Some months later, a *Vertical* journalist arrived in Slovenia to visit his girlfriend. He picked up an ice-climbing guidebook and noticed a couple of routes that Tomaž had opened, commenting to his girlfriend that it was a shame that Humar had died on Nuptse. She said that that certainly wasn't the case: in fact, he lived nearby. The journalist rang Tomaž, went over for a visit and did an extensive interview that was subsequently published in the magazine, correcting the erroneous report. But the mistake left a bad taste in Tomaž's mouth, for he felt it was just another example of the Slovenian climbing community attempting to get rid of him, silence him, snuff him out. To add to the insult, that year there was no 'best alpinist' designation in Slovenia, something that Tomaž – and some others – felt should have been awarded to him and Johan.

The bad feelings intensified when a few climbers downgraded the Nuptse climb to the equivalent of a 'high-grade winter ascent in the Slovene mountains'. He tried to understand their perspective: their beloved hero had died, and the brash upstart had lived. But he defended the route, insisting that the tragedy did not, and never would, cancel the significance of Johan's last climb. Tomaž understood that at least some of this disrespect was not real criticism but rather an expression of grief, for the harshest words came from those climbers who had been closest to Johan. Still, it appeared that this tragedy had significantly widened the chasm between the other climbers and Tomaž. Despite his attempts at understanding their perspective, he was deeply troubled and hurt that they would not respect his own grief over Johan's death. He finally summed it up with: 'The wrong man came back from Nuptse.'

CHAPTER TEN

RETICENT WALL

5 August 2005, Nanga Parbat, Rupal Face

'The day between sky and earth . . . opening the zipper of my sleeping bag . . . with anxiety in my heart, not allowing myself to take a quick glance around. No, noooooooooo! The pain takes all my hopes away . . . again fog, humidity and snow all around me . . . I can't feel my legs! I am still here, trapped in the coffin of ice.'

After a long day on the Rupal Face, Tomaž's condition is deteriorating quickly. It is for this reason, for the first time in his life, and against all his better judgement, that he has broached the subject of a helicopter rescue with Nazir. He knows that rescue from a wall at this altitude is likely to be impossible; it has simply never been done before. But he has heard the most recent weather report and they are forecasting a change. Unfortunately, that change is for the worse. They are now predicting that a major storm is about to hit the area.

Ironically, shortly before, Tomaž's website posted his official philosophy on big Himalayan walls, as well as his views on rescues. The statements were very clear. 'That is what makes mountaineering special . . . undamaged nature, virgin walls and routes . . . If it was easy to get rescued, someone would have tried to climb this route before. All mountaineers who decide to do such a feat know there might be no way back . . .' After taking such a clear and public stand, even contemplating a rescue at this stage must be a difficult process for Tomaž and the entire team.

5 August, 16.00

As he ponders the complexity and unlikelihood of a rescue, Tomaž struggles to recall the details of the rescue advance payment documents that he was obliged to purchase for this expedition. He recollects that the altitude limit for a helicopter rescue is about 5,500 metres. He is now at approximately 6,300 metres, although he can't be certain, since the extreme vacillations in air pressure are affecting his altimetre.

Anda calls their Pakistani organizer Nazir Sabir, who is curiously optimistic. 'I think that the army will be able to rescue him tomorrow,' he tells Anda. Aleš radioes Tomaž immediately to tell him the good news. Tomaž tries to provide a detailed description of his position, explaining that his mobility has diminished even more, for now he is forced to remain clipped to his ice screws to avoid being swept off the wall by avalanches. He explains to Aleš that in preparation for tomorrow's rescue, he will leave all of his equipment and clothing in the snow hole and will keep his knife handy to cut the rope attaching him to the ice screws at the last moment.

Meanwhile, Nazir calls his cousin, Lieutenant Colonel Rashid Ullah Baig, one of the country's best military helicopter pilots. They discuss the possibility of a rescue and Rashid explains that he will need to make some calculations. Some time later, Nazir calls back to base camp, double-checking on Tomaž's elevation. Although Nazir doesn't remember the exact details of the conversation, base camp distinctly recalls that they report Tomaž's elevation as 6,100 metres. Nazir explains that this won't do: it's too high. It must be below 6,000 metres. It will be necessary to change the height on the internet. From that moment on, Tomaž is officially trapped at 5,900 metres.

Aleš is extremely agitated. Tomorrow there may be a helicopter rescue and he will most certainly be involved. He runs around base camp, organising equipment and assembling rescue ropes with weights to stabilise them while they are airborne. The radio springs to life as Tomaž calls down, reminding them of the radio frequency for tomorrow. 'We must be on the same frequency,' he urges them. 'That is really important.'

Nazir has initially informed Rashid that a mountaineer needs to be evacuated from 6,300 metres. Although the official elevation later drops to 5,900 metres, Rashid has made his calculations based not only on the higher elevation, but also on the steepness of the slope. Upon completion, he calls Nazir to say that it will be impossible: the climber needs to be brought down to a safe altitude by a ground party. If he can be lowered to 5,500 metres, an evacuation will be possible.

Nazir calls base camp to give them the bad news – that a rescue is unlikely. He reassures them that Tomaž is a strong, capable climber who will be able to find a way down. Anda is the one who must relay this sobering news to Tomaž.

'He really did everything, Tomaž. He believes in you, your experience, your spiritual powers and God's will. We will pray for you. Conserve your energy so you can find your way out of this. I am sorry I had to tell you this!'

'Anda, I can go nowhere from here, in these conditions I can go nowhere.'

'Tomaž, maybe not now, but in the morning, in the daylight, you will be able, with all your experience, with everything that you have done so far, to find a solution. Nazir also thinks this and believes you will find an exit . . .'

'Do not be so long-winded, Anda, make it short. There are no chances for the helicopter, then? None?'

'For sure none, not now. Nazir asked me to call him back with your response.'

'He is not even going to try?'

'I can ask him, but they assured him they will not fly above 5,000 metres, and they will only do a rescue if they can land.'

Tomaž demands to speak directly with Nazir.

'Nazir, hi, tell me what is happening. Is there really no chance of a rescue?'

'A helicopter pilot told me it is practically impossible for their helicopters to fly that high. Their Lamas are very old and can only go to 5,000 metres. I tried everything but the pilot answered that nobody can fly safely at that altitude.'

'Do you only have old Lamas in Pakistan?'

'The MI-17s and the other helicopters are also unable to execute such a rescue.'

'Nobody will try, for any price?'

'I called many times to different organisations, explained everything and showed them pictures. My experience is telling me that even if they do take off, they will have a hard time rescuing you. If I am completely honest, I am not sure that any machine can fly that high, Tomaž.'

'Okay, okay, I understand . . . so no chance. I am having a hard time accepting this. I hope God will help me, that is all I can say. Thank you for all your help.'

'Tomaž, I really feel for you. I will pray for you. I don't want to disappoint you, but you have to find your inner strength, use your intelligence and trust God's will, like you have done so many times in the past.'

'Nazir, thanks for all your help. I had a lot of hope this afternoon, but this is reality now and it is not looking good. Thanks again!'

'I will be with you and pray for you. Find hope and power. God be with you.'

The radio transmission ends. There is a complete and terrible silence. Base camp has heard the entire conversation and there is nothing they can add. They are startled when the radio comes alive. It is Tomaž. 'I would like to talk to my family. Please.'

They connect him first with his father. Then with his children. He assures them that he is okay. They talk about football, and their next holiday. Then silence once again while he considers his options.

Tomaž is now convinced that there is no solution in Pakistan. But he has no intention of giving up, so he begins flipping through his mental Rolodex: Elizabeth Hawley, the Russian alpinist Valery Babanov, other climbers and friends who might have ideas for a solution or have contacts who could help. Base camp is a flurry of activity as they respond to the suggestions he fires off every few minutes on the radio. They are awake all night, phoning, emailing, and contacting anyone and everyone who might be able to help. They contact Stipe, who grills Tomaž: is there room for the helicopter to hover? What is the terrain like immediately above? What about wind? Is there a possibility that an avalanche could hit a helicopter rotor? As both climbers have extensive experience on rescue teams, Tomaž answers as accurately as he can, and at the end of their conversation, Stipe states the obvious: that Tomaž must be prepared for the likelihood that a helicopter rescue will simply not be possible. Tomaž responds with the truth that is equally obvious to him: he cannot move one metre and survive.

6 August

Meanwhile, at base camp there are only two SAT phones remaining and the other phones are not working well. The team is exremely tense. Tomaž senses the disorder from his frozen perch and tries to regain control: 'Enough of that. Take the notebooks and write things down. You should send all contacts with everybody to Nazir . . .' Maja responds that she thinks it would be better to coordinate the rescue in Slovenia rather than in Pakistan. She senses that Tomaž has lost his confidence in their technical capacity to orchestrate this complex effort, so she suggests that perhaps the most appropriate person to coordinate the rescue would be Viki Grošelj. Her suggestion is met with silence while Tomaž weighs this very important decision. There will only be one chance to choose the right person. A teacher by profession, Viki is one of Tomaž's closest climbing friends back home, and was one of his companions on Annapurna. As one of Slovenia's most successful alpinists and a Himalayan veteran, he is revered within his country and is a superb organiser with a multitude of high-level contacts. Tomaž realises that if anyone can help him now, it is Viki. Finally he answers: 'Okay, let it be Viki.' The call is made.

'I accepted with no hesitation, although I knew the chances were microscopic, that we would have to start from ground zero in all areas, and that we were under enormous time pressure,' recalls Viki. He knows that no mountain rescue team has completed a mission at this altitude on such a difficult wall. And he is also familiar with the rescue capabilities in Pakistan. In both 1986 and 1993 he experienced considerable difficulty in organising a helicopter rescue for some frostbitten team members – and this was from base camp. He is also aware that the Pakistani pilots are not trained for high-angle helicopter rescues, particularly with a winch, something that will almost certainly be required. Professional high-angle rescue teams do exist in Europe and North America, but Nanga Parbat's Rupal Face is thousands of miles from any team capable of doing the job. And even if a foreign rescue team were able to fly to Pakistan to initiate a high-angle rescue, the idea of obtaining permission from the Pakistani government is inconceivable.

Nevertheless, Viki calls Nazir, and after their conversation is somewhat reassured to learn that Nazir has already organised an Alouette – a small, agile helicopter – as well as a very well-respected pilot, to be on standby for the first good-weather day. Unfortunately the Alouette is not powerful enough to actually carry out the rescue, but it's the best that Nazir can do for the moment.

Viki and Nazir strategise about their next step. One option would be to ask the highest-level Slovenian government officials to make a direct approach to the highest-level Pakistani government officials. There could be a slight chance that an official political request of this kind might override the existing regulations. But the request for a rescue would not only break all the regulations, it could threaten the lives of everyone involved.

Still, they decide that this strategy may be worth pursuing. The well-connected Viki speaks to his friend Matjaž Nahtigal, Secretary General of the Office of the President of Slovenia. His phone call produces immediate results. Nahtigal is an intelligent man who grasps the complexity of the problem immediately. Not only does he understand; he wants to help and promises to make some calls. Through his own personal contacts, Tomaž also arranges for the President of Slovenia, Dr Janez Drnovšek, to be informed of his situation. Next, Viki calls on the Slovenian Mountain Rescue Association to find out who, within the European Community, might be capable of executing a rescue of this sort. Who could do it, and who might be willing to try – at exceptionally short notice?

That person is Gerold Biner, the Swiss member of the International Commission for Alpine Rescue (ICAR) and one of the most respected helicopter rescue pilots in the world. Not only does Biner have a lot of experience, but some of it is at high elevations. Curious about the situation, he visits Tomaž's website to get a better sense of the topography and glean more details about the climb and the mountain. After taking a close look at the website photographs, Biner is quietly confident that a rescue is possible. The challenge will be negotiating the international politics and logistics – and most importantly, access to a Lama helicopter, which is the only one he feels can operate safely at such an elevation.

Back in Slovenia, Nahtigal calls Viki back with some good news: President Drnovšek fully supports the rescue effort. His support is a turning point in the operation. The president connects Viki with Renato Petrič from the Ministry of Defence and the Minister of Foreign Affairs, Dimitrij Rupel. Not only that, but Prime Minister Janez Janša is considering a possible intervention with the Pakistani prime minister.

The power-players are moving into place. They appear willing to do what they can. Viki is on the phone constantly, as is his wife. His life is now fully consumed by the rescue and he begins to wonder if it might actually work. But everything takes time, and he senses that Tomaž doesn't have much.

Viki calls Tomaž and assures him that everything possible is being done, but knowing the extreme unlikelihood of a successful rescue, he then quizzes him about the possibility of moving from his precarious position.

'What about going up to the shoulder at 6,800 metres?'

'Considering the situation, it is impossible, not only technically; there is so much snow I cannot move anywhere.'

'I understand. If you have only one plan, if you are counting on the helicopter only, it is not a good idea. We will try what we can and you should concentrate on going down – or up – if there is any chance at all of that.'

'The wall has to avalanche first. I cannot move until Tuesday; I would be avalanched. I was trying to go up yesterday. Had I succeeded I would have been dead now – buried.'

'The situation is very bad for you, but we know everything now. We will try everything we can. Hang on, and take care of yourself!'

Viki realises that the situation is desperate. He will have to move quickly.

The night is quiet up in the snow hole, apart from Tomaž turning on the walkie-talkie to hear messages read to him by base camp – messages from his friends in Slovenia, from friends from abroad, from people he has never met and will never know, from children, from grandparents, and of course from his own children, Tomi and Urša. Bundled in down and fleece, Anda and Maja crowd around the two computer monitors in the mess tent, drinking tea, reading emails to Tomaž, and playing music to cheer him over the two-way radio. Many people are praying for him; others are sending suggestions on how to stay warm; still others have ideas for his rescue. Hundreds of messages pour in from around the world now, for this story has hit the international news. The emails urge him to hang on and to keep the faith, for they believe that he will survive.

But not every message is friendly. The alpine climbing community places huge value on purity of style, aesthetics, self-reliance and integrity. Self-promotion is frowned upon, even though most alpine climbers rely on a certain amount of publicity in order to earn a living. Until now, most climbers critical of Tomaž have kept their comments to themselves, but this rescue attempt and its associated publicity have loosened their tongues.

Perhaps the greatest criticism is that Tomaž's call for a rescue might put pilots in unacceptable danger. For this reason alone, many climbers think that it is wrong. Gerold Biner disagrees: 'We had these discussions 20 years ago. Why should you not save a human life if you can?' Canadian alpinist and mountain guide Barry Blanchard, who was rescued by helicopter when he fractured his tibia on the East Face of Howse Peak in the Canadian Rockies, agrees with Biner, pointing out that when someone dies in the mountains, it's the family and friends left behind who suffer, not the climber himself. Vince Anderson is not a fan of rescue at all, stating, 'Personally, I think that eliminating the risk takes away from the beauty of what we do.' He goes further, stating that if he could, he would completely remove the rescue infrastructure from places like Alaska's Mount Denali and the Alps. Anderson believes that the presence of a rescue service attracts people who shouldn't be in the mountains, for they don't have the requisite skills. His stand is honourable but surprisingly uncompromising, particularly since he earns his living as a mountain guide, taking people with limited climbing skills into the mountains. Stipe Božić has little tolerance for the debate: 'I am a rescuer and I rescue anyone. This criticism is unwarranted,' adding, 'The view from the armchair is always perfect.'

Marko Prezelj, who was openly critical of Tomaž even before the rescue attempt became public, accuses him now of mixing show business with alpinism: 'He's acting like a pop star or like the leader of a religious sect . . . he's creating a silly image of alpinism.' American climber Kelly Cordes refers to the whole affair as 'a three-ring circus'. But in fact even the most critical climbers have used helicopters, either for rescue or access. It's impossible to avoid wondering what they would do in a similar situation: would they rather die for their honour than try to survive? What would their families prefer?

Reticent Wall, Yosemite Valley, 1998

Following his return from Nuptse, and during his recovery from frostbite, Tomaž had ample time to think. As a club board member, he began to feel that the Mountaineering Association had become corrupt and was no longer interested in supporting climbers, other than a select few who were in control of the finances. He believed that there were a number of top-level climbers who did not support or encourage the younger generation, but rather used club money for their own ambitions. He likened them to Stalin – someone who nurtured those who could help them, but discarded them when they were no longer needed. He was further irritated by their claim to be 'pure', as they argued constantly about the minutiae of climbing: alpine style or capsule style, private sponsors or government support, media or no media, leashes or leashless. Tomaž exploded in rage at this holier-than-thou attitude, one which seemed perfectly happy to accept government support for expeditions, yet was highly critical of the private sponsor approach. 'You can't be a virgin and a whore at the same time,' he said. He claimed to know many climbers whose careers – and very lives – were destroyed by these all-powerful, intolerant and destructive mountain club personalities who manipulated the system to suit their own needs and aspirations.

Finally he had had enough, and stated publicly, 'I don't need such a club.' Many accused him of abandoning his club when he no longer needed it. He pointed out that they should think about the next generation of climbers – not just themselves. Nevertheless, finally leaving it was a soul-destroying moment for Tomaž and one that would eat at him for years to come.

He would rant on and on about how dysfunctional the Association was, how unfair it was, how disreputable and even illegal its operations were. But at the core, there was a profound sadness. The club had been his life at one point: it gave him his start; provided him with equipment when he had none and introduced him to his first instructor, Bojan Pollack. He met his first climbing partners at the club, and its social structure defined his youth. But the decision had been made and he had to move on.

At the moment, his climbing options were limited, for his feet were a mess. Recovering from frostbite is a long, slow process, so climbing at altitude was not a possibility, at least not immediately. But Tomaž was an eternal optimist, and so he searched for something positive to take from the Nuptse tragedy and his weakened physical condition. Finally he found it. He had wanted to go to Yosemite for some time, and this was the moment. Until now, he'd always been focused on the Himalayas, but the chance to test his compromised memory capacity on an aid climb might be just the thing. Most didn't see it that way: to consider a huge, difficult rock climb, one should be in peak condition. But Tomaž was resolved.

The route that he chose was Reticent Wall. This 2,700-foot route on El Capitan comprises 21 pitches of climbing, ranging from reasonably straightforward free climbing – climbing without reliance on hardware – to hard, aid-climbing pitches, where various pieces of equipment are used to accomplish the ascent. It is an aesthetically pleasing route, soaring up through the exquisite vertical terrain of the New Dawn Wall. First climbed by Steve Gerberding, Scott Stowe and Lori Reddel over a period of 10 days in November 1995, it was still the most difficult route on El Cap in 1998. The first ascensionists rated the route at A5/5.9, with A5 being the most difficult classification for an aid climb. This grading essentially meant that the climber would need to place protection on very questionable rock features on steep terrain for long sections of climbing. This presented the possibility of falls that could conceivably rip out extended sections of aid protection. As time went on and aid-climbing increased in difficulty in Yosemite Valley, local climbers began looking at existing climbs with the intention of downgrading them in order to preserve the significance of A5 as the top aid-climbing grade. Despite this practice, German climber Alex Huber explained in his book *Yosemite* that Reticent Wall 'is also the only route today that is accorded the full A5 grade'.

For Tomaž, it wasn't the grade of the wall that mattered; his heart remained in the Himalayas. But he knew that climbing a big wall using advanced aid techniques would provide him with valuable training and experience for his next adventure in the highest mountains. It was his first big rock wall and it represented a serious and difficult challenge.

Although he had only resumed climbing six months before going to Yosemite, Tomaž trained hard, first in Slovenia and then in Italy, where he did the first repeat and first solo of Mama Mia, a route in the Val di Mello that was graded A4+. He met the first ascensionist, Thomas Tividar, who was at that time one of the best aid climbers in the world. Tividar coached him on the importance of psychological preparation and problem-solving abilities in contemplating a big aid climb. 'You've got to be able to reason extremely clearly,' he said.

Upon his arrival in temperate Yosemite, Tomaž noticed a distinct chill in the air. The local climbers weren't keen to welcome him to their valley. He quickly learned that Yosemite climbers were 'the best in the world'. Some greeted him with 'You'll fly on the first pitch, man! Take a plane and go home!' Armed with that warning, he proceeded to learn everything he could about the area and the route – anything at all that might help him on the wall. This process wasn't easy. Understandably, the local climbers were put off by this foreign impostor. Here he was, arriving for the very first time in the valley, and planning on climbing the hardest route. Was he mad? If not mad, certainly confident.

His first view of the wall was humbling. He had never before stood beneath such a smooth sweep of golden-hued granite. It took his breath away. Reticent Wall was a potential death route because of its consistent difficulty, the precariousness of the aid placements and the mind-numbing run-outs between solid protection. American Yosemite veteran Steve Gerberding defined it simply as 'death by zippered gear should you fall'.

But Tomaž reasoned that he would have warm weather to bolster him, unlike on the bitterly cold faces he'd experienced in the Himalayas. In the past, he'd hung out on lots of pitons, knifeblades, wooden screws and even fishing hooks. Surely, with all the preparation he had done in his basement fashioning usable holds, plus his recent training, he would be able to manage this wall.

When locals asked him why he wanted to climb it solo, he had a ready answer that provoked even more animosity: 'I'm more convinced than ever that the maximum form of alpinism is solo, because it is here that a person's true ability is put to the test.' Then he proceeded to place Reticent Wall and Yosemite Valley within a global perspective: 'In alpinism, limits don't exist, because the best keep pushing them up, and the Himalayas, where [there is extreme] altitude, still continue to be the stage for the biggest performances.'

Nobody wanted to give him any useful information about the route. Perhaps they thought he would fail. Or perhaps they were simply irritated by the proud Slovenian with the frostbitten feet. Finally he discovered some foreign climbers who were willing to give him precise information.

But before he launched himself on the wall, he needed to become comfortable with the environment. Together with world-cup-ranked climber Matej Mejovšek, and another young Slovenian alpinist, Damjan Kočar, he spent a full month living in the Valley, sleeping on American soil, eating American food, talking to American climbers and acclimatising his hands to American granite. He soon learned that the rock was unforgivingly harsh. It would take longer than a month to toughen up his hands. Tape was the key.

This would not be a lightweight effort. Tomaž painstakingly organised the contents of his three haul bags, which he affectionately referred to as his 'pigs'. Over 100 kilograms of food, liquid and equipment, plus a portaledge. It would take enormous patience and fortitude to haul all that stuff up the wall.

Tomaž soon met up with the world-renowned German climbing brothers Thomas and Alex Huber. Immediately sensing shared values, the Hubers gave him a few pieces of equipment that they thought might be useful. They would have known, since they were already Yosemite veterans, despite their non-American lineage. After a month, Stipe Božić arrived, along with his countryman and fellow cameraman Joško Bojič The two were there to document the Reticent Wall climb for Croatian television, for as Tomaž put it: 'What is not written doesn't exist.'

By now, Tomaž had enough information about each individual pitch that he felt confident to begin. But that confidence was shattered very quickly when he started up the wall. He was completely confused. Pitches graded at a reasonable level seemed impossible for him to climb, while those with difficult grades seemed easy in comparison. Thrown off balance, he didn't know what to expect.

On the first part of the wall he had company, if at a distance, for the cameras were always there. But finally it was time to cut the umbilical cord – the fixed rope that connected him to the valley floor. And with that umbilical cord gone, so too were the cameras. He was now completely alone. Each day was the same: climb, haul, eat, drink, climb, haul, eat, drink. There were many terrifying moments, as he blindly placed aid gear at the far end of a hammer on an invisible hold. He would feel around for some likely protuberance, place the hook, put his body weight on it, and pray that it wouldn't come loose. He didn't hurry. It wasn't a race.

Hauling the pigs took strength. Forcing his mind to concentrate on the details took self-discipline. Trusting the tentative gear placements took self-confidence. But the greatest difficulty lay in the rough granite and its effects on his hands: they ached; they bled; they were ripped apart. Each night he repaired them as best he could, but this hand torture was an entirely new experience. In contrast, his damaged toes performed remarkably well.

Finally he reached the 'lucky 13' pitch, supposedly the hardest on the wall. Tomaž recounted the details of that pitch in his book, *No Impossible Ways*:

I tackle the loose flakes, which remind me of Rzenik back home, with the copper-heads, which I find better than the traditional sawed-off angle-pitons. Next follows wedging the smallest copper-heads into some sort of a scaly black gap, and then hooking up to the next unstable flake. I'm not sure who's holding whom, me the flake or vice versa, but forty metres below me there's a ledge where I'd first break, and another forty metres lower a jagged ramp where I'd shatter.

At that very vulnerable point on the climb, he heard a sound that sent tremors throughout his entire system: a piece of equipment pulling out, or a rock falling? In fact it was Stipe, zipping open a can of beer. He had abseiled down to Tomaž in preparation for the next camera shoot. After Tomaž calmed down, he happily obliged and drank the beer. Another 20 metres and he was at the top. But not for long. His pigs were down below and he needed to haul them up. He spent one more night on the portaledge while his friends and camera crew waited on top.

The next morning he hauled all his gear to the top, and a day later, he and his crew left the Valley. The presence of a camera team elicited some criticism, particularly after an award-winning film was produced of the climb, providing Tomaž with additional publicity. Prezelj referred to the climb as Tomaž's first real 'media project'. But Tomaž was proud of their film.

Those 15 days suspended above the ground on the granite wall had been an intense and formative experience. His hands were in pretty rough shape, but his damaged toes had performed well. He had searched deeply within himself and discovered the self-discipline required to retain high levels of concentration over an extended period of spectacular exposure. He had persevered with the initially strange culture of the Valley and had succeeded in making new friends. He could feel the confidence seeping back: 'I'm in the game again.' And as that confidence grew, he knew what he had to do next. Reticent Wall was 'the last piece in the mosaic', for an unclimbed face in Nepal was beckoning him. Sergeja had searched deeply within herself too, finally realizing that she lived with someone who loved only the mountains. 'I was just his muse and a magnet to draw him home. That wasn't enough for me.'

CHAPTER ELEVEN

DHAULAGIRI

7 August 2005, 07.53, Nanga Parbat, Rupal Face

Tomaž awakens from another night in the hole. A man of action and an intuitive problem-solver, he ventures out to search for some little thing that he can do to improve his situation, but in vain. He is still trapped.

Viki calls with news that he has been inundated with messages from people around the world. Slovenian ex-president Milan Kučan calls and offers to help. Representatives of the [so-called] Religious Army arrive at Viki's door to deliver a message from the Archangel Michael. According to the messenger, Tomaž is in much worse condition than anyone realises, and the only possibility for a rescue is the American special unit. Someone calls wanting to warm Tomaž's feet with telepathy. Another suggests sending him food and drink with a rocket launcher, but cautions that close attention must be paid so as not to start an avalanche with a misguided shot. A woman gets in touch, claiming to have close connections with the French Eurocopter, the helicopter that recently touched down on the summit of Everest. After much time spent communicating back and forth, it turns out that the woman has no such connections.

In Switzerland, Biner learns that the Swiss have a Lama in the Himachel Pradesh region of India, so he immediately calls his contact there, Manjeev Bhalla, about gaining access to it. The prognosis is not good, as Bhalla explains: 'In 50 years they have finally allowed us to go across the Indian–Pakistan border with sugar. The government will never allow a Swiss pilot, flying an Indian helicopter, to rescue a Slovenian climber in Pakistan!'

Shortly afterwards, Biner receives a call from Bruno Jelk, the president of the international rescue organisation ICAR. Having received a heartfelt plea for help from the Slovenian ICAR delegate Danilo Škerbinek, Jelk asks Biner and his team to prepare to go to Pakistan – with their own helicopter. Biner agrees, but this new plan creates an even more complicated set of logistics and politics. Viki arranges visas for the Swiss team. Arrangements are moving ahead, but the weather forecast is not good.

Back at Nanga Parbat base camp, there is some early-morning helicopter activity when the Alouette arrives to observe the weather situation on the mountain and, with luck, to deliver some food to Tomaž. After the first attempt it is forced to return to base camp to refuel, and by the second fly-by the weather has already worsened and the helicopter returns to base camp. Tomaž calls and asks to speak directly to the pilot, asking him why he was unable to fly closer to the site. The pilot answers, 'Because of the fog, but most of all because there was no communication [radio contact], we cannot rescue you.'

Tomaž replies, 'So you will not try again?' The pilot responds, 'There is no chance, really none.' At this point, Tomaž completely loses his temper, for he assumes that it is a glitch in radio protocol, rather than bad visibility, that has destroyed this rescue attempt.

By now, Viki and Tomaž have identified four possible plans of action: Plan A is a rescue by the Pakistanis; Plan B is the Swiss; Plan C is a bit trickier, as it involves NATO helicopters standing by in nearby Afghanistan; and Plan D is even more unlikely, with Kazakhstani pilots ready to do the rescue, should the Pakistani military allow them to fly into the country. This last option is arranged through Tomaž's neighbour in Kamnik, who happens to know Putin himself.

7 August, 11.16

Word arrives in base camp that the Swiss helicopter rescue will not be possible as originally envisaged because of regulations not only in Pakistan, but in each country over which the helicopter would have to be transported. The only helicopter available for the rescue will be a Pakistani one, and the only appropriate Pakistani helicopter is a military Lama. In principle, the military appears ready to act.

Meanwhile, the smaller Alouette returns to base camp to pick up Aleš. They fly past the face to photograph and film Tomaž's location in order to learn more about his position. The photographs are quickly posted on the website. During this manoeuvre, the pilot flies at an altitude of 6,100 metres, which is well above the helicopter's threshold. Upon his return to base camp, the pilot confirms that a more powerful helicopter will be required. But he and Aleš have seen Tomaž and have estimated what is required for a rescue: a rope thrown from a helicopter, and no wind. They attempt another lift-off, this time with food for Tomaž, but the winds are too strong.

7 August, 15.04

Details regarding radio frequencies are exchanged: Tomaž's VHF frequency, set at 149.000 MHz, is reserved for the rescue operation. Up in the snow cave, Tomaž is unable to dry out, but he concentrates on preserving his food, gas, batteries and energy. Meanwhile, base camp continues to read him the notes and emails coming in from around the world. Visitation on the website has exceeded all expectations – and its capacity. The three existent servers are unable to handle the volume, so two more are added.

Tomaž questions his base camp team about the number of hits on his website. They find his preoccupation with the website traffic strangely inappropriate, considering his life-threatening situation. But Tomaž is not concerned about monitoring his popularity on the internet. Instead, he has a strategy: he knows that this rescue is highly unlikely without public

Tomaž's website

persuasion. He is counting on an intricate web of political pressure (post-9/11), national pride (Pakistani and Swiss), and international awareness and pressure built by media interest and internet traffic. The team at base camp, unaware of his strategy, remains confused, but Maja responds to his direction, expressing heartfelt thanks to all those who have corresponded with the website, and encouraging people to continue. Around the world, despite their disdain for what they call 'reality television', most climbers are tuning in regularly. And up in his snow hole, Tomaž prays that his strategy will work.

Up the valley, House and Anderson descend from the Schell route on one of their early acclimatisation climbs, only to learn from both their cook and their liaison officer that something is going on at the Humar camp. Word has spread that 'the Slovenian guy is stuck on the face and there is going to be a rescue'. By now, *Outside* journalist Rob Buchanan has set up at the House camp, and this news excites him. House is openly sceptical: 'It seemed the most ridiculous thing I had ever heard.' He claims that Tomaž is climbing with Aleš, so it is inconceivable that Tomaž is stuck on the mountain alone. As for a rescue – completely out of the question, thinks House. He discounts the tale as 'shepherd gossip' and doesn't even consider visiting or calling the Humar camp to see if there is anything he can do to help. He doesn't feel sufficiently acclimatised, and besides, he reasons, if Tomaž's team wants his help, they have only to send a shepherd up the valley to ask. But Anderson is curious, and that night he wonders if it would be a good idea to wander down the valley the next day to see what is going on.

At Pakistani military headquarters, helicopter pilot Rashid receives an unexpected call from his corps commander, Lieutenant General Salah ud Din, ordering him to undertake the mission. Rashid is shocked, but realises that the order must be coming from a very high level. It appears now that this rescue will be treated like a military mission, attempted at all costs, even their lives. Most significantly, they will be authorised to use military Lamas. After days of denying that they own any Lamas, the military is now agreeing to make them available.

Back in Slovenia, Viki's Herculean efforts continue as he tries to manage the logistics, at the same time making frequent appearances on the evening news. Every night he is featured first on the seven o'clock news, even before the president's regular appearance. By 10 August, both of the two major Slovenian television stations take a full 20 minutes to cover the rescue story. The entire nation has stopped to witness this unfolding event.

Men, women and children, most of whom know little about climbing, tune in each evening to see how their national icon is coping. Viki recalls, 'This was the single biggest event since our liberation. Both sides of the political parties came together to work on this.' A young man from Kamnik, trapped on the Rupal Face, has somehow brought these politicians together in a common goal – to get him home alive.

7 August, 20.22

While Maja works late into the night sending messages to the world, up in the snow hole Tomaž listens to his colleagues and the messages, warming himself with those that express concern and love. His thoughts wander to other expeditions – climbs that ended so much better, despite equal risk. Then he catches himself. He must concentrate on this moment, in this place. Now is all that matters.

Dhaulagiri, 1999

Two years had passed since Nuptse. That tragic expedition changed forever the way Tomaž perceived the great mountains, and altered perceptions of him. Although he gained significant respect and recognition as an alpinist, Nuptse had exposed a few climbers' private feelings towards him – feelings of envy, distrust and misunderstanding – even hatred. Tomaž was still haunted by the fact that he had survived and Johan had not.

Then, following the Yosemite climb, the Reticent Wall film had enjoyed wide and successful distribution, further promoting Tomaž in Slovenia and abroad. He was well known now, often invited to give lectures and to appear at foreign festivals and climbers' meetings. The lifestyle was attractive, although it left little time for domestic duties.

His financial situation had also improved. He earned enough to provide for his family, and he and Sergeja had settled into an uneasy truce. The marriage wasn't what either of them had originally envisaged, but it was still a strong union that supported their two children, and they most certainly still loved each other. Their détente worked reasonably well, except when Tomaž become obsessed with another big expedition. A return to the Himalayas was inevitable; it was just a matter of time.

Although he was aware that this behaviour inevitably hurt those whom he loved the most, he couldn't help himself: first and foremost he was an alpinist.

While the memories from Nuptse still haunted him, another Himalayan temptress, Dhaulagiri, knew nothing about those nightmares. Dhaulagiri didn't care about his self-torment. Dhaulagiri was waiting for him. But this dream was not just about Dhaulagiri, the Himalayan giant – it was about Dhaulagiri's South Face.

The dream didn't begin with Tomaž. Messner had attempted a route on the South Face of Dhaulagiri in 1977 and determined it to be impossible, at least at the time. Tomaž's own mentor, Šrauf, had assembled a team in 1981 and tackled the South Face. They had succeeded, in part, although Himalayan chronicler Elizabeth Hawley determined that they were too far right of centre to actually call it a true South Face route. They climbed approximately 3,350 metres up the face and then veered off on to the shoulder to finish the climb. Šrauf's dream, and his vast experience on the face, informed and inspired Tomaž now as he prepared himself for something even more audacious. Tomaž wanted a line straight up the centre; and he wanted to do it alone. He wanted to follow the most elegant line, the line of a pebble dropping from the summit. The boldness of his vision was overwhelming.

It was spring of 1999 when he began to grasp the complexity of the climb as well as the feeling that Dhaulagiri had 'called him' – almost like a spiritual summons. From April onwards he could barely sleep with excitement and terror. As he began to comprehend the demands of the face, he felt that he must mount the expedition that very autumn. But when? Immersed as he was in astrology, Tomaž struggled to identify the most auspicious time. Finally he found the right date: 24 October, a full moon. He realised that this left him only six months to organise the expedition, arrange the funding, train, and choose a team. He prepared his body and his mind, studying those alpinists who performed exceptionally well at altitude, examining his own past performances, and reading voraciously all he could about physical and mental conditioning.

Attempting the South Face of Dhaulagiri, solo, was what Tomaž called a one-way ticket. He could ascend the face and then cross over to the other side to descend, but he could not reverse his route on the face itself. Failure meant death. Some people thought he had a 50 per cent chance of success. Tomaž thought it was more likely 20 per cent. His old friend and mentor

Bojan Pollak worried that this was too dangerous, even for Tomaž, but he said nothing. 'If we told him not to go, he might lose confidence, and that could be dangerous.'

It was difficult to find a team to accompany him, since most climbers didn't want to witness a death climb. He first asked Viki Grošelj to lead his Dhaulagiri expedition. Viki deliberated and finally said no: 'I decided that I was too young to be a leader. I still had personal goals.' Viki never did understand the final composition of Tomaž's team: 'When I saw how many people he was inviting on this "solo" expedition, it amused me.' But each one turned out to be essential for his strategy. Viki had plenty of expedition experience, and his greatest concern was about who would be the back-up leader or 'right hand' to Tomaž. When he learned that Stipe Božić was going, he was relieved that Tomaž would have the experienced support he needed. Stipe fully understood his role, saying, 'I felt responsible on this trip. I felt that I could help him.' Viki also instinctively understood that the main objective of having a cameraman along was to avoid the Tomo Česen situation on Lhotse. But still he wondered about the size and make-up of the team: 'If I had been leader of this expedition, I would have insisted that half of the people stay at home. He goes solo climbing but he takes nine of the most unlikely people to base camp.' Tomaž had enlisted people whom he trusted, even though they were an odd assortment: his doctor friend Anda Perdan, Stipe, his tower-painting colleague Lado Ogrin, and several other friends. They became known as 'the private horde'. Stipe had a theory about his choices: 'Tomaž wants his friends with him . . . He gets energy from his friends, at least most of the time.'

Tomaž asked the Mountaineering Association for $50,000, but his relationship with its vice-president, Tone Škarja, had somewhat deteriorated. Viki tried to mediate for him, and finally Škarja agreed to give Tomaž $10,000. But a week before he was to depart, there was a serious set-back. Škarja and the Mountaineering Association held a press conference on 3 September at which they announced all four of the Himalayan expeditions they would be supporting that year: Tomaž's was not among them. His expedition was described as being in its 'incipient' stage. Viki felt that the Mountaineering Association's decision was based on Škarja's personal choice, and he was convinced that it was the wrong one.

Tomaž exploded with anger. He knew that that autumn was the right time for him to try Dhaulagiri. Everything was prepared, and most importantly he was ready, both physically and mentally. His anger quickly spent, he mobilised a Plan B, contacting everyone he knew, including an important company, Mobitel. They gave him twenty minutes to convince them to provide support: it took him twenty-seven. Mobitel responded positively, adding significantly to his expedition budget. Viki personally gave him 2,000 Deutschmarks for the trip. Tomaž's oldest supporter, Volkswagen, responded too, not with extra money but with added insurance for his children. Increasingly, Tomaž regarded his sponsors as partners, patrons, even friends. In the years to come, these relationships would prove to be absolutely crucial – even lifesaving.

By 7 September, everything was in place. A handful of Slovenian climbers felt that Tomaž had 'sold out', bringing along his friends and, most importantly, his 'media machine'. He lashed out at these 'purist' detractors, pointing out that almost every one of them had enlisted sponsors for their climbs, perhaps not on the same scale, but money had certainly changed hands. He railed: 'Don't moralise. $1 puts you in the same barrel as $1,000,000. Not only money. If you place one piece in the newspaper, you no longer climb for yourself!'

Tomaž – always a lateral thinker – increasingly viewed the boundaries between climbing and the media as artificial; that far from being antithetical, they could merge and reinforce each other. He had grown up in the age of the internet and understood that the traditional media genres were evolving. Instead of simply bringing a cameraman to the mountain, as so many others had done, he would have a live internet link-up with Slovenia; something that he instinctively knew would be a hundred times more interesting than a film produced a year after the climb. An internet presence would allow the public to follow every move on the climb – while it was actually happening. The older, more experienced Stipe was ambivalent about the presence of the internet: 'At first I thought it was like a game. But it was also dangerous, for it could push you too fast and in conditions that were too dangerous.' But Tomaž was convinced that live transmissions and thorough coverage of the climb were absolutely essential to his efforts, both for his credibility, and now for his very committed partner, Mobitel.

By 10 September, another press conference was scheduled, this time announcing Tomaž's expedition. The reporters were livid, angry, on fire. What was the Mountaineering Association thinking? Why were they not supporting the most exciting Slovenian Himalayan expedition in recent times? What were the politics? What kind of man was Tone Škarja?

Strangely, Tomaž found himself defending Škarja, despite the fact that he had almost been thwarted by Škarja's lack of support. At that press conference, Škarja reassured the public, the press and Tomaž that the Association would cover any remaining expenses. But a few hours later he reconsidered and informed Tomaž that he shouldn't count on that financial support.

After two more days of packing, family activities and frenetic motion, Tomaž was ready to leave. The twelfth of September began with mass with his family. Despite the increased tension brought on by his departure, he and Sergeja still shared some things profoundly: Urša, Tomi and God. Finally it was time to leave. Urša and Tomi pressed him with simple yet heartbreaking queries: 'Where are you going? Why do you have to go, Daddy? When will you be back?'

Tomaž knew better than anyone that the odds of coming home from the South Face of Dhaulagiri were not great. He was as prepared as he could possibly be, but still the climb was extremely dangerous and there would be nobody to help him if he ran into trouble. He looked at those young faces and vowed never again to leave for the Himalayas during daylight hours. He simply couldn't face his children: 'As I wipe away the tears I look back one last time. I see Urša and Tomi standing in the street, waving goodbye. I bite on my soaked handkerchief and howl like a wounded animal.'[1] Sergeja's intuition told her that he would return, and she stated, "He was lucky he did not have to worry about me and the children . . . he knew he had a Lion at home.'

After arriving in Nepal, and several days of trekking, they established base camp on the north side of the mountain, where they would concentrate their acclimatisation efforts on the 'normal' route. Immediately after establishing Camp I, bad weather moved in. By 28 September, Tomaž, Stipe, Tomo Drolec and Vinko Berčič had already completed two acclimatisation climbs. By 10 October, they had reached 6,200 metres and set up Camp II. The weather became more ominous, with lenticular clouds tearing across the horizon from nearby Annapurna. As other teams retreated off the mountain, Tomaž was assaulted by a stream of bad news: first from the Mexicans, then the Swiss, and finally the Japanese. All their reports were consistent: bad weather, dangerous conditions, frostbite, retreat and failure. They expressed shock and disbelief that Tomaž was actually considering the South Face, alone. It seemed inconceivable.

In fact, it seemed unlikely to Tomaž too. As the wind increased to a howl, he fled the mountain, retrieving Stipe from Camp II on the way down. In the deteriorating weather, snow fell constantly as the fog descended upon them, and they struggled through a maze of crevasses, seracs and avalanches. It was a relief to reach base camp, where the enormity of the job ahead of him finally settled in: he had only reached 7,200 metres on the regular route. Now he was headed for the south side to an unclimbed route, alone. Tomaž prayed.

On 15 October Tomaž, Stipe and a journalist flew around to the south side, landing at 3,600 metres. They met an injured Norwegian trekker and loaned their helicopter for an evacuation. The rest of the team headed over French Pass into the Kali Gandaki valley, where they planned to meet Tomaž with provisions. But they didn't know the way and became disoriented. As a result, the Norwegian's porters stepped in, but Tomaž and Stipe lost precious time and energy helping them transport the provisions. It was at this point that Tomaž realised the folly of trying to do too many things: he needed to change tactics. The Kali Gandaki team members now became crucial: Tomaž needed them to act as radio relayers to Stipe, who would soon be on the north side of the mountain. Only Elizabeth Hawley grasped the complexity of this strategy.

Ultimately, it was only Tomaž and Stipe who returned to the base of the South Face, with just enough equipment, fuel and food to pull it off. Together they stared at the wall, and reviewed over and over again what Tomaž would need for his climb. He took three long days to assemble his pack: food, stove, fuel, pitons, carabiners, sleeping bag, a 50-metre five millimetre rope and a few slings. Then he added one more item: one of Tomi's little baby shoes, his good-luck talisman. The night of the full moon, 24 October, Tomaž didn't sleep, for he had made his decision: the next day he would leave. Stipe felt this was a mistake, because as he explained, 'The full moon always attracts avalanches.' Tomaž knew better, since the full moon would provide good visibility, pliable ice conditions and stable ice-seracs.

Tomaž was relieved to have Stipe with him at this moment. Not only was he a very experienced Himalayan climber, he was a trusted friend. He brought an essential sense of calm, solidity and reliability to the scene. What Tomaž didn't realise was the extent of Stipe's anxiety and concern for him: 'I was very confident of his abilities to climb it but I was worried about the conditions on the mountain . . . I felt helpless. It was nerve-racking.'

By noon on 25 October, Tomaž was ready. Stipe prepared a meal, which

Tomaž's nervous stomach promptly rejected. Then Tomaž called Sergeja, who offered him simple words of encouragement that illustrated her trust and confidence in him. He and Stipe reviewed their plan once more. Tomaž offered prayers. Then, at 5.00 p.m., they said goodbye at the foot of the face and Tomaž headed on to one of the highest mountain walls in the world, almost 4,000 metres of loose granite and overhanging ice.

At that very moment, an avalanche cascaded down the central couloir, disgorging ice, snow and rocks. Stipe urged him to delay, but Tomaž said no, he was finished with waiting. He climbed through the evening and by 10.00 p.m., found himself effectively trapped on a ledge. He tried repeatedly to solve the riddle of a slight overhang, but by 5.00 a.m. of 26 October he had radioed to Stipe that he was truly stuck. Although trying to be helpful, Stipe felt impeded: 'When you are at base camp it actually feels much worse than if you are on the mountain yourself.' Tomaž decided to wait during the relative heat of the day, hoping that as the temperatures plummeted with approaching night, the constant flow of water and wet snow would cease. At 5.00 p.m. he tried to begin climbing but the water continued to flow; he tried again at 7.00 p.m. with the same results. Finally, at 10.00 p.m. he was able to make some progress up the ice, but it was short-lived and he realised that he had lost most of a day.

The next morning he began early, soon discovering that the rock spur above him was much smoother and steeper than he had expected and too technical to climb safely with his 30-kilogram pack. He secured it to the face with a couple of ice screws and continued up, rope-soloing until he ran out of Kevlar line. As he began to descend to his awaiting pack, a serac broke loose, pummelling the face with ice, rock, snow and water. Hauling the pack was slow and extremely dangerous, becoming more so as the day heated up and more debris funnelled down over him. Tomaž climbed into the night, feeling pure terror at the dangers over which he had absolutely no control. But he was a very spiritual person, and that spirituality informed his climbing philosophy. He believed that he could communicate directly with the mountain and that the mountain, in its turn, spoke back to him. This approach was one more idiosyncrasy that fascinated his supporters and irritated his detractors.

He was in frequent radio contact with Stipe, who read him emails sent in to their website by people around the world. Although alone on the wall, Tomaž needed human contact, even if only indirect. As this strange climb began to attract more and more attention, Tomaž instinctively appreciated and anticipated the potential of its impact, particularly as the media had begun to follow every step of his progress. By now Stipe too understood the power of the internet: 'In this case it was very helpful, for Tomaž knew that he was being followed. It gave him a voice and he felt responsible to all these people. He felt that he needed to come back alive.' Sergeja too understood this seeming dichotomy: 'Despite his need to be alone in the mountains, whenever he started up the mountain he called and showed that he was vulnerable, that he wanted to come back.'

On the wall, the worst was still to come. By 8.00 p.m., the barrage of avalanches had begun; by midnight, literally tons of snow had fallen down around and over Tomaž. Clinging precariously to his anchor, he was convinced – a hundred times that night – that his life was surely over. Battered and bruised, he was more surprised than anyone when he realised that he was still alive. Life seemed precious – and precarious – indeed.

Another challenge then presented itself. Now that there was a brief lull in avalanche activity, Tomaž needed to move delicately across a 25-metre ice traverse. There was absolutely no way to protect it; he was 1,000 metres up the face; and he needed just a few minutes of avalanche-free time in order to get across without being scrubbed off the wall. He could smell death, but he retained control as he cramponed lightly and carefully across to the other side. Five minutes later another avalanche scoured his tracks. One more gift of life.

After his third bivouac on the face, he awoke on 28 October to the realisation that he had sustained an alarming number of injuries over the past few days. None were life-threatening, but they caused him additional stress as he spent the next 16 hours picking his way through, and over, some of the most horrendous snow and ice conditions he had ever encountered in the mountains. Wet, cold and exhausted, he finally dug a small ledge in the snow at 5,700 metres, ate an unappetising combination of soup, coffee, meat, cheese and tea, all mixed together in some hot water, and collapsed with fatigue.

The 29th dawned and Tomaž was now high enough on the mountain to climb during the much cooler days, so he changed his biorhythms and concentrated on using every possible hour of daylight. This allowed him to make good progress despite the difficult mixed climbing (M7+, 5.9). But that night, at 6,300 metres, a new problem nagged: an infected tooth filling. The pain was acute, so he did the only practical thing: he removed the filling and the associated infection with his Swiss Army knife. The incident was reported on his internet site and absorbed by all his fans.

By the end of the 30th, Tomaž had reached an impasse – he could no longer continue directly up the face, so he had to decide how to escape the wall: left to the Polish ridge or right to the Japanese ridge. Tomaž knew that Šrauf had opted for the Japanese ridge in 1981, and so he chose that too. After what felt like an endless traverse, he suddenly came upon an anchor – it was that of the Japanese from 1978. The surge of relief was overwhelming. He was shocked to acknowledge the stress that he had been under and what a release it was to find this small indication of life. That night he slept on the ridge, confident of the summit.

The next two days were cruel. Tomaž was now exposed to the full fury of the wind. After a couple of attempts up the ridge in a veritable gale, hand-jamming in small rock fissures at 7,400 metres, he regretfully concluded that he would have to traverse back on to the face. There, his progress was slow as he found himself dry-tooling with his ice axes on shattered rock on steep terrain at over 7,700 metres (M5 and M6). Then, with obvious signs of frostbite on his bruised and battered body, he was faced with an open bivouac at over 8,000 metres, equipped with neither stove nor tent. He had now been on the face for eight days. That night he knew he could die. He switched to another dimension: he lowered his pulse to save energy; he 'disconnected' his limbs in order to concentrate his blood flow to his core and head, and he limited his focus to two things: breathing and heartbeat. As he focused, everything else faded away: the pain in his leg from the falling ice, the frostbite that was seeping into his extremities, the pain in his swollen hands, the thirst, the hunger, and the feeling of being terribly alone. Just breath, and his heart pumping blood through his exhausted body. He described this survival technique: 'You live through a computer reset, nothing is important, only yourself . . . In those moments it is as loud as it gets, it starts to scream . . . the noise of silence . . . you do not see and you do not hear anything, you are absent, you do not exist. The wall has its soul. And you have to sneak under its skin, become one with her. Only when you are one with her, when you *are* her; only then you receive. In those times I climb and I am climbed. I caress the rock and get warm from the wall.'

After surviving the night, Tomaž now had to make a decision. He looked at the few photographs he had with him: Sergeja, Tomi and Urša; he recalled the email messages relayed to him from people around the world, all wishing him success and safety; he thought about the 1,700,000 hits on his website in one day. But ultimately, the decision was his alone. He felt with great certainty that if he went on to the summit, he would die on the descent. The summit was not worth his life, so finally he accepted the reality that he had pushed it far enough. He would return to the ridge and descend. 'Dhaula had let me have the face, but not the summit.' After all that he had endured on the face, after all the logistical and financial problems that he had solved in advance of the expedition, and after reaching 8,070 metres, the summit was not to be his.

Even the descent was difficult because of the immense amount of new snow that had fallen while he had been climbing the South Face. He had run out of food and fuel some time before, therefore he was struggling not only with fatigue and cold, but also with dehydration. The original plan had been for a helicopter pick-up at 5,100 metres, so he struggled downward to that rendezvous. The appointed time came – and passed. Unbeknownst to Tomaž, while he had been on the face, riots had broken out in western Nepal and all available helicopters had been deployed to that region. As he waited, he could feel his resolve weakening. His stamina was waning and he could feel himself slipping away. But his teammates, Cene and Tomo, had climbed up towards him and now they assisted him to a tent in the abandoned camp of a French team.

This was the last day of his 'life before Dhaulagiri'; tomorrow would be the first of another kind of life – one that was extremely public, faster paced, infinitely more complex, and ultimately one that would bring him great sadness. The French have an expression that sums it up: *il faut payer* – you have to pay. Tomaž intuitively sensed that his life would now change, although he didn't know the precise cost. He knew that the climb would leave permanent scars.

Finally, on 4 November, the long-awaited helicopter arrived, transporting him to base camp and then on to Pokhara, where his doctor, Anda Perdan, insisted on a complete examination, followed by rest and recovery in Kathmandu. Tomaž would have none of it. He was boyishly deceptive, coming up with excuses to step out of the hotel to run some small errand, knowing full well that he had no intention of returning – not until he and the rest of his team had celebrated appropriately. They ate and drank, danced, whooped and hollered, invited complete strangers to join them, and drank some more. As each day passed, Tomaž appeared more energized. Anda was concerned that he was not recovering from his ordeal on

Dhaulagiri. Tomaž assured her he was, and would promptly go to bed after breakfast to prove his commitment to healing. The celebration lasted four days. Kathmandu somehow recovered, as did Tomaž, and those who participated in the fiesta never forgot that marathon of revelry.

The expedition was both a success and a failure. Although Tomaž failed to reach the summit or to complete his direct line on the South Face, the boldness of the climb, the severity of the route, his decision to do it alone, even his sheer survival, were enough to signal a new era in Himalayan climbing. Of his ascent, Messner said, 'It marked a new watershed in contemporary extreme mountaineering.' Elizabeth Hawley agreed, saying, 'His solo climb on Dhaulagiri I by an unattempted line up the South Face . . . was not a success in terms of having reached the summit – he didn't reach it – but he got very high all alone, and it was a tour de force that very few can match.' The world's response to the climb was intensified by the enormous traffic on his website. A new, much higher level of profile was established on Dhaulagiri, one that Tomaž would never lose.

The reactions were not all positive. Some alpine climbers who freely acknowledged his monumental achievement on the mountain protested against what they viewed as blatant self-promotion on his website. As British journalist and climber Lindsay Griffin said: 'Being British, we do have problems with his media persona.' But it wasn't just the British. The purists felt that there was a certain amount of overdramatisation – even exaggeration – in his story: the close calls, the amount of rock fall, the dramatic tooth extraction. Slovenian alpinist Andrej Štremfelj stated publicly that Belak's 1981 climb was the true first ascent of the South Face of Dhaulagiri, and he went on to speculate that Tomaž's choice of style was motivated by its 'sensational' value, therefore adding to his reputation – and associated market value. That may have been a little unfair, if one counts the number of sensational and extremely dangerous climbs that Štremfelj himself had done in the Himalayas.

Marko Prezelj went further, suggesting that Dhaulagiri was the perfect marketing product for Tomaž, skilfully produced by Mobitel's public relations arm. He too was critical of the manner in which Tomaž represented the climb. He posited that when a climber chooses photos to represent a climb, there are many different possible camera angles: the frontal angle always gives the steepest aspect, and this is the one that Tomaž used. In fact, the photo was from the famed Japanese photographer Koichiro Ohmori's book, *Over the Himalaya*, and was the only one that

Tomaž could find that showed the entire wall – possibly because it was taken from a plane. Some Slovenian magazines even published the photo on which Tomaž had sketched his intended route, rather than the one he finally climbed. Prezelj admitted that printing the photo on which the intended route was marked wasn't exactly a lie, but he insisted that it gave the impression that this boldly elegant line up the centre of the face was the route that Tomaž had indeed climbed, and he added that first impressions were always the strongest. Although Tomaž reported the details of his actual route on his website – the only official report – Prezelj felt that he conveniently allowed these early photographs to perpetuate a kind of myth. Prezelj also insisted that Tomaž needed to place this climb in a historical context, one which included the 1981 climb. According to Prezelj, although Tomaž did reference the earlier climb when he returned from Nepal, he primarily promoted himself and didn't appear to care about the earlier climbers. This is perhaps an unjustified criticism, since it would be natural for a climber to be most interested in his most recently completed climb, rather than dwelling on one done years earlier. The Slovenian climber Silvo Karo thought that the Dhaulagiri climb was an excellent objective, but added, 'He didn't finish it.'

Steve House, although he said nothing at the time, was later sceptical about some of Tomaž's apparent claims of difficulty on the face: 'As for Dhaulagiri, honestly, I don't believe him.' House's problems had to do with two details on the climb. One was Tomaž's alleged report that the mixed climbing at approximately 7,000 metres was M7+ or M8 – an extremely high level of difficulty. He was sure that Tomaž couldn't climb that hard at sea level, let alone at 7,000 metres. He believed that it probably *felt* like M8, but doubted that it actually was. (The official record of the climb, as posted on the Humar website, listed the grade as M7+ at approximately 5,900 metres.) The second issue was with Tomaž's claim to have managed a pendulum move high on the mountain using a single camming device that was inserted between a bit of ice and rotten rock. According to House, 'It just doesn't work. It is impossible to do.' Tomaž replied that perhaps House didn't know how to make it work – but he did. House said that if you were going to report grades at altitude, you had to be scrupulously honest and evaluate them as if they were at sea level, not a particularly easy thing to do, he admitted. This is undoubtedly the most honourable approach, but the problem with challenging the grades on the Dhaulagiri South Face route is that it has yet to be repeated. Surely it must be difficult to downgrade a route on which nobody else has yet climbed. And so the weary, gossipy debate continued.

It wasn't only Tomaž's sins of omission that bothered Prezelj. He was surprised as well that one of the team, Vicenc Berčič, who had also been part of the Slovenian 1981 effort, had failed to mention the earlier climb. He pointed out that shortly afterwards, Berčič was given a job at Mobitel, and wondered if there was a connection. Tomaž said that some time later, Berčič had done an in-depth interview with the country's most important newspaper, *Delo*, and spoken extensively about the 1981 climb. About the job, Tomaž had an answer as well. After the expedition, Mobitel had offered Tomaž himself a job. Although he wasn't interested, he told them that one of the team members – Berčič – didn't have a job and could really use one. They hired him, and he continues to work there. Tomaž saw this as nothing but a good-news story, claiming that the steady job changed Berčič's life. He was baffled by Prezelj's objections.

Maria Štremfelj, wife of Andrej and an accomplished Himalayan climber, had further criticism: 'He broke the unwritten rule in climbing . . . that climbers should do things without publicity, without revealing every moment of what you have done.' She pointed out that even before he left for Nepal, he spoke a lot about the climb, about what he would do, the mountain gods, his chances of success, and even more tastelessly, his chances of survival. She felt that he exploited the media, leaving out important details, adding that this seemed to be the modern way, a style that she did not approve of. But even Maria and her husband had been on high-profile climbs with abundant media attention. Prezelj thought that the media hype went well beyond what the climb deserved, saying that 'Humar put alpinism on the yellow pages, and he enjoys it.' Others suggested that these comments were simply jealous voices from alpinists whose climbing exploits were near to or equal to Tomaž's, but whose public profiles were sadly deficient.

Prezelj summed it up with: 'My impression is that it is just another solo climb, close to the Šrauf route.' Tomaž, when he heard this assessment, simply shrugged, saying, 'The climb is what it is – that's all.' His climbing instructor from earlier days, Bojan Pollak, was watching all of this debate and finally came to the conclusion that the negative comments were fuelled by envy. He categorised it as a special national style: 'In Slovenia, people like to put people up on a pedestal, but even more, they enjoy knocking them down.' Perhaps the Česen débâcle had simply whetted their appetites and they were hungry for more.

Stipe Božić filming below Jannu East.

Tomaž belaying Aleš on seracs on Aconcagua.

Anda Perdan, praying at Base Camp at Jannu.

Tomaž belaying Aleš on ridge of Cholatse, April 21, 2005.

Aleš Koželj on the summit of Cholatse, which he climbed with Tomaž and Janko Oprešnik, April 23, 2005.

Aleš and Tomaž bivouacking at 6850 metres on Nanga Parbat's Rupal Face during their acclimatisation climb on the Messner Route, July 17, 2005.

Tomaž and Maja Roš relaxing on a short trek between Thasering and Nanga Parbat base camp, 2005.

Tomaž greeting Steve House when he arrived at the Rupal Face base camp on Aug 1, 2005. Aleš looks on.

Tomaž kissing the grass upon arriving at base camp after being slung by helicopter from the Rupal Face.

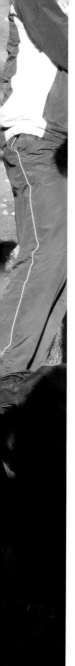

Tomaž, in obvious pain and distress after his nine days on the Rupal Face. He can hardly believe that he is in base camp.

Tomaž, embracing his Sirdar, Javed, after his rescue from the Rupal Face.

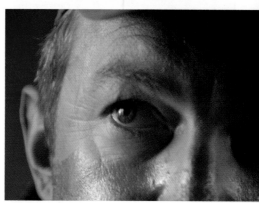

Portrait of Tomaž Humar taken below Lhotse's South Face on Nov 5, 2006. He had just climbed Baruntse and was returning over the Ama Lapcha Pass.

Tomaž, with Himalayan historian Elizabeth Hawley in Kathmandu, after climbing Baruntse in 2006.

Rock island on
the South Face
of Annapurna at
5,000-5,800 metres.

View from the
Annapurna's East Ridge
down towards the
second bivouac site.

Nevertheless, the international climbing media heaped praise on his accomplishment and Tomaž returned home a hero. Unbeknownst to him, the public relations arm of Mobitel had invited Reinhold Messner to Slovenia to be at the airport when he arrived. Perhaps surprisingly, even to Mobitel, Messner said yes, adding: 'At the moment, Humar is the greatest high-altitude climber of the world.' Messner went on to point out that he knew this wall, and fully acknowledged the seriousness and danger it had presented. In fact, he had retreated from the wall in 1977. Older, more experienced climbers thought that Messner showed up less for Tomaž's sake than for his own. They suggested that Messner's climbing career was finished now, and that he was cunningly strategic in keeping his climbing profile alive, even though he was no longer active. Tomaž had done something even more outrageous than what Messner had accomplished in his own brilliant career; therefore it was good for him to be seen with the new superstar.

Škarja had his own opinion about why Messner showed up, alleging that he had perceived a rival in the former Slovenian star Šrauf, and had never publicly acknowledged his achievements. But the younger generation didn't threaten him and this was why Messner was in Ljubljana congratulating Tomaž, just as he had done for Tomo Česen before he was disgraced. Prezelj, on the other hand, believed that Messner was invited to the celebratory homecoming because 'when Messner put his blessing on the climb, the local climbers could say nothing. It virtually stopped all . . . criticism of the climb. The only comments accepted at that time were glorifying "holy" Tomaž.' In order to silence the critics, Viki protested vehemently that there was never any conspiracy to bring Messner to Slovenia. Messner allegedly made only one stipulation to his appearance in the country: there would be no questions about Česen. Apparently he didn't want to deal with his earlier lapse in judgment.

The scene at the airport was pure madness. The children were there with Sergeja. There was Messner, most of the Slovenian climbers, politicians, representatives of Mobitel, Tomaž's parents and Tone Škarja – the man who had withdrawn his support for the expedition. One of Slovenia's more experienced climbing veterans overheard Škarja say that within a few weeks everyone would have forgotten this climb. But at the same time, he made an effort to take some credit, professing that the Association had supported Tomaž. Even though he still considered Škarja to be a remarkable man and a tour de force in the mountaineering community, Tomaž was furious.

The media became frenzied in their attempts to cover the story. The reporters were well aware that the entire country had supported Tomaž on this climb; they had followed him step by step up that face; and they were ecstatic that he had returned alive. He had been transformed from a climbing figure to a national hero. Journalists clustered around him, fawning over him and giving him ever more publicity. His face was now on every newspaper and appeared at the street-corner kiosks and in magazines. His story enlivened breakfast conversations in households across the country. His appeal was multifarious. He brought something fresh and unspoiled and heroic into the lives of ordinary people: the image of some-one brave and generous, yet with a saintly smile that somehow embraced them.

The public loved his smiling, upbeat character. Perhaps it reminded them of another Slovenian folk hero, Kekec, the young shepherd who was the star of a number of family films. *Srecno Kekec* (*Good Luck Kekec*), was released in 1963 and immediately captured the hearts of all Slovenians. When Tomaž arrived home after Dhaulagiri, throngs of people completely unknown to him called out, 'Welcome home!' The actor had finally been called for his role, and he shone effortlessly in his performance, capturing the hearts of the public much like the young shepherd had. But like his climb, this performance was irreversible, a one-way ticket.

Although his Slovenian climbing counterparts criticised Tomaž, well-respected climbers from around the world lauded him. This young Slovenian with only eight Himalayan climbs to his credit had pulled off the most futuristic climb in a decade. Viki marvelled at the strategic approach to his climbing career: each ascent was more difficult than the last, laying the foundation for the next. American climber Ed Webster, whose Everest East Face expedition in 1988 was a landmark climb for its time, suggested that Tomaž's Himalayan achievements had set a new standard in difficulty and danger: particularly danger. American extreme alpinist Mark Twight also acknowledged that Tomaž had raised the bar, stating in an *Outside* magazine article: 'Climbers are not prepared for that kind of difficulty, in that length of time, in those conditions. The great evolutionary steps in climbing take place because of people expanding their psychological capacity. We can improve our gear and our training, but it doesn't matter unless you can see with enough clarity what is possible. The rest of us just aren't seeing what he is.'

The climb was nominated for the Piolet d'Or. This time the entire process was clouded in murky controversy as the prize went to French climbers Lionel Daudet and Sébastien Foissac for their ascent of the South-East Face of the Burkett Needle. Jean-Claude Marmier, one of the founders of the award, who had resigned from the jury in disgust the year before, was particularly vocal in his criticisms. He alleged that, whereas the French team had accomplished 'an interesting ascent', it was, he insisted, 'at a standard that we have seen recorded two or three times a year in the *American Alpine Journal* for the last fifty years'. Others pointed out that Tomaž had failed to reach the summit and, that worse, his expedition had had an inordinate amount of media coverage, something true of other nominations too. Still another voice on the jury chastised Tomaž for having 'gone too far' on the Dhaulagiri climb, despite the fact that he maintained enough control at the end to turn back from the summit, rather than tag the top and die. This presented an interesting juxtaposition to the Piolet d'Or decision of 1997, when they awarded the prize to a climb where two team members died. Once again, it appeared that the prize depended less on the values of the originators of the award and more on the make-up of the jury that particular year. Regardless of the outcome of this particular award, the climbing world stood in awe; if not completely unanimously, very close.

The response was intoxicating. Tomaž could do no wrong. He was wined and dined. Life was a party. Somebody always picked up the tab. The press was always on the lookout for a photo opportunity, or a quote, and his celebrity grew. One of his favourite expressions from this time was 'Don't think; don't look down; and don't fall – just push, push push.' Then he would slyly add, 'And drink only when necessary.' People pressed to be near him. His circle of friends expanded and moved to the highest possible levels, including the President of Slovenia. Shortly afterwards, the President gave him the Honorary Emblem of Freedom, the country's highest honour.

When Tomaž drove around in his Golf car, with its sides emblazoned with his oversized name and face, everyone would stop to stare. There were endless opportunities to go out, to socialise and, more frequently, to drink. A naturally sociable person, Tomaž began to lose perspective and, finally, control. As Sergeja described it, 'Our marriage became madness.' The grin pasted permanently on his face fooled almost all, but Sergeja knew better: 'He had a wonderful smile before, but it is different today . . . the wind has lashed his face too many times...also mine.' He hardly slept. He was invincible. Nothing could hurt him. The world was his, and he had only to choose the next pleasurable moment. But he also used his fame – and his time – for a multitude of charitable works. Within this whirlwind of activity, his family would be there for him: of that he was sure. And for a time, they were.

CHAPTER TWELVE

THE FALL

8 August 2005, 07.55, Nanga Parbat, Rupal Face

Base camp vainly attempts to contact Tomaž in his snow hole. It has rained all night in the valley bottom and has been snowing above 5,000 metres. Due to a thick mantle of fog, they are unable to see anything other than the base of the mountain. The helicopters will almost certainly not be flying today. Tomaž has only four remaining batteries; base camp suspects – and hopes – that he is saving them. But the mood is desperate.

8 August, 10.23

Tomaž finally radioes to report that he was up most of the night digging, in order to keep the heavy snowfall from completely burying him. Once morning arrived, he promptly fell asleep. He is cold and wet and worried about frostbite. Anda instructs him to take some aspirin to thin his blood, and above all to keep moving. At this point, it's all she can suggest.

Thousands of miles away, Biner prepares to leave Switzerland for Pakistan. He calculates the fuel and power requirements for the rescue and assembles the equipment: two-way radios, including special radio-equipped helmets for the rescuers; 100-foot, 150-foot and 300-foot lines with anchor ropes and weights; a special cargo-hook safety system as a secondary backup; and his personal equipment. He plans to do an initial reconnaissance flight past Tomaž's snow hole in order to take a closer look at the scene, and then return with a rescuer on the end of a 150-foot line. If, on the reconnaissance flight, Tomaž shows no signs of life or movement, two rescuers will be flown in on the end of the line. Under no circumstances will the rescuers leave the line: they will be attached to the helicopter at all times. Upon arriving at the rescue site, the rescuers will clip Tomaž on to the line: nothing will be left for Tomaž to do, for he could be unconscious or confused and he must be kept under control.

An extremely important factor will be the communication link between the rescuer and the pilot. The rescuer will have a much better view of the scene and will need to pass on these crucial details to the pilot, whose view will almost certainly be limited. Finally, the single most critical moment will be when the belay line connecting Tomaž to the mountain is released or cut. If this is not done quickly and precisely, the entire effort will end in disaster.

Viki has cancelled all arrangements to transport the Swiss helicopter, and is now focusing his efforts on getting the Swiss team to Pakistan. He frantically searches for possible flights and then calls base camp to say that the flights have been arranged and the Swiss are on their way, a message that is duly passed on to Tomaž.

8 August, 12.22

The all-important weather forecast has arrived, and there is hope. Although the very immediate forecast is for blowing snow, high winds and virtually no visibility, there may be a three-day opening of relatively good weather during which the storms are scheduled to move away from Nanga Parbat. Only three days. This break is likely to be followed by another storm. It's imperative now that the helicopter be here tomorrow morning, if not to actually rescue Tomaž, at least to drop him some supplies. This is the new plan.

At the same time, Rashid is on the phone to Nazir Sabir for clarification on certain details. How steep is the wall? He learns that it's 75–80 degrees. How high is Tomaž? Unfortunately, he's at around 6,300 metres. How large is the space around the climber? Certainly not enough to put down a single helicopter skid. What is the terrain like around the site? A sheer drop on one side and a deep ravine on the other, both of which have avalanches running down on a regular basis. This explains why nobody has gone up to get him, and why he hasn't attempted to descend on his own.

Rashid thanks Nazir for the information and then gets to work. After checking the weather forecast, he concludes that the rescue attempt must take place immediately, for he doubts that the climber will survive another storm. He does a quick appraisal of the situation and decides that a classical hoist operation will not work, based on the weight of additional crew members and the power limitations of the helicopter. Because of the prevailing temperatures on the wall, the actual density altitude of the rescue is likely to be over 7,000 metres, which would make it impossible to pick up a 70-kilogram load, the approximate weight of the climber.

Rashid comes to the conclusion that their only hope is to place a long rope close to Tomaž's cave and instruct him to attach himself to it. This is not an ideal situation, because when the helicopter arrives at the site there will be an enormous amount of rotor wash and a lot of loose snow blowing around. What if Tomaž is unable to see? What if he is unable to hook himself to the line or detach himself from the line that connects him to the wall? Even more importantly, how will the helicopter manage to reduce its weight in order to hover at this impossible elevation? And even if all that is possible, how will they get Tomaž back to base camp without him dying from hypothermia? In flight, the winds on the suspended climber will be around 60–70 kilometres per hour. With the current prevailing tempera-tures on the mountain, this would expose him to a wind-chill factor of lower than -30 degrees Celsius for at least 10 minutes. Rashid worries that even if they can somehow get Tomaž off the mountain, they might kill him flying back to base camp.

Rashid is struggling with high-angle helicopter rescue problems that have been solved years ago, and techniques that have been practised and perfected countless times before by experienced rescue teams. But he does not have the luxury of this knowledge. He thinks he must solve these problems alone.

In order to understand better just who it is they will be dealing with, Rashid asks Nazir some questions about the climber. He learns that Tomaž is experienced; he has endurance and strength; he has done many rescues himself, and he has faith and confidence in the Pakistani rescue effort. This is good news, because with the strategy that is developing in Rashid's mind, it will be absolutely critical that the climber be fit enough to clip himself to the sling rope. This will be the only possible way.

As for the helicopter itself, Rashid has unwavering confidence. The Lama SA-315 has the world's highest altitude flying record, having flown to almost 12,800 metres. Tomaž is much lower, so in theory the actual flying shouldn't be a problem. But Rashid is well aware that the altitude record was set in a completely different situation, since the helicopter was flying forward, not hovering, and with only one pilot (this rescue will certainly require two, for this is military protocol). The altitude-record Lama had been stripped of everything but the bare essentials in order to get its weight down to 850 kilograms. This rescue helicopter will need some of those essentials, and Rashid doesn't think he will be able to reduce the weight much below 1,200 kilograms.

Rashid continues working well into the night. Having calculated the weight and balance equations, as well as having gained an understanding of the terrain in which they will be operating, he calls Lieutenant Colonel Ubaid ur Rehman, the commanding officer of the 5th Army Aviation Squadron (known as the Fearless Five). This is the squadron that operates in the formidable mountain ranges of the most northerly regions of Pakistan. The colonel agrees with Rashid that it is an almost impossible mission. But they have orders. They agree that they will use two Lama helicopters and one MI-17 in a supporting role. The main purpose of the second Lama will be to scout the exact location of the climber on the wall, as well as to function as back-up in case something happens. The MI-17 will be there primarily in a support role, particularly for fuel.

Rashid and Major Khalid Amir Rana are both from the 8th Army Aviation Squadron, one of the most decorated squadrons in the military. Their motto is 'We fly where eagles dare.' They will fly one of the Lamas from the army aviation base in Rawalpindi to Astore, a village about 15 miles from the base camp. At the same time, the second Lama and the MI-17 will fly in from Skardu to meet them in Astore. From there, all three will continue on to base camp. Rashid's helicopter will be stripped of all but the most important essentials, and the plan will be to sling a rope in to Tomaž and, hopefully, sling him out. Rashid knows that temperatures are crucial, so they agree to take off as early as possible: 04.30 at the latest. With the plan, the people and the helicopters in place, Rashid settles in early for a restless night of very little sleep.

But it is not only rescue details that occupy Rashid's mind throughout the wakeful night. His head is full of memories – memories of his family, his early days in the Pakistan military as a pilot, horrific war memories high on the Siachen glacier, risky rescue missions and, above all, memories of his beloved brother. There is possibly no other person in the Pakistani army who is better prepared and more perfectly suited to do this rescue than

Rashid; not only because of his military experience but because of painful personal reasons.

As a child, sandwiched between two sisters, Rashid yearned for a brother. Finally, when he was eight years old, his prayers were answered and his brother, Masood Ullah Beg, was born. Although much younger, it wasn't long before Masood became Rashid's most cherished family member. Rashid grew up to be an exemplary student and a model cadet in the Pakistani army, graduating with distinction. It was at his graduation ceremony that Masood declared that his dream was to follow in his older brother's footsteps. Rashid soon moved into aviation and Masood followed suit. Although Rashid was proud of his brother's ambitions and skills, he worried about him. It was dangerous having two brothers flying risky missions in the highest-elevation war in the world. While fighting on the Siachen glacier, Rashid had already survived many close calls and had seen a number of helicopters and friends tumble to their fiery deaths. At Masood's aviation school graduation ceremony, Rashid was torn between pride at his brother's achievement and fear for his safety.

Masood was one of the very best graduating pilots and so was invited to perform low-level aerobatics at one of the special graduation ceremonies. Then, on the day of the rehearsals, Rashid received a call from the chief flying instructor with devastating news: Masood had crashed and been killed. Rashid remembered the moment clearly: 'Time stopped. My heart stopped. The sip of tea travelling down my throat tasted like acid.'

Rashid was now the only remaining son, and was therefore responsible for informing the rest of the family, making all the arrangements for his brother's funeral and trying to hold the shattered group together. The next day he flew to his home town with his brother in a coffin, a tragically macabre repeat of so many other flights from the Siachen with dead comrades as cargo.

Masood's death shattered the entire family, particularly Rashid. It was this loss that prepared him, more than anything else, for his attempt to rescue Tomaž. He had experienced first-hand what it was like to lose a precious family member. As he explained, 'Although time heals the wound, it does not cure the deep scars that remain for ever.' After Masood's death, Rashid became even more religious than before. His respect for human life increased and he found himself taking greater and greater personal flying risks if a single life could be saved. Nazir Sabir has told Rashid about Tomaž's children, and about everyone praying for his safe return. As Rashid finally drifts off to sleep that night, he knows that he will do anything possible to protect Tomaž's family from the anguish that he and his own family continue to endure.

8 August, 18.47

Tomaž struggles with the constantly falling snow, digging himself out as best he can and vainly attempting to stay dry. He melts some snow for water, but only half a litre. He has so little gas left that he must conserve it carefully. However, he knows that half a litre is not sufficient up here. Rehydration is absolutely essential to prevent frostbite, but he simply can't run out of fuel. He hears Anda's pleas to drink, drink, drink. He sips a little of the precious life-giving liquid and prays for better weather.

The messages relayed from base camp are encouraging, but in a way, also meaningless. They come from people in comfortable places, warm places, dry places. They don't know what this is like. Tomaž is increasingly fearful for his life. Once again he considers the possibility of leaving the hole. But it hasn't stopped snowing. The conditions are as dangerous, if not more so, as when he made the decision to stop. He would need at least one day of good weather for the mountain to stabilise, and then another to begin his descent. He needs to be plucked out of this death hole. But he knows he won't die here. He refuses. He would rather die trying to escape.

A message from Messner is relayed from base camp, saying that Humar is one of the best and toughest mountaineers and that he will succeed – if the weather improves. Of course, Messner is one of the very few people who actually *does* understand the situation, so naturally he would include that proviso. He encourages the team to continue with their helicopter rope rescue plan, as he feels it has the best chance of success.

Email traffic is out of control; 57,000 messages, and more than 7,000,000 hits on the website. Tomaž is encouraged by the numbers and hatches a plan to raise money for charity: he asks that each SMS messenger contribute one Euro to a charity back home. This somehow takes his mind off himself. Then a recurring concern crowds out all others: radio frequencies. He calls base camp immediately to warn them that it is critical that he be on the same frequency as the helicopter, when and if it arrives.

He talks a bit more with Maja, trying to convey to her what it's like in the ice coffin. He has just dug himself out of yet another avalanche. His ice shelf is covered in snow, and each time an avalanche descends on him he digs out a U-shaped tunnel, with his head facing out. This provides him with the fastest response time for the next avalanche. Of course he doesn't have a shovel, so he digs with his hands and elbows. But the snow is so wet it's freezing to his body. His toes are now blue. Then, with a start, Tomaž realises that he is using precious batteries. He closes off abruptly, something he hates to do because once again he is alone. Alone with his thoughts.

He remembers a conversation years ago with the American alpinist Jack Tackle, an Alaskan specialist with dozens of extreme ascents of the northern giants under his belt. But the conversation Tomaž recalls is not about an ascent but a rescue. Trapped on a small ledge more than 450 metres up the North Face of Mount Augusta, Tackle had been hit by a briefcase-sized rock that broke both his back and his neck. His partner, Charlie Sassara, retreated alone off the mountain and back to base camp, where he initiated a rescue. The following day, a Pave Hawk helicopter slung in a para-rescue specialist, and despite some split-second changes to Tackle's anchor tie-ins, he was successfully slung off the face. But the story didn't end there. Because the helicopter had needed to dump most of its fuel in order to manoeuvre close to Tackle, no sooner had he been plucked off the face than the dashboard registered 'no fuel'. The helicopter raced towards an HH-C130 fixed-wing aircraft, managed a docking and refuelled in mid-air, before finishing the rescue mission. The story ended well and Tomaž draws a certain amount of strength from it, before drifting off into a nervous slumber.

The Fall, 2000

Amid the media whirl, the socialising and the fame, Tomaž had a new project. He was building a house for his family on the edge of his home town, Kamnik. He had searched diligently for the right location, perched on a hill above the Kamniška Bistrica river, with a splendid view of the Kamnik Alps and the bucolic farms below. Above the site, lush green meadows rolled gently up towards the sky, perfectly framed by a picturesque traditional wooden hay-drying structure. Most importantly, the site lay tucked up against a mature beech forest, full of mushrooms, foxes and squirrels. It was perfect.

Sergeja was excited, too, for finally she would have a home for the family. The land itself had been costly, since its location alone dictated a premium price. They planned a spacious home, with rooms for each of the children, space to entertain and a large office for Tomaž. This home was something they would be proud of. But how would they pay for it? A few climbers, envious of Tomaž and his high-flying ways, developed theories about how it would be done. These theories ranged from 'washing money' for the government, to huge gifts from his sponsors, to the best of all: an outright gift from the President. Some were convinced that it was Mobitel, funder of the hugely expensive Dhaulagiri expedition, that had paid for the construction of the house. All the while, Tomaž was enjoying an extravagant and indolent lifestyle. It was soon common knowledge that he had 'barrels of unclean money' in his possession, all directly given him by the President. Tomaž howled with laughter at this and asked, 'Why then was I giving two slideshows a day to make the money to build this house?'

Tomaž had learned how to build from his father and had already built an entire house, so naturally he took on this project himself, with help from friends and family. They began construction in the autumn of 2000, and by October the basement concrete was poured and the floor joists were in place. Late in the day on 30 October, Tomaž was working with his electrician to finish some remaining chores. As the light faded, he was moving across the open floor joists at his usual breakneck speed. Beneath him was three metres of space above the concrete floor of the basement. For a Himalayan alpinist, three metres was nothing at all, and equally spaced floor joists on a horizontal plane did not present a problem. Yet in a split second of lapsed concentration, he slipped and fell like a stone to the concrete below.

Upon regaining consciousness, he sensed immediately that he was in trouble, for his right leg was lying on top of him at an angle that appeared abnormal. Likewise with his left foot – it didn't seem to be attached in the normal manner. As his body was overcome with shock, a strange sensation of relief flooded over him. Finally he would be able to stop – stop running, moving, arranging, dealing with everything, socialising, arguing and planning. At some subconscious level, he accepted that this accident was necessary in order to prevent complete self-destruction.

Yet he also knew that he needed to get to a hospital – immediately. He was bleeding uncontrollably, and he could feel the life force oozing from his body. His electrician summoned the emergency unit from Kamnik, which dragged Tomaž out of the basement, crammed him into an ambulance and rushed him to the hospital in Ljubljana, about 30 minutes away.

Despite the adrenaline surging through his body, waves of pain now washed over Tomaž. This pain was different from that which he knew so well: the bite of extreme cold, the assault of falling ice blocks, the numbing pain of creeping frostbite. This new pain was more elemental – deeper, perhaps more serious. He didn't know the extent of the injuries, but he feared the worst.

Upon arriving at the hospital, the on-call trauma team summoned two of Slovenia's leading traumatologists to perform emergency surgery. After first assessing the nature and seriousness of the injuries, they decided that two separate operations would be required: one for the left heel and one for the right femur. The surgeons administered a spinal block and began with the heel. Entering from the side, they found a substantial amount of crushed bone material. They inserted a nail to stabilise the larger break and then added a Kirschner wire structure to bring some stability to the many smaller bones floating about in the heel. Then they closed it up and moved on to the bigger problem – his thigh.

In order to stabilise this extremely large and severely broken bone, they needed to introduce some fairly intrusive hardware. The largest of all was a Küntscher nail, a long piece of metal that they drove into the marrow of the bone and down its entire length. Because they could see that Tomaž had big strong bones, they chose a particularly thick version of the nail. In the process of inserting it, a four-centimetre piece of bone on the medial side was broken off. They then fixed the upper and lower parts of the femur with screws in order to hold the entire structure together. During the reconstruction, a complication emerged when an embolus, a small piece of bone marrow, cut loose, entered Tomaž's bloodstream and began to travel. It would be several days before the seriousness of this development would be revealed.

Tomaž was conscious during these hours on the operating table, although his mind was not lucid due to the massive amounts of painkillers administered to him. Throughout the night his family stood by, waiting for the results. As dawn approached, the operations were finally finished. Sergeja was watching over him, overcome with sadness. But she also, like Tomaž, felt a slight sense of liberation that he would now be forced to put a stop to the madness that his life had become. For some time now Sergeja had felt a premonition that something terrible would happen to Tomaž. She didn't know what, but she knew that his life was out of control and that if he couldn't bring it back into alignment of his own free will, some higher force would do so for him. In fact, she regarded his fall as a gift from God: 'He had to fall into darkness to see the light again.' Maybe now he would stop and think about his life. Maybe he would concentrate more on his family.

Then Dr Anda Perdan, his Dhaulagiri expedition doctor, arrived. Anda carefully observed his medical treatment, initially noting simply that the surgeries had been completed quickly and efficiently. Only later, after double-checking with other bone specialists, was it confirmed that the heel, in particular, should not have been operated on so quickly. As Anda described it, 'The heel is like a sponge.' With so many small bones floating loose, it would only be a matter of time before it would become infected. Another concern was the size of the Küntscher nail placed in his femur.

Heavily dosed with anticoagulants to prevent the possibility of embolisms, Tomaž was soon moved into the intensive care unit. By 1 November, the doctors administered a blood transfusion to counteract his low red blood count, the body's principal method of delivering oxygen from the lungs to body tissue. His haemoglobin was also abnormally low, indicating a level of anaemia. The following day they stepped up his Fragmin medication to the more powerful heparin, both designed to stop clots forming within the blood vessels. This was a particularly dangerous situation for Tomaž because he was completely immobile, a condition that greatly increased the risk of a certain kind of blood clot known as deep vein thrombosis. If a clot formed, it could break off and travel to his lungs, causing pulmonary embolism. The strengthened medication indicated the doctors' growing concern.

On 6 November, they moved him from the intensive care unit into an ordinary trauma unit room. Here they began giving him light exercises that he could perform in his bed, as well as fitting him with a wheelchair. At this point they changed his medication back to Fragmin, a less potent formula of the blood-thinner heparin. This adjustment was nearly fatal. By the next day Tomaž was having difficulty breathing and was spitting blood. Intensely in tune with his own physiology, he sensed that something sinister was taking place in his body. He could feel an embolus travelling up towards his lungs and he became increasingly agitated. He eventually became so insistent with the medical staff that both Viki and Stipe arrived to try and soothe him. The doctors prescribed medication to calm him. They did not believe his self-diagnosis. But that night, Tomaž could feel pain in the right part of his lung. Still he could not convince his doctors, so in a rage he threw his bedpan to get their attention. Even this didn't work.

As he continued to cough up frothy sputum, Tomaž knew that not only was there an embolus in his lungs, he might even be in the early stages of pulmonary oedema, and if it was not addressed, he would die. Finally he took matters into his own hands, in his own way, lowering his oxygen level by 50 per cent in order to set off the alarms on the machines that were monitoring him. This biofeedback technique was one he learned on expeditions, and it served him well at this moment, for the medical technicians came running, and shortly afterwards, administered the lung scans that he had been demanding. They found pulmonary emboli in the lower portion of both lungs, as well as an embolus in his upper right lung. The X-rays and CT scans also revealed pneumonia. The doctors immediately put him back on heparin to further thin his blood, and moved him back into the intensive care unit. Here he remained for another 12 days. Strangely, despite his Himalayan experiences, Tomaž had never experienced pulmonary oedema, a common problem at altitude.

In addition to this scare, Tomaž's injuries were presenting other problems. The wound on the lateral side of his heel had opened up and was seeping. He also felt a constant throb in his right leg, and the vein was partly open. Despite the complications, once the immediate lung emergency had been solved, the doctors moved him out of the intensive care unit. He immediately tried to do some light rehabilitative exercises, relying heavily on strong painkillers to dull the throbbing ache.

Meanwhile, Reuters news agency had picked up on the story of his accident and it quickly spread around the world. Online newsletters and mountain websites carried the news, and climbers everywhere wondered if this would be the last of the überclimber. HimalayaNet carried the story in their newsletter: 'Tomaž Humar last year pulled off a mountaineering feat hitherto considered impossible – a solo ascent of the southern face of the 8,167-metre (26,795 feet) Dhaulagiri in the Nepalese Himalayas. But the house proved more than a challenge for the 31-year-old. The patient is feeling well and will stay in hospital another 10 days, but full recovery might take several months.' In fact, it would be much longer than several months and even then, 'full recovery' would need to be precisely defined.

Then Tomaž was hit by another blow: his world-class standing with the

Mountaineering Association had been mysteriously withdrawn. He had not been informed of this directly; it was his accountant who had noticed the termination of the small stipend that was one of the benefits of this elite status. Tomaž was furious, believing that ravenous hyenas were moving in to finish him off when he was down. He had no intention of accepting the insult, so he informed his lawyer, who enthusiastically took up the cause on his behalf. It took some time and an enormous amount of effort, but eventually his world-class status was reinstated.

On 8 December, Tomaž was moved to a rehabilitation centre called Terme Laško. The luxurious health spa is located in central Slovenia in the village of Laško, perched on the left bank of the Savinja river. The healing waters of Laško's hot springs were well known even in the time of ancient Rome, and now, in addition to catering to wealthy 'wellness' clients, the spa boasted an entire wing devoted to therapeutic and rehabilitative programmes for post-injury patients. Tomaž was given an exercise regime to begin the process of mobilising his broken body. Part of the regime was aquatic exercise, but with Tomaž there was a problem: the wound on his heel refused to heal and there was a persistent brown seepage from within. The physiotherapists wisely refrained from allowing him in the thermal waters, fearing even worse contamination. Unlike Anda, who was worried about this obvious infection, his surgeon was confident that it was a normal reaction.

His heel was not the only problem, for his leg was causing him constant pain. He experienced paraesthesia along the entire front side of his thigh, a tingling sensation that occurs when pressure is placed on a nerve. Most people have experienced some kind of paraesthesia, usually described as 'pins and needles', when the anaesthetic slowly wears off after dental work. When pressure to the nerve is relieved, the feeling usually dissipates, normally in a matter of hours. But this paraesthesia had lasted weeks now, suggesting the possibility of nerve damage in his leg. As a result of these multiple symptoms, the physiotherapy was slow and his leg was unresponsive. The process was unbearably frustrating for Tomaž, whose entire being was focused on rehabilitating as quickly as possible. Patience was something he was beginning to learn.

During this stressful period, he began writing his innermost thoughts in a small book that he kept at his side, his 'Dream Book'. Thoughts like: 'Risk gives you more pleasure than victory'; 'Everything is personal if you are a person'; and one that applied rather aptly to the moment: 'When you are ill you have one problem. When you are healthy you have many problems.' Then one day he wrote a strange little entry that for Tomaž was a major victory: 'Iron 20 – Hallelujah!' His blood iron count was finally approaching normality.

Meanwhile, his friends and family continued building the house. By 23 December, Tomaž had begged his medical team for a chance to return home for Christmas. He had one more visit to the Ljubljana hospital, where they operated on his heel in order to clean up the wound. Although they cleaned it thoroughly, the treatment proved to be superficial and temporary, for the problem was deep inside the heel. Back home at last, Tomaž could still put virtually no weight on it, so he was confined to the living room sofa and his wheelchair. Still in enormous pain, and frustrated by the slow rate of progress with his rehabilitation, he was nevertheless relieved to be home. Sergeja consoled him, but the long hours of forced inactivity on the sofa gave him ample time to think, and there were many dark moments – moments when he could see no future for himself other than a wheelchair and chronic pain.

Yet out of this darkness and at times deep depression something positive emerged, for it was while Tomaž was bound to his 'red Ferrari' wheelchair that he and his father finally grew closer. Devastated by the accident, his parents were initially confounded; after all those years of them worrying about his climbing, Tomaž had managed to hurt himself while building a house – something that Max could do in his sleep! The irony seemed too cruel. They promised him that if he would just walk again, they would never, ever nag him about climbing. They prayed constantly, not just for his recovery, but that he might have a more stable life and spend more time with his precious family. For Max it was unbearably painful to see this son of his, this troublesome yet amazing son, so like himself in temperament and spirit, beaten down this way. If he could have absorbed his son's pain he would gladly have done so. Tomaž could finally fathom the full extent of his father's love, uncluttered now by arguments and strife.

With his keen interest in alternative medical care, Tomaž contacted Nataša Pergar, a respected biotherapist and author, whose speciality was auras. Nataša began by teaching him to pay more attention to his body in relation to all its parts: mind, emotions and spirit. She worked with him on meditative exercises to enhance his intuition and to locate energy blocks that might prohibit his healing. Of course his body was severely traumatised, so she taught him to focus on these 'diseased' areas during his meditations, searching for an answer through self-healing. They used instruments such as voltmetres to measure his energy field, not only in the injured areas but also in the more emotional experiences of worry, grief, anger or love. She taught him to use his intuitive intelligence to find clues to open these blockages and to see his individual organisms in an integrated relationship, able to exchange energy and information in order to promote healing.

Nataša was particularly interested in Tomaž's personal energetic field. Using biofeedback and other devices to measure his biofields, the subtle electrical fields associated with an organism, she helped him become more aware of, and more involved in, the process of increasing his own electrical intensity. She taught him to be firmly grounded, like the beech trees outside his home. These tools helped him begin to feel that he had a stable base from which to launch his healing process. He desperately needed this stability because his clarity of thinking and his self-assurance were badly damaged. After all, for months his body had been flooded with intense levels of painkilling drugs. What he needed above all was clarity of vision, a feeling of safety and greater self-awareness.

Nataša helped him become aware that he needed, now more than ever, to avoid being with people who would distract his energy from the healing process. As her work continued with Tomaž, it evolved into more of a scientific experiment than just a therapist-patient relationship.

Using ancient medicinal practices, Nataša expanded Tomaž's under-standing of what was possible. They began using gongs to create harmonics that would stimulate and balance the various levels of his human energy field. Together they looked for energy emanating from the earth, energy that could circulate throughout his cells and organs and tissues, clearing out the old negative energy and replenishing it with new, healing energy. She helped him to find and increase his own high-frequency patterns, closely associated with his level of spiritual awareness. This life force is part of many ancient traditions and philosophies: the Chinese call it *chi*; the Hindus refer to it as *prana*; and the Masai call it *ngai*. Nataša's job was to translate this life force energy into something that resonated for Tomaž.

As he became more aware of his own body, he began to sense when there were unhealthy energies within his system, and how to deal with them. This was accomplished primarily through his chakras, the Sanskrit word meaning 'wheel'. He learned that the natural directional flow of life force entered his body at his seventh chakra and flowed down through his head and neck, along his back through subtle channels on either side of his spine, and then into the first chakra at the base of his spine. All of this contributed to the aura around his physical body that could protect and shield his energy system, provided it was in good shape.

As a clairvoyant, Nataša could easily see Tomaž's aura. She could see when it was whole and brightly coloured, and she also saw it when it was dull and grey and torn around the edges. She worked hard to help him develop a healthy, vibrant aura to protect him from destructive environmental influences and heal him from within. If he could develop a greater awareness of his aura, and consciously work to strengthen it, he would be able to detect negative energy disturbances trying to manifest themselves within him, such as the injuries that simply would not heal.

Nataša and Tomaž made progress, but it was slow, and when Anda arrived to visit him she was shocked at what she saw. Almost two months after the accident, he was still suffering from an extremely high fever and his heel was swollen and red. It was obviously still infected, but why? She cleaned the wound diligently and gave him antibiotics to try and control the infection. Finally she convinced the head of plastic surgery in Ljubljana to X-ray the heel. They could see the problem immediately, for bone fragments were still floating about and were the obvious cause of the persistent infection. But by now the heel was so inflamed that they could do nothing but try to control the infection.

Anda knew the Slovenian medical community quite well and she knew that Tomaž had been given the very best care by the top physicians in the country. After all, he was a national icon. Their surgical work was at stake, as were their reputations. So it was with great sensitivity that she began enquiring about a second opinion for his prognosis, for she was convinced that those bone fragments had to be removed.

Instead of returning directly to Terme Laško to continue his rehabilitation as planned, Tomaž went back to the Ljubljana hospital for another round of X-rays. There they discovered that his femur was still not growing together. In fact there was an alarmingly wide gap between the two sections of broken bone. This was devastating news. After two and a half months, the bone sections were not even touching, let alone meshing. What could possibly be wrong? At first they thought it was because Tomaž was unable to put weight on his leg, due to the persistent numbness. But upon closer examination they realised it was because the metal pin that had been used to replace the first pin (the one that was too thick) was now too long. There was absolutely no possibility of the bones meeting and meshing, for the pin was keeping them apart. Now the surgeons would need to go back into his leg, remove this second pin and replace it with a third. The only other option was to remove a bit of bone from his hip and place it in the gap, in the hope that it would take. To add to this complication, they discovered major damage to a blood vessel near the injured femur. Probably traumatised during one of the two operations, this injured blood vessel increased the possibility of yet another embolus, for blood tended to collect in the damaged area and clot. Assuming that Tomaž would eventually become more active, the possibility of a clot moving through his veins to his heart or lung was very real. They would now need to put him on stronger anticoagulants once again. The whole situation was a nightmare.

The heel was not much better. Anda had been observing it for weeks, and each time she cleaned it, she discovered secretions and a very wet, angry-looking scab. At times the secretions were foul-smelling, suggesting massive infection inside the heel. The wound was frightening to observe.

Still, Tomaž retained his focus and optimism. It was at this point that he and Anda decided that they needed to go outside the country for their next surgical interventions, which were clearly necessary. They received considerable criticism for this decision, and as Anda recalled, many accused Tomaž of being 'too good for Slovenian doctors'. Deliberately and thoughtfully, she explained the real reason: 'In the end, Tomaž chose not to go with another specialist in Slovenia because . . . this would have placed too much pressure on this doctor.' Anda supported him in this decision. In fact, by this time she was so frustrated with the level of care he was receiving in the trauma division of the Ljubljana hospital that she wrote an uncharacteristically strongly worded letter of disappointment.

But at least one of the Ljubljana surgeons understood the seriousness of the situation and supported their decision to go outside the country for treatment. To that end, this unnamed medical practitioner arranged for Anda to obtain all the original X-rays so that she could copy them in order to have a complete medical record. She sent the X-rays first to a traumatologist in Munich, who then suggested one of the best in the world – Professor Gert Muhr in Bochum, Germany. Another medical friend suggested a heel specialist in Dresden – Professor Hans Zwipp. Now both Tomaž and Anda travelled to Dresden and Bochum to see the specialists and to have additional X-rays and examinations done.

Professor Muhr described what he had seen and what he felt needed to be done, first suggesting that the surgery be done in Slovenia, since they had excellent traumatologists. Anda explained the sensitivity of the situation as best she could and convinced him that they would prefer him to do the surgery himself. He agreed, but then asked Tomaž why he didn't walk. After all, it had been more than six months since the accident. Tomaž explained that he simply couldn't. In fact the muscles in his buttocks were by now completely atrophied. But it wasn't the buttock muscles that were the problem; it was the constant pain in his femur. He could not bear to put weight on that bone. Professor Muhr soon discovered that it was not pain from the bone, but rather pain from a nerve. When they had dealt with this pinched nerve and put a local block on the pain emanating from it, the situation improved almost immediately. There was still some residual swelling from the months of interference, but that too was remedied by another round of medication. For the very first time, Tomaž and Anda could see some progress. Tomaž could finally put weight on his leg, and he was ecstatic. To Anda's horror, he was so excited that he immediately got on his bicycle and began to ride.

They headed back to Slovenia and waited for word from Professor Muhr regarding the next operation. Finally they had a date – 16 June. Now they had another problem: who would pay? Obviously Tomaž could not afford this costly procedure in one of the most expensive countries in Europe. He hadn't worked in months. Mobitel had generously offered to pay, but Tomaž refused, since he felt this would be an overextension of their generosity. He was constantly amazed at their concern for him throughout the entire process, for they never asked about his future plans as a climber but rather stayed focused on his recovery. It didn't feel at all like a traditional sponsorship arrangement. In fact, the relationship had moved well beyond that, into the realm of deep friendship.

Ultimately it was up to Anda to solve the financial dilemma, and once again her sensitivity and diplomatic skills saved the day. She returned to the hospital in Ljubljana and requested a meeting with the director of traumatology, a man who was also in charge of the country's health insurance. What she needed from him was very simple: a signature, a signed document stating that the next surgery must be done abroad. After the meeting, and with some careful negotiating on Anda's part, he promised to sign the document, with the result that most of the expenses were subsequently covered by the health insurance.

There were two operations: one in June on the thigh, and the second in September on the heel. The first operation was to remove the pin that connected the two sections of his femur. During this operation they discovered that between the two sections of bone a new piece of material had begun to grow. But this growth was not bone. It was a completely useless substance that resembled soft cartilage. Tomaž's body had courageously tried to bridge the gap, but with the wrong material. After removing the too-long pin and the useless cartilage, the surgeon pushed the bones together as closely as he could and extracted some bone material from Tomaž's hip, which he then inserted into the still-existing gap. The end result was that the damaged leg was about three centimetres shorter than the other, but at least it now had a realistic chance of healing.

Now Tomaž could gradually begin to put weight on his right leg. This was a major breakthrough. It was at this point that they discovered that the big toe on his right foot was also broken. With all the other injuries, this one had simply been overlooked. The physicians dealt with it promptly. Immediately after these operations, Tomaž began physiotherapy treatment in the unit attached directly to the hospital. It was here that he met the irresistible force of a woman he called Hilda, his physiotherapist and constant companion over the next few weeks. The German philosophy was to start physiotherapy as early as possible and train as hard as possible. At first it seemed like fun. Hilda gave Tomaž a high-tech bed with all kinds of levers and a remote control with which he could manipulate his suspended limb. The entire contraption looked like a giant toy. But he soon discovered that the mechanism was a trick: 'It was a kind of perpetual mobilé situation with weights attached to my leg. The only way to make the pain leave was to keep moving the leg, yet each time I moved the leg, another wave of pain would come, over and over and over.' Accompanied by howls of pain, he participated in this sado-masochistic activity for a minimum of 20 minutes per day – to start. The routine was increased substantially each successive day.

Standing guard over the entire procedure was Hilda – an unyielding character, absolutely inured to the pleas of her patients. Even Tomaž couldn't convince her to go easy with him. Her colleague, Frank, would stand beside the pool, arms akimbo, ordering him: '*Schwim, schwim, schwim!*' Tomaž would moan: 'I can't I'm so tired.' They ignored his complaints and kept him moving for the allotted time. The indestructible force from Slovenia had finally met the immovable German wall.

The sessions were particularly rigorous for this unruly patient, and with good cause, for the physiotherapists later told Anda that they 'were preparing Tomaž for the mountains – not for the office'. When the sessions ended, Tomaž returned home with a vastly improved outlook on life. He was finally able to see some progress in this long recovery process. The black cloud began to lift. Back at his home on the edge of the forest, he started to test his newly healing leg on crutches. What a thrill it was to finally emerge from the red chariot that had so dominated his life. But it was a painful process, not only for Tomaž but for anyone standing by to watch. As his movements were still clumsy and awkward, he would take out his frustration on his crutches, bashing them around, trying to make them go faster. Grunting and storming about, he forced himself to walk, first on level ground, then on steeper and more uneven terrain, and finally into his beloved Kamnik Alps. Here he could absorb the energy that was his life force – the energy of the mountains. Here he finally began to feel elemental joy in his being once again. As his crutches become almost too battered to be safely used, he began to ride his bike. Now he could see some real progress in his rehabilitation. After hundreds of days flat on his back, after weeks confined to his red Ferrari, after hours of complicated surgery and even more hours of diligent and painful physiotherapy, after stretching his mind and soul as far as he could to embrace alternative solutions, and after many setbacks, he could finally see some results – and they excited him. For the first time in months he began to imagine a comeback. But first he needed more work on his heel.

Back he went to Germany, where two more operations were required to fix the mess. The first was simply to remove all the loose pieces of bone. Professor Zwipp then inserted a massive dose of antibiotics to rid his heel of the infection as well as ensure that no new infection crept in. After a few days he operated again, this time inserting two metal pins to secure the heel. In order to facilitate Tomaž's ongoing physiotherapy and exercise pro-gramme, Zwipp also gave him a special boot designed to keep his weight off the newly mended heel. Now Tomaž could walk without crutches, albeit with a horrendous lurching gait. But the important thing was to move. And move he did, for he now had a goal. Finally he allowed himself to dream about his future – about returning to the mountains.

During those long months of therapy and training, Tomaž was deliberately low-key about his medical experiences in Germany. For the sake of the medical professionals in Slovenia who had helped him as best they could, he wanted to keep quiet about having left the country for surgery. He even implored the media not to report on that part of the story. For the most part, he was successful. Anda did not completely agree with him on this issue, for she felt that it was important for every citizen to become more aware of their right to a second opinion. She felt that their biggest oversight was to have delayed seeking one. So many costly and painful mistakes could have been avoided. Had Tomaž not secured that second opinion, he most definitely would have been confined to a wheel-chair for the rest of his life.

Some people questioned Anda about her devotion to this sometimes difficult patient. Surely she had other equally important patients on whom to spend her time. Anda tried to explain her motivation: 'It took a lot of my time and energy, but from the first time I met him and on our first expedition [Dhaulagiri] I knew he was someone I just had to care for. He had an extraordinary feeling for the mountain. I don't want to put him on a pedestal but his relationship with it was almost spiritual. I felt I knew what climbing meant for him. And when there were all of these complications, I couldn't abandon him. I couldn't.'

Anda would accompany him on almost all of his future expeditions. There is absolutely no doubt that had it not been for her, Tomaž would never have climbed another mountain. Tomaž often said that he had been given a second 'ticket' after the accident. The one person who personified that ticket was Anda Perdan.

CHAPTER THIRTEEN

AFTER THE FALL

9 August 2005, 04.15, Nanga Parbat, Rupal Face

Rashid arrives at the army aviation base in Rawalpindi for the pre-flight inspection. Unbelievably, the tail rotor hydraulic dampers have developed a leak and need to be replaced. They make the repair as quickly as possible but it isn't until 05.45 that they are airborne. En route to their first destination of the village of Dashkin, they fly up the Indus valley past Nanga Parbat's Diamir Face, which is partially visible in reasonable weather. But upon turning into the Astore valley, they are immediately hit by rain and low cloud and have to turn back. They revise their flight plan to the village of Jaglot, where they wait for the other helicopters to join them.

9 August, 08.30

Tomaž wakens from an uncomfortable night on the face to a feeling of increasing panic. He recollects his thoughts:

*I feel unease in my heart, I do not allow myself to look . . . no, noooo!!!
Pain chases the hopes away . . . it is foggy again, moisture, snow . . .
For a moment I indulge in the hope that this may just be a bad dream
. . . the reality hurts. I'm still trapped . . . trapped in the icy coffin.*

*The valley is filled with fog and I cannot see further than about a
hundred metres into the grey whiteness. When the snow starts to fall,
the view shrinks to a few metres of whiteness, whiteness in the foggy
snow. It gives the impression that it will never stop.*

The smallest move in my soaking wet clothing reminds me of hopeless cold, right to my bones. In order to conserve energy I do not allow myself to shiver any more. Shivering would have warmed me up for a moment or two, but I am aware that this survival technique saps the energy, takes away days of living, and I want to live, to live one more day, even if it is my last one . . . to live in pain and peace, morning after morning, day after day, evening after evening.

How many days are left for me? How long can I hold on? Until when? I am searching for the answers, some meaning, a message in the labyrinth of thoughts, hope, and sometimes hopelessness. But I cannot ask myself the right questions any more. I cannot think any more. In times like this I turn myself off after a few deep breaths. I leave. I go to a timeless world, a world with no space, no pain, no thoughts.

How many blessings have I been given? I can still not fully comprehend; the story is still not completely finished.

Tomaž calls in on the radio, his voice severely strained: 'This isn't a bivouac any more, it's pouring all over me and everything is freezing!' Last night in the snow cave was the worst yet, with the snow sifting in around him, narrowing his small tunnel to a slot, despite all his efforts to keep it clear. The temperature hovered around –5 degrees Celsius, not just in the air, but in his sleeping bag as well. He is losing this battle. Again, Anda encourages him to drink as much as possible. Tomaž no longer shields his team from the facts: his gas is low, so half a litre of fluid is all he can manage. Anda is horrified: she knows this is not enough.

Tomaž asks about the forecast. Will there be any improvement? In fact, it does appear that the clouds are breaking up after this morning's downpour, and the visibility is improving slightly. They can see as high as 4,500 metres as the mountain reluctantly reveals itself. The forecast promises more stability later in the morning, bringing a note of optimism but also reinforcing the need to hurry. The prevailing weather patterns seem to offer brief moments of respite from the storms, but only in the mornings. With that in mind, base camp radioes the rescue helicopter team to see what time they will arrive.

The pilots respond that they will arrive with their Lama helicopters as soon as the weather improves. But only to base camp. They will then have to wait until the face is completely visible, for it would be suicidal to head towards the wall in any other conditions. Nazir calls base camp to assure them that the pilots are Pakistan's very best. Base camp press for more details: who are they? Upon learning more about the pilots, they provide details to Tomaž. The lead pilot will be Colonel Rashid Ullah Baig, a pilot for 12 years, a flying instructor and the commander of the Chumnik Soviours unit, a group of 20–30 army pilots. To assist him on this mission, Rashid has chosen 40-year-old Major Khalid Amir Rana as his co-pilot. Each has over 3,000 hours of flying experience.

Back in Slovenia, Viki contacts the Swiss team, asking them to bring a pilot, even though they don't have permission to bring a helicopter. He's confident that they will be able to fly a Pakistani helicopter once they arrive. Gerold Binder is not so sure: 'From my experience in India, I know that I will never have a chance to sit in a Pakistani army chopper and act as a pilot.' But he also knows that his rescuers will feel more comfortable if he is in the helicopter with them. By now it is obvious to Biner that the Pakistani army is not overly enthusiastic about a foreign team doing this rescue. He understands this and does his best to be sensitive to the situation. He is confident of his ability to do this rescue mission, even in bad weather conditions. If the Lama has good clean fuel, he knows he can get Tomaž safely off the face. But his big concern now is with the Pakistani pilots, for they have no experience at human cargo slinging.

He urges Viki to ensure that the Pakistani pilots are not informed that a Swiss team is on the way. He is sure that this information will place added pressure on them, possibly forcing them into a situation for which they are not prepared or equipped. Despite his request, the Pakistani pilots do learn that the Swiss team is on its way; now they will be pushed to their limits – and beyond. Surely this is the worst possible situation: national pride, as well as several lives, is now at stake.

9 August, 10.28

A message arrives in base camp from Viki. Astonishing news. He has heard that a permit has just been issued for the Swiss helicopter. Nazir's request to the Pakistani Foreign Minister has produced the desired result. Sadly, it's too late. The Swiss team is on their way, but the helicopter will have to be a Pakistani one. In his heart Viki knows this scenario is unlikely. What kind of miracle would allow a Swiss pilot to fly a Pakistani military helicopter? 'I was paralysed by the thought of how small the chance of a successful rescue really was,' he later admits. But the message he gives to the team and to Tomaž is that 'the Swiss are on their way'. This message, repeated day after day, is beginning to irritate Tomaž, for he feels manipulated, certain that he is not being told the entire story.

Despite the reasonable forecast, the weather has again worsened. There is now a drizzle at base camp, and for the fifth day in a row, it's snowing steadily at the bivouac site. Tomaž radioes base camp with panic rising in his voice: 'What's with the rescue? Why aren't the helicopters at base camp yet?' They have no answer for him. The last message they received was that there were three helicopters at Jaglot, 18 kilometres from Gilgit and 20 minutes' flying time from base camp. Two of these are Lamas and the third is an MI-17 fuel-delivery helicopter. They continue calling Jaglot, asking when the helicopters will lift off. The answer remains the same: when the weather permits.

Everyone at base camp is frustrated beyond belief. They are caught between Tomaž's radio calls demanding information and action, and the reality of the rescue team's impossible flying conditions. Nothing they can do or say will bring the helicopters more quickly. They are at the mercy of the weather, and the weather appears to be merciless.

Meanwhile, the pilots are not wasting their time in Jaglot. While they wait for a break in the weather, they fine-tune their strategy and double-check everything. Finally, at 14.15 they receive word from base camp that the cloud bank has lifted and the Rupal Face is visible. All three helicopters start their engines and they're off.

9 August, 15.00

The helicopters arrive in base camp! There is excitement and fear in the air. The wall is again shrouded in fog, but arrangements have to be made – and quickly. First they contact Tomaž, who at the moment is in a snowstorm and can see no obvious clearing. Back at base camp the pilots and Aleš closely examine the photos taken two days before. Rashid is taken aback by what he sees in these more detailed photos: 'My worries were magnified a thousandfold.' What he now sees more clearly is the true steepness of the wall and the minuscule platform on which Tomaž is trapped. Most troubling of all is the cliff looming above the site, on top of which is precariously perched a pillow of powder snow. As Rashid stares at the photograph, a silent terror engulfs him as he imagines the effects of his rotor wash on that mushroom of snow. If it cuts loose, Tomaž, and perhaps the helicopter itself, will be buried. Even if the helicopter isn't hit by the avalanche, the downdraught alone could catapult it down the face. Upon closer examination he sees deep ravines on each side of the site which will make it very difficult to judge the approach. And the steepness of the slope presents the final problem, for there will not be enough room to allow the rotor clearance. The spot on which they need to deposit the rescue rope is about 12 feet square. They will need to be light enough to hover for a number of minutes, yet retain enough power to lift a live 70-kilogram cargo. They will then need to descend almost 10,000 feet to base camp.

Rashid quickly does some more calculations, based on the detailed photos. The rotor diameter of the Lama is 36.15 feet and is located approximately 10 feet above the sling hook. In order to have rotor clearance on the 75–80-degree slope, he will need to use a sling rope of about 90–110 feet. Yet that troublesome rock cliff looming over Tomaž is not more than 80–100 feet above the rescue site. The rock feature is very clear on the photos. He recalculates the numbers and determines that the sling rope length cannot exceed 41 feet. This should leave him enough room to hover over the site, yet still provide about 30–50 feet between the top of the spinning rotors and the protruding rock cliff and snow mushroom. But in order to get close enough to the wall for Tomaž to reach the swinging rope, Rashid realises that he will have to fly in – and under – the black rock; he will literally have to tuck his helicopter under that rock outcropping.

Stipe spoke earlier with the pilots via satellite phone, urging them to use a 100-foot line, which would give them a much better chance of swinging the end of the line in to Tomaž's snow cave. But now that the pilots have examined the photos, they decide to shorten the line to 30 feet.

The pilots are worried, and base camp senses their concern. Everyone is tense. Rashid glances up from the photos and for the first time looks around at the people whose lives he has entered. 'I could feel their helplessness. Their eyes spoke of the despair they buried deep inside. I did not find a single soul there not praying for his [Tomaž's] safe return.' Rashid is not referring only to Aleš, Maja and Anda, for a number of locals in the valley have congregated at base camp and all are concerned about the drama that is unfolding before them. Rashid recalls, 'May he be a porter, a reporter, an under-training army soldier or a local shepherd, everyone loved him like a real brother.' Rashid speaks the same dialect as some of the locals in camp, and as he converses with them, many burst into tears. All express their hope and confidence in the Pakistani army. Rashid, in turn, urges them to pray.

How can he back down now? Everyone is counting on him. They get to work. Rashid and the other pilots, together with Aleš, prepare ropes and weights to sling in to Tomaž. Aleš is worried that the weights will hit Tomaž and injure him. The pilots assure him that they will be in constant radio communication with Tomaž and he will be well aware of their arrival. He will not be at risk from the weights swinging at the end of the lines.

The rescuers are rigorous with their questions: what is the night temperature at the bivouac? What is the morning temperature? What colour is Tomaž's clothing? Does he have any kind of flag that he can wave at them? Does he speak English? Is he still physically able to attach himself to the sling rope? Does he have carabiners? Then they review, once again, the radio frequencies. This is a critical detail. The helicopter, base camp and Tomaž must all be on the same frequency. The timing must be perfectly synchronised.

Officially, Tomaž is trapped at 5,900 metres. But he knows the elevation is higher; Nazir Sabir knows; and the pilots know. However, they cannot acknowledge it. They know that this rescue is higher than is authorised, but their order has come from the top – from President Musharraf. So they continue.

Maja contacts Viki to tell him that the helicopters are there. Viki is elated. He is immediately connected directly to Tomaž, reviewing the details, particularly the radio frequency. While Tomaž and Viki talk on the radio, Anda approaches Rashid. Her eyes are serious, concerned and careworn, and she quietly asks him, 'What are the chances?' Rashid wants to be honest but he can't be, so he exaggerates the probability of success. 'About 10 per cent,' he says. Anda slowly walks away to deal with her thoughts in private.

Then they wait for the weather to improve.

9 August, 15.30

Tomaž excitedly radioes base camp: the weather is clearing immediately above his position and he can see the ridge emerging from the murk on the left. Not only that, it has stopped snowing and the wind has disappeared. He screams for the helicopter. The crews run, and after a few last-minute instructions they are off, the second helicopter five minutes after the first.

As the upper part of the mountain opens up, base camp strains to see. Aleš is glued to the telescope, Anda to the radio. The two Lamas begin the steep ascent towards Tomaž. At 5,300 metres, they encounter clouds. Climbing higher immerses them in thick, almost whiteout conditions. Now a new cloud emerges from the right, threatening to obscure the site completely. The pilots have made radio contact with Tomaž. They are near him. The fog has obscured the scene from base camp, which is frantic to know what's going on. Then they hear the devastating radio transmission: the helicopters are returning – without Tomaž. Back at base camp the pilots explain that as they approached the bivouac site, the fog completely obscured it. They could not get close enough to Tomaž to attempt a rescue – or even to drop supplies.

Tomaž and his team are shattered. Rashid recalls, 'I could feel him disappointed at our performance, but we were helpless against nature.' But nobody, not even his co-pilot, knows Rashid's private thoughts at this moment, for as he turns back after the unsuccessful attempt to pluck Tomaž off the face, his thoughts are of his deceased brother Masood: 'I thought, what could I do if Masood was there in place of Tomaž? How far could I go?' He realises that whatever effort he would have made for Masood, he is now prepared to make for Tomaž. He is completely committed to making this rescue work.

At base camp they consider their next steps. Rashid promises a rescue the following day if the weather improves. Arrangements are made to call the pilots at 04.30 to inform them of the flying conditions. This will allow them to be there by 05.00. The pilots assure base camp that today's flight is a valuable one, for they have firmly established the whereabouts of the site, they have established communication between the helicopters and Tomaž and they have seen the conditions of the pick-up spot. They are confident they can do it.

As they leave, the entire mountain briefly shows its face, as if to taunt them.

Viki has been monitoring the goings-on and is devastated that the rescue wasn't successful. He calls Nazir Sabir and reviews the protocol for the next day. They run through the details once again. Everything must go perfectly.

The Swiss have arrived in Islamabad, but Nazir reiterates to Viki that there is too much at stake with the military; the Pakistanis must have first chance at the rescue. If they don't succeed, then the Swiss will be brought in. Viki understands, but it makes him nervous. The Swiss have so much more experience. He is convinced they could do it quickly, efficiently and safely. But they will have to wait. Once again Viki informs Tomaž that 'the Swiss are on their way'. By this time Tomaž realises that something is amiss. For two days now he has been told this. Each time he has been given a time frame: in 12 hours; in 10 hours; within 20 hours. Each time his hopes have been raised, only to be dashed yet again. How can it take the Swiss two days to fly to Pakistan? He knows that the facts are being kept from him, but he doesn't have the heart to challenge Viki. Besides, deep down he hopes that it's true and that the Swiss really are on their way.

Tomaž decides that it's time to speak with his father, Max. Base camp arranges the call for him and then moves away from the radio in order to give him some privacy. At first they discuss what Max is hearing on the news. Tomaž urges him not to believe everything he hears and assures him that he is okay. They move on to the garden, the cats, normal, everyday topics. The underlying message is concern and love for each other. At the end of the call, Tomaž promises Max that he will not die in this cave. What he doesn't say is that he may well die trying to escape.

Then it's time to talk with his children. Once again base camp arranges the call. Shortly afterwards, Tomaž receives an SMS message from Urša and Tomi that nearly breaks his heart: 'Father, we know that you are strong enough. You will survive. You will bring the shoe back.' They are being brave on his behalf. Finally he receives one more message, this one from Sergeja, with whom he has had no contact whatsoever during the entire ordeal: 'I know you very well. You will survive. Be strong.' This is a very emotional moment for Tomaž, for he realises that despite their troubles and bitterness, there is still a capacity for compassion, a gift that Sergeja has just given him.

In Gilgit, where the helicopters have landed for the night, the pilots have no time for rest. They don't want any mistakes tomorrow, so they spend the rest of the evening practising high-altitude training manoeuvres. They check and recheck the helicopters and they review their calculations yet again. This turns out to be a valuable exercise, for in the process, they slightly modify their plan.

Rashid recalls a search that he conducted in 1995 when two Korean climbers went missing while descending the 7,708-metre Mount Tirchmir. They had disappeared somewhere between the summit and their highest camp at 7,400 metres. While flying over the summit, Rashid had the unusual experience of attaining a pressure altitude of 7,730 metres, which translated into almost 8,900 metres of density altitude. This was achieved because of the low temperatures at the time. He knows that every metre of pressure altitude gained provides added manoeuvrability and power, so could be important in the success of the rescue.

He speculates that this greater density might also be found on the Rupal Face if they take advantage of the cool, early-morning temperatures. But there is a complication. Together with those early-morning low temperatures there is also a very good possibility of a downdraught on the steep slope. This downdraught, known as a katabatic wind, is likely to be flowing down the face in the early morning, due to the heaviness of the cool air. If it is strong enough, it could completely nullify any advantages provided by the cooler air.

However, Rashid also knows that when the sun shines on a steep slope, exactly the opposite happens; an anabatic wind blows up the slope. Yet as soon as the temperature rises from the effects of the sun, the density of the air will also lessen. He and the others calculate that there might be a small window of opportunity between the time when the sun first hits the slope and the moment the air temperature rises. Within this window – perhaps as much as 30–60 minutes – they might have the benefits of both the greater air density from the cool temperatures and the updraught of the anabatic wind. With these new strategies in mind, they agree to fly early in the morning and hopefully be at the site just as the sun hits the slopes beneath Tomaž. They feel cautiously optimistic.

Meanwhile, up in his cave, Tomaž prepares himself. He changes his anchor rope and attaches the lightest one he has, just in case there is a problem in the morning. He tidies up around his hole to ensure that nothing is loose, for he knows that if the helicopters actually get close to him, the rotor wash will be terrific. He is as ready as he can be. The snow continues to fall, sifting down around him and into every part of his cave. There is nothing left to do but dig. One last night of digging – he hopes.

That night, an enormous series of avalanches rumble down the great Rupal Face. Aleš is awakened by the roar and senses impending doom. He has been suppressing his stress for days now. He knows he is doing everything possible to get Tomaž off this mountain but he doesn't feel anything is working. As the only technical climber at base camp, he feels an enormous amount of responsibility. But at the same time he feels helpless. He knows Maja is trying to help him, giving him ample opportunity to do interviews with her for Slovenian television, but he is simply not interested. His entire focus is on Tomaž, on the face, on the helicopters, on the rescue. He is the unsung hero of this effort. And on this night, Aleš feels as if the mountain has come alive. 'That night I was afraid,' he later recalls.

Shishapangma, North-West Face, 2002

Professor Muhr had told Tomaž while he was in Germany that it would be at least six months before he could remove the metal from his leg. But looking back at the accident, the many setbacks and the long-delayed but gradual recovery, Tomaž felt that he had been given another chance – another 'ticket' as he described it: 'And once you get it, you have to use it . . . You simply have to go.'

When Tomaž began planning his first post-accident climb, he knew he would need a relatively straightforward objective since his leg and heel would still be full of metal. He wasn't ready to tackle anything terribly technical, but rather he needed a chance to get back into the mountains to test himself at altitude. Since he had now experienced pulmonary problems for the first time – in a hospital – he was worried about a recurrence in the mountains. He chose Shishapangma, the lowest of the 8,000-metre peaks, with an elevation of 8,046 metres. Located completely within the Tibetan region of China, Shishapangma was the last of the 8,000-metre peaks to be climbed, in 1964, by a Chinese expedition. The Tibetan name translates as 'crest above the grassy plain', and its broad expanse offered the least technical 8,000er on which Tomaž could test himself.

Even though Shishapangma was known as one of the easier 8,000-metre peaks, with vehicle access to a base camp at 5,000 metres, the mountain still demanded respect. Many climbers ran out of energy as they traversed the immense summit ridge, trying to reach the true summit. The mountain certainly had its lethal qualities. More than 20 climbers had been killed during its relatively brief climbing history, including one of the most experienced of all, the American alpinist Alex Lowe. So it wasn't without concern that Tomaž prepared himself for Shishapangma. This would be an important test: would he ever be able to climb in the Himalayas again?

Although he would have preferred to climb alone, he eventually joined a team from Kazakhstan in order to keep his expenses down. For Shishapangma he had two main concerns: the performance of his leg, and the possible recurrence of pulmonary embolism. Once again, Anda would be with him to monitor any dangerous symptoms. He was not worried about his general conditioning, because after the final round of surgery on his leg and heel, he had trained diligently, running, riding his bike, ice and rock climbing. Still, his heel was not completely healed, for he could not move it in one direction.

Upon arriving in Kathmandu, Tomaž found it impossible to ignore the troublesome political situation. Following the massacre that had taken place the previous June, when the drunken Crown Prince Dipendra had slaughtered his parents, two siblings, two aunts, two uncles, a cousin and finally himself, the country had degenerated into a period of instability. Prince Gyanendra, who was initially appointed regent immediately after the massacre, soon took on the mantle of king. But Gyanendra had some massive problems to contend with: the Maoists were staging uprisings in many of the poorest regions of Nepal and the general populace was in a heightened state of nervousness and confusion. Gyanendra dealt with this in his own way, dissolving parliament, firing the prime minister and basically governing alone. His firm approach kept the large cities and towns reasonably quiet, but there was ample evidence of military patrols, desperately trying to maintain control. Their presence created a decidedly unsettling feeling.

Tomaž soon left Kathmandu and crossed the border into China to join the Kazakh team, a high-powered group of four climbers with considerable experience in the Himalayas. In fact, for them this was just one more stop along the way to the fourteen 8,000-metre peaks. They arrived soon after Tomaž and met up with him at advance base camp at 5,600 metres. While they were getting organised, they encountered more than ten teams in various stages of retreat from the mountain; their reports were not very encouraging. The winds up high were ferocious, and they would not let up. Thus far, only six individual climbers had reached the summit.

Convinced that the weather would change, Tomaž and the Kazakh team began their acclimatisation work, climbing up through the ice falls, hauling equipment and establishing a second camp at 6,900 metres. After returning to their advanced base camp, they rested for three days and then began their summit attempt. In three days of climbing, they reached the massive summit plateau, but the wind was so strong that they were blown completely off their feet while trying to climb the exposed ridge leading to the summit. They hunkered down and waited for some improvement.

Finally, on the night of 25 October, there was a slight easing of the wind's ferocity, and so they started off again. Eleven hours later they were at the top. The entire section of the plateau between the central and main summits had exposed them to wind they had never experienced before. It took all their efforts to avoid being blown off completely. They remained on top just long enough to document their ascent and then retreated as quickly as possible to their camp at 7,200 metres, where they could escape the relentless wind.

The climb accomplished, Tomaž assessed the status of the 'machine', the name he gave his body: leg worked okay, heel was a little inflexible, lungs worked just fine, motivation was better than ever. This was the most important – motivation. He headed back to Germany to have the metal removed from his leg and heel and then began thinking of the next project. It was a big one: the Rupal Face of Nanga Parbat. Perhaps it was a bit premature to attempt this face so soon after his accident, but his motivation was as strong as it had ever been. So he headed to Pakistan to attempt the highest face in the world. The weather was bad the entire time and conditions on the mountain were impossible. This, combined with illness, made this first attempt a failure, but at least he had a good look at the mountain and gained a sense of what he would be faced with on his next try.

His rehabilitation was going well and he could feel himself becoming stronger every week. But there were other troubles that threatened to invalidate all this good progress. Although they still lived in the same house, Sergeja had finally learned to live her own life. Tomaž was seldom there. Even when he had been in Slovenia because of his accident, he spent most of his time at the hospital or at physiotherapy, absorbed by his recovery. And now that he was feeling healthy and regaining some of his lost confidence, he was focused again on the Himalayas, rather than his family. Even their spirituality, something that had previously bonded them, was now something they experienced alone. Only two years earlier, Sergeja had described Tomaž as 'the cross' that she had been given to bear, a burden she had seemed willing to accept. 'I need this. He's my therapy. Hard therapy . . . By carrying this cross, I grow spiritually.' But that cross had become too much – for both of them.

For years now, they had been arguing and fighting about almost everything: money problems, his constant absences, his wild lifestyle, her new and different friends, their infidelities. But always they had stayed together because of the children. Like many couples in deteriorating relationships, they thought the children would benefit from their remaining together. Urša and Tomi became their shield. Much of their anguish and acrimony was exposed before them, creating even more tension. Tomaž and Sergeja avoided being alone together, for their bitterness was then impossible to ignore. Tomaž admitted that they were probably no longer in love, but he was sure that they still loved each other. Each of them was dissatisfied with elements of their own individual lives, and these personal disappointments became the seeds of their discontent with each other.

They did less and less together. She joined him less frequently in the mountains, an understandable development, for he raced around like a madman when he was training, maintaining a pace that no normal human being could match. But sometimes he enjoyed a slower pace, picking mushrooms and simply observing nature. This too he did without Sergeja, for she was no longer interested. Instead, she spent more time in coffee shops, enjoying urban life with her new friends. She liked to shop and she enjoyed good restaurants. She wanted a normal life, one not completely dominated by the mountains. Eventually, Tomaž became convinced that her friends were turning her against him. It was obvious that she was fundamentally, desperately despondent. Photos of Sergeja revealed a woman with a deeply troubled soul. Their relationship seemed beyond the point of repair.

Finally, Sergeja left Tomaž. The first time was a shock to both of them, but her departure was short-lived and soon they were back together, making up for lost time and vowing to make it work. However, the reunion was unsuccessful and she left again. Tomaž clung to the belief that their marriage could be repaired and he tried to convince Sergeja to return. But his behaviour belied his motivations, for he spent most of his time alone, in the forest.

They tried once more, for two months. Then they went on a short holiday together, trying to leave the past behind them, wipe their memories of all the hurts and insults and begin anew. No more secrets. For three weeks they tried. It was like a honeymoon. But when they returned home, Sergeja left again. The third time, it was final. Through it all, Tomaž was convinced that if he just tried hard enough, he could make their relationship work. A few years later he reflected, with great sadness in his voice, 'My big sin was to try and keep Sergeja.'

Throughout this traumatic, emotional turmoil, Tomaž continued training, for he had another lover: the mountains. Shishapangma had provided him with good feedback on what he could do at altitude, but he was not interested in easy 'walk-up' climbs at altitude. He was a 'face' man. So he spent the early part of the winter ice-climbing as much as possible. It was on one of those days that he met Aleš Koželj, another Kamnik climber. Much younger, Aleš certainly knew who Tomaž was, but he didn't know him personally. It was a curious scene. Aleš had gone out for a quick ice climb after work, and there he found Tomaž, rope-soloing an ice fall. Tomaž clearly had the confidence to get up the climb, but he was concerned about the descent. So he had brought along a rope which he planned to use to abseil down. His legs were still rather wobbly and he didn't dare risk another fall. Aleš joined him and they finished the climb together. Walking back to their cars, Aleš was astonished. 'He was walking like a cripple,' he recalled. It was true: Tomaž had mastered the art of climbing on technical terrain much more quickly than he could navigate relatively flat ground. His lurching gait was difficult to watch. But Tomaž didn't care; in fact, he was ecstatic. He was training!

Aconcagua, 2003

At this time, Aleš was planning a trip to the South Face of Aconcagua, at 6,962 metres the highest point in the western and southern hemispheres. Aconcagua is located on the border between Chile and Argentina, about a day's walk from the nearest settlement, Punta del Inca. An often-climbed peak because it is one of the 'Seven Summits' (the highest peaks on each continent), it has a number of different approaches and routes. The north slope is quite gentle, providing an easy 'normal route' to the summit. The steep and massive south side is glaciated, forming a cornucopia of gulleys, couloirs, faces and arêtes for the qualified climber. Its two summits are separated by a kilometre-long ridge.

Aleš's original partner was to have been another Slovenian alpinist, Matej Mošnik, but he had developed knee problems. So Tomaž joined the climb, a change that Aleš would later claim was crucial to their performance on the face. Of course Tomaž preferred to climb solo, and on this topic he and Aleš had some long and serious conversations. Some people thought that he preferred to climb alone because he was assured of getting all the glory. He maintained it was not that: it was the pain of losing a partner that held him back. Tomaž's Nuptse climb had somewhat soured his appetite for climbing with a partner: the entire experience had been too tragic for him. He suggested to Aleš that he was willing to give it a try as a twosome, but if the feeling wasn't right, he would climb solo. Aleš agreed.

They travelled together to Argentina in late November of 2003. They briefly visited the city of Mendoza, where they organised their food supplies and soaked up the ambience of the wide leafy boulevards, the abundant local wine and the almost impossibly beautiful Mendoza women. Difficult as it was to leave, they finally did so, beginning their trek in to the mountain from the tiny ancient settlement of Punta del Inca. They headed around to the steep south side of the mountain, for their chosen route was up the 2,500-metre face, to the left of the 1982 Slovenian route to Aconcagua's south summit. They had no internet, no media, no sponsors, not even a walkie-talkie. But they did have a rope, and they intended to tie into that rope together.

The mountain is well known for its warm temperatures and rotten rock, and the duo soon became intimately acquainted with those endearing traits. They began climbing on 17 December, and shortly thereafter Tomaž was hit in the shoulder by a rock. Soon they approached a section they had hoped would be an ice fall, but due to the warm temperatures it was instead a waterfall, with small rotten remnants of ice to remind them of what they might have enjoyed in cooler temperatures. To capture their attention even more, along with the falling water came falling stones. The waterfall was obviously not an option, so they traversed around the feature, gained the snowfield above, and eventually found a place to scratch out a bivouac inside a crevasse. This effort took them two days.

On the third day they came across a steep ice fall with some vertical and overhanging sections. Four pitches long, the last portion became increasingly tenuous as the ice grew thinner and as they became uncomfortably aware that water was running directly underneath them. Climbing delicately and as quickly as possible, they still failed to reach the top of this section in one day and were forced to carve out an uncomfortable bivouac site on the steep ice. Thus far, the conditions on their chosen line were abysmal. Surely they would improve.

The fourth day provided more excitement – and real danger – as they crossed the aptly named 'Traverse of Death' to gain the next snowfield, which was shaped curiously like a swallow. The traverse was nightmarish, with warm rotten snow perched precariously on steep, smooth rock slabs. It was impossible to create safe belays, so once again they were forced to climb carefully and delicately, although still roped together. No mistakes were allowed. Then there was a huge bang, and a giant rock hurtled past Aleš. If it had touched him he would certainly have been killed instantly. With no other choice, they carried on, climbing until they reached a snow mushroom crowning a tall pillar of rock. It was in this mushroom that they dug out a bivouac site for their fourth night on the mountain, their ice axes rammed hopefully into the brittle rock.

The next section was primarily rock – or some semblance of rock. In fact it was completely rotten, almost dust in its composition. Nevertheless, it was vertical dust and it needed to be climbed. After some additional mixed climbing of dust and ice, they reached a ridge that led to the final snowfield. Here they were faced with a completely new surface: black ice riddled throughout with air pockets. It turned out to be climbable, and topping out on the black ice section at 2,400 metres, they joined a route called the Sun Line route, first climbed in 1988. By now the temperature had plummeted, so they spent their fifth night attempting to stay warm atop their new route – unsuccessfully, as Aleš experienced frostbite in both his hands and feet.

The following day they continued across the long ridge to the summit, which they reached at 6.00 p.m. On the summit Tomaž retrieved from his pack a memento of one of the most painful moments of his life, pulling out a green glove formerly belonging to his friend Johan, who had died on the summit of Nuptse. After seven years, the glove symbolised to Tomaž that he was finally ready to climb again with a partner. They named their route Mobitel Swallow, Johan's route. Their descent was lightning-fast and they were down at the normal route base camp in two and a half hours.[1] For Aleš it was a great accomplishment and the fulfilment of a dream. It was Tomaž's first technical climb since the accident and he now knew that he was back.

Later that year, the climb was described in *Alpinist* magazine as 'one of the best alpine climbs ever'. That autumn, Aleš and Tomaž were nominated for the Piolet d'Or for their new route on Aconcagua. It was Tomaž's third nomination, and Aleš's first. This was a particularly controversial year for the prestigious prize, and although Tomaž didn't expect to win, he was even more surprised at the posturing and arguing that went on at the prize ceremony. As usual, it was the continuing disagreement between 'pure' and 'tainted' alpinism. In the end, a Russian team led by Alexander Odintsov won the prize for their 'heavy' ascent of the North Face of Jannu, over a much 'lighter' ascent of K7 by Steve House. House protested loudly and walked out of the ceremony, later writing a formal criticism of the award process, as well as of the Russian climb, claiming that they had used excessive technology to get up the route. Since climbing was basically an activity done for one's own personal satisfaction, House felt that this 'immoral' approach only diminished the experience. Odintsov was taken aback by the criticism, stating that 'In Russia all styles exist side by side: Himalayan, capsule, alpine.'[2] For House, it was uncertainty, not success at any cost, that was the most interesting aspect of climbing. Many felt that House had gone too far, suggesting that his climbing achievements spoke more much eloquently about his ethics than he ever could by ranting in public about a prize. Italian alpinist Simone Moro agreed in principle, saying that it was unfortunate that competition between climbers often manifested itself in criticism, rather than simply going out and climbing in better style. Prezelj was more in accord with House, for he felt that ethics were of the utmost importance: 'In alpinism, if you take ethics away, there's nothing on the other side.'

The British climber Ian Parnell withdrew from the competition that year, as did an Italian threesome the following year, citing philosophical differences with the ethics of the committee. Controversy swirled around the award like the Himalayan wind, mostly due to the non-quantifiable nature of alpine climbing accomplishments. Because of the inherently subjective approach to the act of climbing, each year the award recipient was determined, primarily, by the make-up of the jury and their own preferences and styles.

Tomaž's comment on the award was direct: 'Awards are like haemorrhoids; at some point, every asshole gets them.' This may not have been a completely honest statement, at least concerning the Piolet d'Or, for his own career had benefited greatly from winning it. Although many climbers dismissed the prize as a publicity stunt, there was always massive controversy within the very climbing community that claimed to be so completely uninterested in prizes.

Jannu, 2004

Back in Slovenia, Tomaž had a personal mess to clean up. Sergeja was gone and he needed to deal with the practical aspects of that separation. He moved some things to his father's house and burned many other painful reminders of his departed wife. But Urša and Tomi were relieved to be away from the constant turmoil and simmering anger. They could finally enjoy both of their parents, although separately. Then Sergeja and Tomaž began divorce proceedings, which were protracted, hurtful and unpleasant. It was during this time that Tomaž came close to completely losing his bearings. He had believed in marriage for life, and this divorce cut him to the core. He saw himself as a complete failure, and yet he still loved Sergeja. When things became irreconcilable between them, he thought that his base value system was under assault. He couldn't believe what they were doing to each other, and on both sides there was almost inconceivable pain.

The only aspect of his life that retained some semblance of sanity and routine was his climbing. In the summer of 2004 he was preparing for yet another ascent, once again to Nepal. His objective was Jannu, also known as Khumbhakarna. Located near Kangchenjunga, third highest peak in the world, its main summit is 7,710 metres high. Jannu, roughly translated as 'sleeping goddess' is considered a very holy mountain. Tomaž's objective was the forbidding East Face, which tops out on the east summit at 7,468 metres. Every team but one that had tried to climb the East Face had been Slovenian, and none had succeeded.

Tomaž sometimes boasted that he could put together an expedition in three weeks. His choice of companions was always interesting, the selection guided by instinct. He never knew what the magical combination might be for each trip: sometimes he was looking for someone with mountain experience, sometimes for a joker, or it might be for someone with good energy, or great sensitivity. For Jannu, he once again invited his good friend and cameraman Stipe Božić. In fact it was Stipe who had suggested the climb to Tomaž, for he had seen the face on his previous expedition to Kangchenjunga: 'I thought it could be a face for Tomaž.' Also on the trip was his loyal doctor, Anda Perdan, and Nataša Pergar, the psychic healer on whom he relied for her astrological expertise. He needed both heavenly and earthly support for this effort, although he intended to do the climb alone.

On 4 October the team flew by helicopter to Tseram, from where they moved all of their equipment by yak up to the Ramzea plateau. It took another two days and 30 porters to transport the camp up to the Yalung glacier, which was located at the base of Kangchenjunga, as well as the base of the East Face of Jannu. The poor weather, which had been obscuring their views, suddenly improved, revealing a spectacular but disappointing scene: their porters, who had already departed, had not carried the equipment high enough. For the next two days, the small remaining team was forced to move all of that equipment one kilometre closer to Jannu.

By 11 October, they had assembled their base camp at the foot of the East Face. Their first act was to invite a lama travelling through on his way to an Indian expedition's base camp at the foot of Kangchenjunga to perform the sanctification ceremony known as a puja. According to local Buddhist beliefs, every man who enters the kingdom of the gods must pray for their mercy. Since Jannu is considered one of the most sacred peaks in the Himalayas, it was clearly required here. First the Sherpas built a small chorten and mounted a number of strings of brightly coloured prayer flags, strung out in four directions. Every flag had a prayer written on it, and with the ever-present winds, these prayers were transported upwards and released to the gods. The flag-mounting exercise was followed by the burning of leaves on the altar, and as the smoke ascended, the gods were appeased. They next offered food and drink, and finally they threw grains of rice into the air as an offering to the gods. Then everyone gathered round for a sacred feast.

Tomaž and Stipe then headed off towards the left side of the face to scout out a very important aspect of the climb – a safe descent route. There they were faced with a curious scene: a wall of vertical granite slabs interlaced with a labyrinth of cracks crammed with grass. The only way they could climb this unusual surface was with ice axes! They managed to reach the top of this section and fixed a rope for further explorations as well as for the descent.

For the next two weeks they explored various options on the face, acclimatising in the process. Tomaž had studied detailed photos from a 1992 attempt and was shocked to see how drastically the nature of the face had changed. There was much more black ice now, and the face was threatened from above by huge mushrooms of dangerously unconsolidated powder. On their second night on the face, the two men found a good bivouac site on top of a ridge at 6,750 metres. That evening they sat back and marvelled at their position, basking in the late-afternoon sunshine and gazing across the Yalung glacier at the towering peaks nearby: Kangchenjunga, Talung and Cabru. It was a strangely peaceful moment in a truly spectacular environment, and the climbers' hearts were filled with joy.

Continuing up in the days to come, they searched for weaknesses in the face, placed bivouac tents for the actual climb and attached fixed lines where needed. Finally, on the 19th, they both descended to rest and prepare for the final climb. Now feeling strong, Tomaž felt ready for the face itself. Nataša had encouraging words about the timing, for she had observed Tomaž's aura and announced it was 150 metres wide. The time was surely right.

They endured a stint of bad weather, but this was predicted to clear up by the 26th, so on the morning of the 27th, Stipe accompanied Tomaž to the base of the face and said goodbye. Tomaž began by crossing a glacial amphitheatre feature, which was blanketed in chest-deep snow. Underneath that snow were countless yawning crevasses, some more than six metres across. He felt his way across the dangerous terrain, sometimes crawling to avoid falling in, and at other times leaping uncontrollably across openings that appeared to have no bottom, and no feasible snow bridge.

Approaching an ice and rock pillar at the southern end of the face, he was confronted with about 30 metres of overhanging rock and ice. Partway up he was hit by an ice pinnacle, but was not seriously harmed. Late that afternoon, Tomaž established a bivouac in a vertical crack at about 6,000 metres. In order to continue, he had to climb a suspended 20-metre ice feature topping the crack. Half way up, the bottom broke off, leaving him hanging precariously on one axe. It took him an entire day of delicate climbing to ascend the next 200 metres, where he established his second bivouac.

Tomaž was then faced with a series of overhanging rock cracks, each about 20 metres high. For each one, he would need to climb inside the crack, and then up and over the lip. It was impossible to create any kind of self-belay system, for the rock was polished granite, offering very little friction for his equipment. This was as hard – or harder – than Dhaulagiri. He managed to complete this tedious bit of climbing, but the problems continued, for next he found himself before a series of mushroom-like snow ridges 'so beautiful that even Michelangelo could not have painted them'. This next stage turned into a nightmare of intricate weaving amongst the mushrooms, all the while dodging avalanches. At 6,200 metres he discovered a rock ledge where he thought he could create a bivouac. Unfortunately, the ledge was so narrow that he was forced to spend the night suspended, half on, half off his little ledge.

The following day, the 29th, was more successful, as he was able to climb quickly and efficiently. In six hours he made his way up a 70–90-degree face as far as a narrow couloir, which he soon discovered consisted of black ice under a thin layer of light, powdery snow. Each step upwards had to be first cleared of snow, and then carefully climbed. There was no escaping the couloir, for each side was flanked by steep, unconsolidated powder-snow slopes topped with cauliflower-shaped cornices – graceful, overhanging crests of snow, formed by the wind: beautiful to look at, but deadly to tread upon.

Despite taking three falls, he finally reached the top and then traversed 20 metres to the right, where he tunnelled through the snow to dig a hole in one of those precariously perched mushrooms. He stashed his gear in the snow hole and tried to scout a route beyond, in preparation for the next day. But in four hours of searching, he gained only 25 metres. He returned to his hole for a cold and worrying night. The weather had deteriorated and 100-k.p.h. winds now howled around him. But he retained his enthusiasm and was confident that he could climb this last remaining section of the face the next day. He would then be in position to reach the shoulder of the south-east ridge, which would lead more easily to the top.

But that was not to be. On the morning of 30 October he began threading his way through the mushrooms. Five separate attempts through five different couloirs brought him absolutely nowhere. After four and a half hours, at around 7,000 metres, he finally gave up. It was simply too dangerous. 'If I had been a bird I could have flown those last 20 metres.' It was a bitter disappointment. He was cruelly close to the ridge that could have led him to the top. Nevertheless, he recognised the futility of throwing himself at the mushrooms again and again, so reluctantly, and with some relief at his decision, he headed down.

The descent was a continuation of the nightmare: heavy snowfall, gaping crevasses and avalanche debris obscured his tracks. After several frightening falls, he finally arrived in advance base camp after dark. He spent one more night on the face and then descended the rest of the way to base camp. Asked if he would return, he said no, the face was too dangerous in its present condition. As he described it, the face had become 'harder and harder, riskier and riskier as I went higher and higher'.

Although Tomaž neither completed the face climb nor reached the summit, he considered the climb an extremely positive and valuable experience. Jannu was another piece of the puzzle, for it had presented him with conditions he had never encountered before. He had climbed light and fast, negotiated the complex route-finding, managed to thread a way through the mushroom labyrinth, and retreated with his life intact. It provided him with one more high-altitude, extreme-conditions experience, one that he was convinced would serve him well in the future. But it was an effort so intense that he went immediately to India for a spiritual retreat rather than returning to his now empty home.

Cholatse, 2005

Six months after Jannu, in April 2005, Tomaž was back in Nepal. This time it was for a 6,440-metre peak in the Khumbu region called Cholatse. A startlingly jagged and savage-looking peak, Cholatse wasn't climbed until 1982, when Vern Clevenger, Galen Rowell, John Roskelley and Bill O'Connor ascended its south-west ridge. Its snow-fluted summit ridge is long and complex, making it difficult to find the highest point. Tomaž's plan was to do a new route on the North Face.

For this effort, he brought with him his Aconcagua climbing partner, Aleš Koželj, and Janko Oprešnik (Zumba), his partner on Annapurna and an outstanding aid-climber. Of Zumba, Tomaž said, 'I admire his "sick" [dangerous] style, especially his solo climbs, most not repeated . . . I learned a lot from him.' At the same time, the famous young Swiss climber Ueli Steck was attempting a solo climb on the same face of Cholatse.

The Slovenian trio first acclimatised on nearby Cholu. In nearly perfect weather, they reached the 6,083-metre summit on 13 April. They felt strong, in high spirits and ready for their real objective. The weather forecast deteriorated slightly, but they decided to launch themselves on to the North Face anyway, heading up on 19 April after a few days of rest. Their very first challenge was to climb an elegant 60-metre ice fall that Tomaž referred to as their 'dessert'. Unfortunately, the quality of this first part didn't continue, and they were soon faced with a full range of ice, from solid to rotten. A curious section of terrain reminded them of the Slovenian Julian Alps where they had trained: large, almost vertical frozen grassy mounds were interspersed with rock and ice. On these, they simply used their ice axes in a dry-tooling technique.

After their first bivouac, the dreary weather forecast came true and they were stuck with snow, fog and dropping temperatures. On steepening rock and ice, avalanches were frequent since the new snow had not consolidated. During one of these, Tomaž managed to lose one of his gloves. By mid-afternoon on the second day they realised they needed to stop, so they dug a snow cave and set up their second bivouac.

In the distance, both Everest and Lhotse were capped by ominous cloud formations that did not bode well for the weather. With this in mind, the trio decided to alter their route slightly and try to reach the north-west ridge a bit earlier than originally planned. Here they found another interesting challenge: huge snow mushrooms with unstable bases and towering caps through which they must navigate. Zigzagging through the mushroom maze, they searched for a way up, trying to avoid the constant spindrift of avalanching snow. Finally they were forced to dig into one of the giant mushroom structures and construct their third bivouac. They were starting to run out of food and gas; the weather continued to deteriorate; and now Zumba was feeling the altitude.

On the fourth day they pushed on, floundering amongst the mushrooms, at times swimming in the deep snow. By 4.00 p.m. they were on the top. Since Zumba was still altitude-sick, they decided to bivouac on the summit and begin their descent the next morning. This turned out to be more difficult and dangerous than the ascent. They began early, searching for a route down the south side of the mountain. They descended some distance down the south-west ridge and then began a series of abseils down the South Face under ominous-looking ice seracs. Abseiling as quickly as possible in order to minimise the time beneath the unstable seracs, they made good progress. Tomaž led the way, abseiling first and constructing new belays at the end of each abseil. But at one point, in his haste, he lost his concentration, forgetting both his ice axes before heading off on one of the last abseils. Unfortunately, the 70-metre ropes were not quite long enough to deposit him in a place where he could safely build the next belay. He would need to down-climb, yet he had no ice axes. For his moment of inattention, he was forced to remove his spare gloves carefully, and use his hands as tools to climb down about five metres of vertical ice and rock to a place where he could build the next belay. Aleš brought the two forgotten axes with him when he descended. Now it was Zumba's turn.

Zumba abseiled down to near the end of the ropes and began down-climbing to Tomaž and Aleš. Directly above the two climbers, he suddenly slipped off the end of the ropes. He screamed, alerting the climbers to reach out and grab his hand and part of his rucksack. Luckily they were able to hold him, but it was a very close call. By mid-afternoon they had reached the base of the South Face and were safely off the mountain.

In the meantime, Steck had also completed his climb, reaching the summit on 15 April via the North Face French route, with a new variation above 5,900 metres. His report of the climb indicated that the 1,400-metre face was 'very difficult – 37 hours of technical and sometimes dangerous climbing'. Tomaž's climb was reported in *Alpinist* magazine as a new route, with his photo of the mountain on the cover. He called the route Yarchagumba, after a rare Nepal flower. However, it was later stated that his was not a new route, but rather a variation of a climb done in 1984 by four American climbers. The confusion appeared to come from the topography of the north side of the mountain, where two similar faces, the North Face and the North-East Face, are separated by a shallow prow. Some time later, it was finally confirmed that Tomaž had indeed climbed a new route. Regardless of the controversy, the climb had provided Tomaž with what he needed: additional experience at altitude and a good acclimatisation climb to prepare him for the business to follow later that summer – the Rupal Face of Nanga Parbat.

CHAPTER FOURTEEN

RESCUE

10 August 2005, Nanga Parbat, Rupal Face

Base camp is awake by 4.30 a.m., ready and alert, cautiously optimistic that this is the day Tomaž will be saved. They gather outside their tents, talking quietly amongst themselves, peering at the sky. As dawn begins to break, the mercifully clear sky blushes a gentle pink from the rising sun. But the mountain is completely sheathed in fog. How can this be? Mornings are supposed to be the clearest. They wait, and slowly the fog begins to lift. Small patches of blue appear as a slight breeze rips promising gaps in the fog bank. They radio the pilots. Please come, if you can.

Rashid has been awake for hours and has already offered his morning prayers. This morning he has been very specific. He asks his God to be with him in his effort to rescue Tomaž, and if he succeeds, he implores Allah to bestow blessings upon his brother's soul. If he doesn't succeed, he knows that the Swiss rescue team is standing by in Islamabad and will be in base camp by this afternoon. The pressure is enormous. The pilots warm up the helicopters. By 05.00 they are airborne.

10 August, 05.45

Where is Tomaž? Base camp has been radioing him all morning and there is no response. Is his radio dead? Is he sleeping? Has he been buried by an avalanche?

Suddenly the air reverberates with the roar of helicopters. They land briefly while Rashid takes a last glance at video footage of the rescue site. Then, looking up at the mountain, they see that the sun is shining directly below Tomaž's snow hole. They're off.

Lieutenant Colonel Ubaid ur Rehman and Major Mueen ud Din are in the lead with the search ship, and Rashid and Khalid are close behind them in the rescue ship. This weather is exactly what they have been hoping for. The rescue site is still in a cloud layer, but they're convinced that the anabatic wind will quickly push that cloud higher.

The search ship moves in close to the face to determine Tomaž's exact location. While they are searching, the rescue ship carries out an additional hover check to ensure that everything is working at 6,100 metres. The helicopter seems stable enough, but Rashid notes that the pedals that control the tail rotor are at their limit. They are really pushing this helicopter to hover at this altitude. Meanwhile, the cloud cover is lifting, but oh so slowly.

The radio jumps to life as the lead helicopter announces that they have spotted Tomaž. They usher the rescue helicopter in to the exact spot and then exit carefully.

Tomaž wakens with a start. His silent world of ice and snow is suddenly alive with the deafening roar of helicopter rotor blades and the chaos of swirling snow. After digging all night in order to keep himself from being buried by sifting snow, he has slipped into unconsciousness in the early morning hours. The helicopter approaches him and then backs away. The altimetre reads 6,347 metres, 300 metres higher than previous estimates and 700 metres over the allowed helicopter limit.

Tomaž is screaming into the radio now, and Aleš yells back: 'Why didn't you call? What's wrong? The helicopters are on their way.' The pilots confirm that they see him, dressed in red and waving madly. Tomaž quickly checks his bivouac site and reviews all the steps discussed the previous day to be absolutely certain that he is ready to catch the rescue line. Everything looks good: he is still attached to the two ice screws that secure him to the wall by a loose sliding knot known as a Prusik hitch. This will allow him to lean out to the rescue rope without falling off his airy perch. At the same time he double-checks his carabiners: one to attach to the rescue line and the other securing him to his anchor. It is this second carabiner that he must unclip – immediately after attaching himself to the rescue line with the first one. His knife is attached to his harness, handy and easy to grab should he need it. Hopefully he won't. He reviews each step: reach, grab, clip, unclip. All of this must happen in seconds. He's ready.

The helicopter approaches again. Rashid places Tomaž at the nine o'clock position in his sight lines. He inches the helicopter very slowly to the left. The collective pitch indicator reads .98, which means that 98 per cent of the power is being consumed, just to maintain this hovering position. There will probably not be enough residual power to pick up an additional 70 kilograms. Rashid moves in a bit closer. He feels that he is running out of power. Suddenly he senses the effect of the anabatic wind. He can feel the helicopter gaining strength, and a quick look at the gauges confirms it: they are now using only 95 per cent power and the tail rotor pedals are no longer at their limit. With this advantage, they must move in quickly with the rescue line.

They drop the rescue line, which is simply a series of ropes tied together with a large bag of rocks at the bottom for ballast. The helicopter approaches more closely, tilting somewhat. The rotors seem only inches from the wall and the rotor wash creates a blizzard of blowing snow. There is now no visibility. How can the pilot see the wall? How can he see where Tomaž is located? Tomaž is completely blinded by the snow as he leans out from the wall as far as his sling will allow, flailing wildly at the ropes with his ice axe. Aleš yells over the radio: 'Please don't kill him with the weight.'

The pilots take turns at the helicopter controls while, at the same time, passing their only oxygen mask back and forth between them. They are using oxygen to avoid becoming hypoxic but they can't keep the mask on for more than a few seconds because it quickly fogs up. Because they are hovering, there is very little air movement in the helicopter and the interior of the cabin is full of steam. Despite the fog, the inside temperature of the cabin is -8 degrees Celsius and both pilots are shivering, unable to turn on the heat because the heater will consume too much power.

Rashid tries to keep Tomaž in his line of sight. He can see that he is desperately trying to reach the ropes with his ice axe. They have now been hovering for five minutes. Suddenly the ice axe makes contact with the ropes. Then they're gone. Tomaž reaches out again and again but he can no longer make contact.

As a last resort, Rashid pulls the helicopter back from the wall in order to make a fresh attempt. Tomaž sees the helicopter pull away and his heart sinks. But Rashid has no intention of giving up. He returns to the wall, swings forward, and stops the helicopter just short of the wall. This creates a swinging motion in the ropes, bringing them slightly closer to Tomaž. He reaches out with his ice axe, touches the ropes once more, and this time he makes contact. He yanks them towards him with a magnificent surge of adrenalin and immediately clips his carabiner. He's on!

Khalid is on the controls and he announces to Rashid that he can feel the load from Tomaž. At that very moment Tomaž gives Rashid the thumbs-up signal. To Rashid, this signal means that Tomaž has attached himself to the rescue ropes and has disconnected himself from the belay on the wall as had been discussed earlier on the radio; the thumbs-up signal is a clear indication that everything is ready for the helicopter to begin the descent to base camp.

Tomaž is securely clipped to the rescue ropes hanging from the helicopter, but he has not unclipped from the wall. He knows that he must unclip this carabiner immediately, so he reaches down to undo it. Then his Prusik sling catches on the edge of his open carabiner and it simply won't come loose. But this is critical – he absolutely must unclip himself or everyone will die. In a split second he changes tactics: he will cut the cord connecting him to the wall. He reaches for his knife, but his hands will not function. He cannot make his fingers work.

Rashid can see none of this, for the wall is a sea of white rotor wash. But he has seen the thumbs-up sign and he orders Khalid to pull up. Then, as Rashid recalls, 'the nightmare began'.

Still fixed to the wall, Tomaž feels the rescue lines go taut as the helicopter slowly moves away. He is pulled off balance, falling headfirst into the snow. The helicopter is straining, but as the rescue lines tighten, the line to the anchor holds firm. Tomaž will either be split in two or the helicopter will be pulled down – or both.

At this point the helicopter has been hovering for a full 10 minutes at over 6,000 metres. The low fuel warning light begins to flicker and the rotor vibrations are threatening the giant snow mushroom perched just above the rescue site. They have been extremely lucky up until now, but time has run out. They know that Tomaž weighs 70 kilograms and they have calculated that at this elevation the extra weight will translate to a collective pitch rise of .02 or .03, or about 2–3 per cent of the helicopter's total power capacity. But the dials show them something else entirely. As Khalid begins to pull up, the indicators show that the collective pitch rise is twice as much, using approximately 5–6 per cent of the helicopter's total power. They have nothing left. Khalid announces grimly, 'Sir, it is not pulling out!'

Then things get worse. The helicopter begins to sink and then to vibrate. Rashid is sure that they are approaching a vortex ring state, similar to a stall in a fixed-wing aircraft. They will most certainly fall out of the sky. He looks out of the window and sees that the sling rope is fully extended and at full tension. Rashid understands immediately what has happened: Tomaž has been unable to detach himself from the wall. At that moment both pilots know what their next move *should* be: jettison the load. This is the protocol that they have been taught, and it is the logical thing to do. Rashid recalls the moment: 'But it was not a load. It was a living man who had struggled for life over many days. We would rather die up there with him than go down empty-handed.'

This was not a rash decision made on the spot. The previous night, the two pilots had decided that if something like this occurred, they would not operate the emergency release switch, and they had turned it off and taken out the circuit-breaker. Despite their training, and against all the protocols of any rescue mission anywhere in the world, they had decided to stick with this climber to the end.

The helicopter dips once more, steadily losing power. Rashid grabs the controls and moves slightly to the right. The rotors are getting dangerously close to the wall. At that moment he feels a distinct jerk. The helicopter feels much lighter. Khalid shouts that Tomaž must have been dropped, because he can no longer see him. Rashid shudders to think that after all of this effort and danger, they have lost their load. He refuses to believe it.

While Tomaž has been wildly flailing about, desperately trying to detach himself from his belay anchor, his Prusik cord suddenly rips and he's off the wall. The tension on the rescue line catapults him uncontrollably into space, directly towards the helicopter. Tomaž recalls the sensation: 'Like a bungee, I was flying up to the window of the helicopter.' Rashid sees him out of the corner of his eye and instinctively adjusts the angle of the helicopter again to prevent Tomaž from flying against the wall or, even more seriously, into the helicopter rotor blades. Tomaž is swinging wildly now and it takes a couple of minutes to stabilise both him and the helicopter.

The second helicopter closes in to observe Tomaž's condition and confirms by radio that he is waving his arms and seems to be okay. With this information, Rashid begins the descent to base camp. He asks Khalid to take over the controls as he tries to collect himself. Despite the freezing temperature inside the cabin, Rashid is running with sweat. He looks over at Khalid and observes the same. They have just pulled off the impossible. It is miraculous that they are still in the air, flying steadily down to safety. Rashid looks at his watch: it is 06.30.

Up the valley, House has been searching the sky with his binoculars. Aware that helicopters are in the air, he first assumes that the military is conducting manoeuvres, but he can't understand why they are using high altitude Lamas. When he sees a human cargo at the end of a rescue line, he realises that the rumours are true: there really is a rescue taking place. He is astounded.

At Tomaž's base camp they are screaming, crying, dancing around as they watch through the long lenses of the telescope and the video camera. The tension has been almost unbearable as they monitored the operation – 10 minutes of hovering by the Lama. It was unthinkable that Rashid could hold the helicopter at that elevation for so long, so close to the wall, so carefully positioned. But he did. Not only that, he managed to stabilise it when the rope broke. Aleš could see the helicopter lurching dangerously, and although he didn't know the reason, he knew that something had gone terribly wrong.

The dot in the sky grows larger. The helicopter approaches base camp, and below that helicopter is a rope, and at the end of that rope is a body. It is certainly Tomaž, but what kind of shape will he be in? They wait.

After what seems like hours, the helicopter is there, hovering above the green swampy ground, slowly and gently lowering its human cargo. Finally Tomaž is down. His legs crumple beneath him as he fumbles with the carabiner attaching him to the rescue line. He manages to unclip himself and collapses to the ground. The helicopter lifts and lands a short distance away. Military personnel approach Tomaž. Then Anda runs towards him. Tomaž is weeping as he touches the earth in relief. He tries to walk but wobbles. 'Thank God. Thank God,' he repeats. In an incredible effort of self-restraint and professionalism, Maja holds back, filming the entire scene. Finally she embraces him. Aleš helps him over to a rocky bit of dry ground and helps him remove his pack and then his frozen wet clothing. Aleš is concerned about frostbite and immediately focuses on the boots, gently removing them and calling out, 'Anda, bring him some dry shoes.' Anda replies, 'Yes, I will and he needs a sleeping bag under him. Give him something to drink.' Tomaž is bent over and obviously in pain.

After shutting the helicopters down, the pilots bow their heads in prayer, thanking Allah for giving them the strength and courage to endanger their lives in order to save another. Then they slowly approach the group. Everyone is weeping and laughing uncontrollably. Tomaž somehow rouses himself to walk over to Rashid and Khalid. He embraces each of them in turn, weeping quietly, thanking them for saving his life. They are stoical. At this moment, Rashid is thinking not of Tomaž, but of his brother, hoping that somehow Masood is aware of this happy moment. Then Tomaž stands with them in order to have their photo taken by Maja, who says to them, 'You are the real heroes.'

Tomaž stumbles back to his rocky perch and collapses once again. He rubs his frozen hands together and bends his head, as if seeking relief. Anda arrives with the medical kit and some hot liquid, for he is extremely dehydrated. She speaks softly to Tomaž and he becomes emotional. Then he feels faint and nauseous and lies back on the sleeping bag to regain his equilibrium. He has held it together for so many days up in that hideous hole, and now, finally, he can let go. Anda rubs his feet lightly and tucks them back into the sleeping bag. She doesn't want to do too much too fast. She hovers protectively.

Dozens of onlookers have quietly lined up nearby, watching, squatting on their haunches, observing an event such as their valley has never witnessed. Members of the military approach and suggest that Tomaž should be flown immediately to Islamabad. Tomaž feebly begs: 'I have to stay here one more day.' He explains in a weak, hoarse voice that he cannot face the onslaught of media attention in Islamabad. He needs to be in seclusion for one more day, together with those closest to him.

Maja is filming everywhere, trying to capture the moment, the tension, the drama. She approaches Rashid and Khalid and asks them some questions about the rescue. They politely decline to be interviewed. 'We are military. We have to follow the protocol.' Maja persists. 'Can you describe the rescue, please?' They don't answer. They need permission to appear in front of the camera.

Anda and Aleš remain close to Tomaž, talking quietly to him, ensuring that he is warm, dry and comfortable. They give him more liquids. Somewhat revived, Tomaž sits up and begins to talk. He describes the horror of the hole. Once again his emotions overwhelm him. His voice is harsh and low, barely audible. He keeps raising his painful hands, attempting to breathe warmth into them. He stands up, loses his balance, sits down again. Then he reaches to his pack and awkwardly searches for something – he finds it, attached with a carabiner. It's Tomi's tiny baby shoe. Tomaž thanks God he can fulfil his promise to bring it back.

Maja calls Stipe to tell him the good news. Anda calls Tomaž's father and then passes the phone to Tomaž. Once again he becomes emotional as he speaks very softly into the phone. Then they call Viki. Anda too becomes emotional, saying to Tomaž, 'Everyone was praying for you – the whole world.' Tomaž's answer is pathetic in its simplicity: 'I just wanted to climb. I didn't want all this.'

With Tomaž safely off the mountain, the Swiss rescue team, now in Islamabad, receives a call from the Pakistan army informing them that the rescue mission has been successfully completed. They are completely and utterly stunned. Then, the aftermath begins, starting with the practical implications of an expensive and very risky multinational rescue effort. Payment is a rather complicated affair. The Swiss costs are eventually covered by Mobitel, Tomaž's loyal partner of ten years, and the Slovenian government pays for the equivalent of three airline tickets, funnelling their support through the Slovenian army to the Pakistani army. Tomaž pays the rest.

Many observers later say that the rescue effort placed too much of a burden on the inexperienced Pakistani pilots. The Swiss worry that this one spectacularly successful rescue will increase the pressure to do even more difficult rescues in the future. The high-profile operation places the Pakistani rescue association in the international limelight, and they subsequently make serious efforts to improve: they participate in international conferences and training programmes, honing their skills and impressing their international colleagues in the process. Gerold Biner later reports, 'I have to revise my opinion . . . I was amazed at both of them . . . very openminded and absolutely highly skilled pilots. The Pakistan army can be very proud of them . . . they demonstrated a well above average flying capability!' Both rescue pilots are awarded the Medal of Bravery by President Musharraf and the Gold Medal for Bravery in Slovenia.

Outside Pakistan, reverberations are felt within the Slovenian army as well, for they begin to discuss response strategies for a potential similar situation in their own mountains in the future. The European Association of Mountain Rescue initiates a special unit equipped for swift rescue operations – anywhere in the world.

In addition to these changes, the whole world analyses the rescue, as well as Tomaž himself. 'What was he thinking, exposing his children to this kind of stress and media attention? What about his parents? They must have suffered terribly.' Climbers begin analysing the previously invincible Slovenian hero. Some speculate that Tomaž simply lost his nerve up on the face. Certainly his personal life was in a shambles at home, for he was just coming out of a messy and protracted divorce; perhaps this dulled the sharp edge of his confidence. Tomaž is quite sure he did not lose his nerve – not on the Rupal Face. 'Up there, I was in a safe box. I controlled myself.'

Many, however, believe that Tomaž's biggest mistake occurred long before he set foot on the mountain. Maria Štremfelj feels he never should have begun the climb in those questionable conditions, and she places this responsibility squarely on Tomaž's shoulders. 'He wasn't going on a holiday at the coast. He went to the Rupal Wall and everybody knows that the weather changes a lot on the Rupal Face.' Looking back at the entire experience, Tomaž disagrees that he made a mistake and wonders if some of the armchair judgements are not a bit harsh: 'My misfortune was that the promised north wind never came: the mountain never gave me one chance.'

Others place the root of the problem in the early departure of some team members. At the end there were only four: Tomaž, Aleš, Maja and Anda. Tone Škarja doesn't know why Stipe and Nataša left, but he is convinced that their leavetaking affected team morale. He knows from experience that when morale is bad, nothing goes right, pointing to an earlier Annapurna expedition where 'nobody wanted to work,' he recalled. But the important fact, according to Škarja, is that Tomaž has survived. He doesn't feel that the rescue will damage Tomaž's reputation nearly as much as some people think. 'People were just happy that he survived,' he says. Simone Moro feels that the rescue might even produce a positive effect, for it proves that Tomaž is 'human', that he too has limits.

Many climbers are not as kind as Moro, and they express harsh criticism for the entire expedition: for its media strategy, for the rescue, and for the performance of its star climber. Although Prezelj admires the fact that Tomaž attempted to solo the face, stating that 'soloing is the purest form of the sport', he adds, 'Soloing is pure only when you are alone on the climb. If you involve others on radio or camera, that somehow changes the experience.' He feels that Tomaž's Dhaulagiri climb combined alpinism and show-business, but with Nanga Parbat it was simply show-business. His assessment of the climb is uncompromising: 'As an alpinist he should not have gone on the face. It was a bad decision. As an alpinist, Tomaž failed.' Steve House agrees with Prezelj, and went on to say (to that same *Outside* reporter at his base camp) that Tomaž's defeat resulted from the overwhelmingly commercial nature of his own expedition, describing him as 'less a cutting-edge alpinist than a careerist profiteer'.

With the efficiency of heat-seeking missiles, the remarks from Karo,

Cordes and others hit their mark: 'Humar chose only dangerous walls – not technically difficult walls; he went up on to that wall and sat there deliberately waiting for a rescue and the associated media attention; it was all a staged event; he pulled a stupid stunt, endangered others' lives; he should have been a man and died up there.' American alpinist Mark Twight is quoted as saying, 'There is now one less place in the world where true personal autonomy is required, where there is no safety net . . . An alpine-style ascent of a Himalayan summit meant more on August 9 than it did on August 11.'[1] He adds, 'Personally, I think this rescue fucked the evolution of alpinism in a way that no other single act could have done.' Rashid is so outraged by the quote that he writes to the magazine protesting against their treatment of the story.

The editor of *Alpinist*, Christian Beckwith, is also very critical, stating, 'Alone or with partners, alpinism at its best is conducted in a wild environment with complete self-reliance. The amount of media attending Humar's attempt created an atmosphere in which hype became more important than adventure, help appeared an easy radio call away, and the subsequent rescue was reduced to something resembling a reality television show. This media coverage may also have influenced Humar's original decision to begin his climb regardless of the poor conditions and short weather window, which in turn put the lives of the rescuers at risk . . .' Beckwith goes one step further in an attempt to rally like-minded alpinists with a passionate and heartfelt letter:

We, the undersigned, believe that Tomaž Humar's Nanga Parbat expedition and the rescue that finished it provide a false impression of Himalayan climbing. Media coverage of the expedition should acknowledge the regrettable decisions leading to the attempt and refrain from popularising the expedition as heroic or as representative in any way of the best in high-altitude alpinism . . . Furthermore, we believe that motorised technology such as helicopters should have no place in the highest mountains; they should remain a wilderness in which men and women can discover the capabilities of the human spirit without artificial safeguards. We owe this to all the men and women who have died on their climbs, committed to the consequences of their decisions and self-reliant to the end. And we owe it to the future of high-altitude mountaineering, the cornerstone of which, we hope, will always be adventure.

Ultimately, Beckwith refrained from sending the letter.

One has to ask if those most critical could justifiably have expected all those people who were trying to keep Tomaž alive to stop – simply in order to retain a sense of adventure as defined by *them*. Would the price not have been too high? Tomaž listens, reads and reflects on the criticisms directed at him. Finally he responds with a biblical reference: 'The person who is innocent should cast the first stone. These people are trying to eat my soul. They can eat my body, but not my soul.'

Meanwhile, the general public sees things differently. Even Prezelj agrees that although the expedition was a failure as a climb, 'He came home a hero.'

The 'real hero', Rashid, has a different perspective on the whole affair. Not as concerned about the climb, he is more impressed with what he saw at base camp: 'The amount of happiness and joy that hovered over the entire base camp, engulfing every soul, cannot be defined in words. Only those who have experienced it can understand how noble it feels to have a soul back into life when the jaws of death have almost closed in on it. Where words finish up, expression diminishes, eloquence fades away, only tears speak. They spoke the universal language of the soul.' For Rashid, the expedition and the rescue are not about failure, or shame, or marketing. They are about life.

Rashid feels that Tomaž came back from Nanga Parbat for a reason, saying, 'I have no doubt that Almighty Allah wished to grant Mr Tomaž another lease of life, and he made us instruments in the process.' Although he and Tomaž speak to different Gods, they are in agreement on this. Rashid insists that it was divine control that turned the tide of the rescue. Even though he and his team had calculated as best they could, and taken every eventuality into consideration, he points out a few details that appear to have benefited from a higher intervention. 'We were planning on -5 degrees and we got -8 degrees.' This gave them the much-needed added air density. 'We had hoped for sunshine below the rescue site.' They got that, and much more, for not only did they have sunshine below, but they had thick cloud above, creating an even stronger updraught. Even more astonishing, the rope that secured Tomaž to his anchor had a holding strength of 500 kilograms. The helicopter at full strength could only exert a force of 250–260 kilograms. And yet the helicopter was able to pull back and snap the line. 'Where did the rest of the force come from?' asks Rashid. It could have been a slight updraught, or his skilful manoeuvre as he pulled the helicopter to the right. Rashid admits that any of these things could have happened, but he adds: 'Call it a miracle, good luck or whatever; the fact that it came at that particular point in time when the helicopter had started to sink was nothing short of Divine Hand.'

Throughout the swirling discussion, literally tens of thousands of people were simply relieved that the rescue succeeded, and genuinely grateful to have Tomaž back alive. They had adopted him as their own. They didn't moralise or preach or take credit. During those ten days in August when the entire Slovenian nation watched the evening news with bated breath, devouring each small development on the Rupal Face, their thoughts and prayers were focused on one thing – the return of their home-grown hero from the biggest mountain face in the world.

CHAPTER FIFTEEN

CINDERELLA RISES

11 August 2005, Nanga Parbat, Rupal Face

In his first email message out to the world, Tomaž referred to 10 August, the day of the rescue, as the day he was reborn:

> I'm thanking [everyone] for a new birthday: the crew members, everyone involved in the rescue, both in Pakistan, Slovenia and other parts of the world, political support, Pakistani army and members of the helicopter team. And to all who have sent me positive thoughts, have prayed for me and believed in a happy ending. My original intent was to climb the slope, but at the end the mountain showed us the way and triggers compassion towards fellow man. Life is beautiful! Thanks, for bestowing it upon ourselves. Tomaž.

Finally it was time to leave the mountain, first on horseback as far as Tashering and then on to Besham and Islamabad. As the team suspected, interest in the rescue had exploded, and while the team was recuperating at base camp, Nazir had been busy doing media interviews – 17 of them so far – with journalists from the BBC, AP, Reuters, the *Guardian*, *Dawn* and many other members of the foreign press. Shortly after the team arrived, they met Rashid and Khalid for an emotional reunion, and then Nazir, to strategise about the media: there were many requests – too many – and they would need to make choices. One of their first tasks was to attend a press conference at which journalists from around the world quizzed Nazir on the logistics of the rescue, questioned Rashid on the technical aspects, and of course interviewed Tomaž – the man who was reborn. Both pilots were now nicknamed 'the brave eagles', and were national heroes in Pakistan.

Soon politicians were asking for meetings with the team, first the

Pakistani minister for foreign affairs, then the minister for tourism, and finally, amidst great security, Prime Minister Shaukat Aziz. At the conclusion of each meeting, in gratitude, Tomaž presented his host with an ice axe.

Then they learned that even President Musharraf wished to meet them. The visit was to take place within the presidential palace on 16 August and the security was sure to be rigorous. Musharraf's invitation extended to the entire team: Tomaž, Aleš and Maja, as well as Nazir Sabir and both rescue pilots, Rashid Baig and Khalid Rana. Tomaž knew that he had to show his gratitude, for this had been a military exercise controlled from the top. When Slovenian President Janez Drnovšek called Pakistan to press for cooperation, it was with President Musharraf that he spoke. Without Musharraf's agreement, the rescue would never have happened. And now he wanted to meet them.

Crammed into two cars, they proceeded towards the presidential palace through numerous gates and checkpoints. Each stop sign loomed larger than the previous one, demanding obedience. Towering concrete walls guarded each checkpoint, effectively controlling any unwanted visitors. They were searched carefully, and frequently. Finally they were inside the palace, waiting for the president to appear. The meeting room was spacious and elegant, with beautifully upholstered sofas and chairs placed throughout the room, and sumptuous Persian carpets. Tomaž sported a new shirt, provided by Nazir. Sparkling white in honour of the visit, it showed a number of telltale creases since it was fresh from the box. Each team member dealt with their nervousness in their own way: Tomaž attempted to break the tension with jokes; the pilots were stoically silent; and Maja adjusted and readjusted her video camera.

After waiting some time, there was a slight flurry of movement and President Musharraf entered the room. He walked directly up to Tomaž and shook his hand. After they greeted each other, Tomaž first thanked him and then, referring to Rashid and Khalid, said, 'They did a good job.' Both pilots saluted. The president responded first to Tomaž, saying, 'This mountain is known as a killer mountain. We are glad you are safe.' Then, turning to the pilots, he added, 'I compliment you both on doing a great job.' Tomaž went on to describe what the 'two brave eagles' had actually done, attempting to give the president a better understanding of the skill they had demonstrated. The president listened attentively and then explained to Tomaž where those skills had originated: 'Our helicopter pilots are maybe the best in the world because we have a confrontation with India on the Siachen [glacier] and they fly in these mountains.' Tomaž acknowledged the president's comments but added, 'They have more than experience. They have guts and courage.'

Then the president asked, 'Will you try to climb Nanga Parbat again?' The question caught Tomaž off guard, but he answered, 'I might, if I could get another permit. But the next time that I come to Pakistan, to more fully express my gratitude I would like to build a small hospital in the Rupal valley on the southern side of Nanga Parbat.' The president promised to cooperate by finding a doctor for this region of more than 3,500 people.

The president next turned his attention to Nazir Sabir: 'Can you tell me something about the logistics of this rescue?' Nazir explained that the rescue was an important milestone for mountain rescue worldwide. The president agreed: 'The success of this rescue is very important – it is the most difficult ever attempted in Pakistan.' Finally, he summed up by saying how happy he was to meet Tomaž and how exceptionally proud he was of the pilots, and spoke of his intention to honour them both properly and officially at a future date.

He then presented Tomaž with a gold watch, which symbolically had begun ticking on 10 August, the day of the rescue. To reciprocate, Tomaž had a gift for the president. Amazingly, the team had been allowed into the presidential palace, and this private presidential sitting room, with an ice axe: one can only imagine what the security guards must have thought.

Finally it was time to return home to Slovenia. On Thursday 18 August, Tomaž and his team said their goodbyes, loaded up their gear and headed to the airport. The flight took them to Dubai, Frankfurt and finally Ljubljana, giving them a brief respite between the media flurry in Islamabad and the welcome they were sure to receive back home.

Ljubljana airport was a mob scene. Inside and out, people crowded around, pushing to get close, to welcome Tomaž, congratulate him, shake his hand. First in line were his children, Tomi and Urša, relieved and thankful to have their father back. Then his parents, overwhelmed with emotion as they embraced their son. Video cameras, flashbulbs, friends, strangers, politicians, children, all pressed closer.

Slovenia, 2006

Marko Prezelj observed that upon his arrival home, Tomaž was treated like the leader of a religious sect. As Prezelj described it, 'He had *followers*.' Although Tomaž scoffed at the idea, there appeared to be some truth to it. Even a year later, complete strangers would approach him, describing their pilgrimage to the Basilica of St Vid at Brezje to pray for him during the rescue. All begged for an autograph. What was it about this man that could elicit this kind of behaviour? These people who approached him with such reverence were not stupid, ignorant sheep, but normal citizens. There was something about Tomaž – his approachability, his humour, his optimism – that spoke to them and offered them something they needed. Ultimately, he seemed to give them hope. Many Slovenian climbers felt irritated that he had this following, but what harm could it do?

For once in his life, Tomaž realised he had had enough – enough of media and criticism and crowds and adulation. Needing to regroup, he gathered those most precious to him – Urša and Tomi – and headed south to the Croatian coast, ignoring all telephone calls and refusing all interviews, despite the clamour from around the globe. While in seclusion, he had a sense of what was being said, but for a time he savoured his children's company and the fact that he was still alive to enjoy them. He thought, too, about his survival: one more time, he had come back. First it was Kosovo, then Nuptse, Dhaulagiri, the wheelchair, and now Nanga Parbat. His passion for living was more intense than ever.

After his return from this brief hiatus, Tomaž was inundated, smothered, almost drowned in phone calls, emails and letters asking for interviews and appearances. For ten days his face had dominated the evening television news. Now he was learning to say no. If he wanted to have any kind of private life, to see his children, to manage the still-painful separation from his former wife and to rebuild his business so that he could make a living, he had to say no. Equally as important, he realised that he must refrain from reading everything that was being written about him, something he referred to as 'their' game. As long as he refused to play, he felt that he was in charge. He knew that his most serious detractors saw him as a kind of pop star or cult figure. In fact, he had even been called 'the Michael Jackson of Slovenia' by Silvo Karo. Tomaž laughed, responding, 'I am popular because I'm sincere. That's why people care about me. I'm not popular like a pop star. I'm one of the people.'

Tomaž referred to his return from the Rupal Face as his birthday, a second chance, a gift of life. The next question was what he would do with this gift. He could settle down and become more of a family man, or he could continue climbing at a very high level. He could expand his humanitarian efforts, helping people less fortunate than himself. He could even become president. The decisions of this dynamic, sometimes tortured individual would surely be driven by his fundamental values, be they honesty, hard work and kindness, or pride and ambition.

His options were endless, as were the opinions of those who would advise him. Bojan Pollak thought that he should set up a climbing school and guiding service. Others recommended that he go into politics. Many politicians had already approached him and his face is known to most Slovenians. If you send him a postcard marked Tomaž Humar, Slovenia, it will arrive at his home. But Tomaž understood the responsibility of elected power, and although it didn't frighten him, he was wary of the compromise he knew was part of the package. As he explained, 'Normally politicians are in the middle of the road – I am not like that. If it's yellow, then I say that it's yellow. In the western world all politicians are in the middle: middle right, middle left, Middle East! But when you look at the programmes, they are all the same: support children, help poor people, better quality, lower prices. It is just votes.' But most people agreed that if Tomaž Humar, national hero, wanted to run for president, he would be elected.

Instead, Tomaž returned to his roots – the towers. He doesn't paint them himself any more, but hires an ever-evolving crew of climbers to do the work. His job now is to find the projects, negotiate the contracts and supervise the work. The details are endless and the standards high. On any given day he places a hundred phone calls, buys paint, negotiates with suppliers, rearranges transport for a worker, inspects towers, argues with inspectors and back-fills for workers who have left because the weather is better for climbing. In the evenings he pores over spreadsheets provided for him by his accountant. Everything must be double-checked and analysed: Is there room for profit? Can expenses be cut? With dozens of simultaneous projects, at times it is chaotic. Undoubtedly his fame attracts good contracts, but the work still needs to be done well. He may be hired the first time based on his name, but the second time will depend on his performance.

It is not only the towers that keep him running. He gives slideshows, to raise money for charity, and to corporations as motivational presentations. He arrives at a convention centre, meets the organising party, inserts his DVD and begins: youth, learning at the feet of the masters, apprenticeship in the Kamnik Alps, bigger and bigger objectives, failures, success, tragedy, learning from mistakes; all of these lessons are illuminated by his own personal stories. He stresses a long-term perspective: look at a project from a distance, not just for today. The rooms, packed with businessmen, erupt in spontaneous applause. The question periods go on and on. After he's finished, the organisers press him to stay for a drink, for lunch, for coffee. But no, Tomaž has to go. During one presentation, 30 calls have come in on his mobile. There is a problem at one of the towers and a crew has run out of paint. He has to run. Thank you very much. See you next time.

His parents watch in wonder. They are thankful that he is back home and working, and they can see that he is paying his bills. But they are flabbergasted at the whirlwind pace. Tomaž laughingly recalls a time when he was still taking his phone messages at home, some of which would end up with his parents. A man called one day and asked if Tomaž could repair his car. His mother said no, he could do many things, but not repair cars. Tomaž was horrified and reprimanded his mother: 'Mother, if somebody calls me about curving bananas, I can do that too. Don't turn anything down.' This can-do attitude has him running, painting towers, fences and bridges, repairing façades and balconies, felling trees, hauling firewood and, occasionally, repairing cars.

There might be an easier way of making a living, and his private backers might even support him outright as a professional climber, but he insists that is not what he wants. 'I can't just be an alpinist,' he says. 'That's not enough for me. It's not complete.' He claims there is much more to life: family, a real home, good food and travel.

Back on Nanga Parbat, events had been no less tumultuous than those in Tomaž's personal life. Less than a month after Tomaž's spectacular rescue, Steve House and Vince Anderson climbed the magnificent Rupal Face on a route near Tomaž's chosen line. After weeks of acclimatisation and patiently waiting for good weather, the pair headed up on 1 September. With the absolute minimum of gear and a remarkable stretch of clear, calm weather, they ascended the face in impeccable style. It was a bittersweet moment for Tomaž: although he himself hadn't reached the summit, this proved that his goal was justified – it was not just a dangerous wall, but an objective worthy of other world-class climbers too.

The Slovenian press mistakenly reported that House's team had left base camp without attempting the mountain. When it became clear that they had reached the summit, the newspaper *Delo* published a photo of Tomaž and House shaking hands, alleging that it was a picture of Tomaž congratulating House. In reality, this was the photo taken at the beginning of August when House passed through Tomaž's camp. House felt that this was gross manipulation of the facts, and he wondered if the impetus had come from Tomaž. Tomaž, in turn, cited others as the instigators of the entire newspaper débâcle.

To add to the controversy, House made a planned visit to Slovenia soon after his climb, accompanied by his parents, whom he wanted to introduce to his hosts from the post-high-school year spent in Maribor. While there, he was asked repeatedly to do interviews. He refused, citing privacy and exhaustion as reasons. After his parents left, his girlfriend arrived and they headed to the coastal climbing community of Osp. He was again approached by journalists, and finally he agreed to an interview with *Delo*. House was very particular about the choice of journalist, for he was well aware of the sensitivity of doing an interview about his successful climb on Nanga Parbat, particularly after the massive media attention given to Tomaž's rescue. Apart from a mistaken reference to him as the 'owner of a company called Patagonia', House was pleased with the accuracy of the article. As he expected, there were immediate reverberations from the interview. Some Slovenian alpinists, critical of Tomaž, laughed at the irony of it all: in a few short weeks, the wall that had threatened the life of Slovenia's national hero had been 'conquered'. Those who supported Tomaž considered it petty and small-minded for House to come to Slovenia and speak to the press about his climb. A few months later, House and Anderson were awarded the Piolet d'Or for their magnificent achievement.

There was some talk within the climbing community about what the American team could have done to help Tomaž. Tomaž told a reporter, 'The Americans' base camp was close to ours . . . they were perfectly aware of the situation I was in. What they did and what they didn't, and – most of all – why, is something you have to ask to Steve and Vince, not me.' Anderson pointed out that if it was too dangerous for Tomaž to descend from his snow cave, would it not have been too dangerous for them to ascend those same slopes? When Slovenian newspapers published accusations that House did not offer to help Tomaž, House was offended but chose not to respond. The behaviour in both camps posed questions about the brotherhood of climbing and the spirit of cooperation.

The perceived competition between Humar and House initiated new discussions about the existence of rivalry within the elite community of Himalayan alpinists. Although what they do is in essence a physical activity, it is also highly creative and structureless. There are rules, but they are not absolute, and they are certainly open to interpretation. Nuance takes on great importance. Within this culture of ambiguity, strict competition is difficult to imagine. Still, amongst this small group of top-level climbers there exists an enormous amount of ambition and competition, with winners and losers. The British climber Ian Parnell added clarification to the general topic of competition when he wrote in *Alpinist*: 'Human beings are innately competitive, and mountaineers are no exception; but their most prized contests haven't been between climbers, but with nature in its most dramatic forms.'[1] Vince Anderson was more pragmatic about competition within the world of alpinism, simply stating, 'It's not negative – it's healthy.' Tomaž had a different perspective: 'We are all in competition,' he said, 'but with our weaknesses. Gandhi won because he conquered his own weaknesses.'

Tomaž struggled to retain a sense of equilibrium and to distance himself from the entire discussion about competition. But he could not ignore it completely. A top tier of Himalayan climbers *does* exist, influencing one another with their abilities and projects: Simone Moro, Marko Prezelj, Steve House, Denis Urubko, Valery Babanov, Ian Parnell, Ueli Steck, to name a few. These are the climbers who guard their next projects fiercely. They are the ones who are nominated, year after year, for the Piolet d'Or. Their names grace the covers of climbing magazines. Tomaž now had to evaluate his situation honestly: was he still a member of this group?

Certainly in the past he was regarded as a serious player. Reinhold Messner expressed an optimistic view of Tomaž's future in an interview with Xan Rice for *The Observer*:

The absolute limits of endurance shift outwards for each generation of mountaineers. There may be no higher mountains to climb, but great challenges remain. I hope someone can make the traverse of Lhotse and Everest, which has never been done before. It's so long at high altitude and you would need to carry so much food and gasoline to survive. It would take seven to ten days and there must be no rest and no prepared camps – pure alpine-style climbing. Maybe Tomaž Humar, the Slovenian climber, can do it. It was too difficult for me.

Messner's opinion undoubtedly carried a lot of weight, but Steve House was ambivalent about Tomaž as an alpinist: 'If I look at his climbing résumé and consider all of his climbs, I would have to say that yes, he is a world-class alpinist. If I just look at Dhaulagiri and Nanga Parbat, I would have to say no.' House didn't believe all of Tomaž's claims in terms of difficulty, and once that credibility was destroyed, even on a small point, it was difficult to regain. Whether or not Tomaž would be a player in the future, House said, was 'up to him'. House didn't believe that the rescue would do any permanent damage to his reputation, but added, 'He can never erase it. It will always be there and I'm sure he's sick to death of talking about it [Nanga Parbat]. I know I am.' Vince Anderson agreed that Tomaž's future as a climber was in his own hands: 'I would hope that he had an epiphany up there, that he would climb in the future with no media, no circus. That would be good.'

Tomaž's nemesis, Marko Prezelj, was highly critical, although he made some attempt to restrain himself: 'I don't express my opinion openly in Slovenia because it's not a tasty opinion.' Of all the climbers in Slovenia, these two probably dislike each other the most. Prezelj even discounted Tomaž's Kosovo war experience as 'good packaging'. But as for Tomaž's future, he commented only that he 'respects Humar as a show-business person and also as a climber, but not as much as the public does'. In contrast, Tomaž openly admired Prezelj as 'one of the best climbers. I respect him so much.' But he added in a critical tone, 'I would not go to drink a beer with him.' With these two climbing stars, such statements were as close to a truce as one could hope for. Stipe was quite philosophical about the alpine world and its stars and their opinions of each other, bringing his experience and maturity to bear: 'There are many kinds of characters within the climbing community. We carry our characters with us. We are all different. Not all good climbers are good characters.'

Although Tomaž expected negative reactions after Nanga Parbat, the intensity surprised even him. But his response was pragmatic, as he stated, with no visible sign of emotion: 'The alpine world is much clearer now. There are no more masks.' Despite his efforts at emotional disengagement, he nevertheless struggled with anger towards those he felt were against him, even while he instinctively knew that this suppressed emotion was damaging to his health, a mental and spiritual pollutant. He was undoubtedly hurt by some of these remarks, saying, 'We all have the right to defend our dignity – not to attack.' When he heard that climbers were saying that 'Humar is finished now,' he lashed back: 'The story is not over yet . . . One swallow does not bring the spring.' And inevitably he retreated and retrenched, becoming somewhat hermetic as he tended to his wounds, gathering his strength and healing.

As he reflected on all the battles that he had fought – with Škarja, the Mountaineering Association, his club, his parents, the army – Tomaž insisted that he had come out on top: 'I refused to play their game. I moved to the forest. I disappeared. I play *my* game.' Italian alpinist Simone Moro wasn't convinced that disappearing into the forest and refusing to play the game was the best strategy. He thought that the criticism surrounding Tomaž had two sources. The first was based on his rather original personality, which Moro felt most climbers were simply unable to tolerate: 'Many climbers are not so intelligent or so culturally minded as to be able to accept his differences.'

But Moro also believed that Tomaž brought some of the criticism upon himself. Like Tomaž, Moro is a professional climber. He understands the demands and the requirements of maintaining a public profile. He believed that Tomaž failed to maintain his credibility by not training publicly with other climbers. Instead, he appeared to prefer to train privately. That was fine, Moro said, if you are not a professional climber, but if you make the decision to 'join the game', then you have to 'go public'. For Moro, that meant rock climbing and training on mixed climbs with other people; proving that he could perform at a very high level. 'Not everyone believes Tomaž when he says that he has climbed M8 or M9 at altitude because they haven't seen him climb M11 at sea level. If he says he climbs 6a at 7,000 metres, they don't necessarily believe him because they haven't seen him climb 7c at the local crag.' Tomaž responded that he climbs best under pressure and his style is more complex. Because Tomaž's big Himalayan climbs were almost always solo, Moro felt that he more than most needed to prove himself on the training grounds to maintain his credibility. It was this nagging doubt that climbers had about his abilities that fuelled the criticism. Moro added that it was not only a matter of proving yourself: by training in public, climbing hard, trying hard, sometimes falling off, you proved that you were a human being, not some kind of superman or prima donna.

Despite the internal fighting and intrigue, it is an accepted fact that Slovenia has produced many of the world's leading climbers in the past 20 years. It's hard to imagine what their impact would have been if some of those leading alpinists had lived a bit longer. And it's even harder to imagine what this small country might have achieved if the climbing stars could have learned to tolerate each other a bit more.

Rejection by the Slovenian purists was perhaps unavoidable for Tomaž, as a result of his stepping ahead of the crowd and promoting himself. The controversy probably tells us more about the climbing community and their values than it does about Tomaž himself. The disposition of most alpinists is somewhat reserved and introverted and the Slovenians are possibly even more reserved than most. Throw a flamboyant character like Tomaž into their midst, and it's natural that he would be ostracised. Any group of specialists, whether they are climbers, musicians or neuro-surgeons, judge the behaviour of their peers much more critically than the general public does.

Sometimes that heightened criticism is fuelled by jealousy. Viki believes that this was the case with Tomaž: 'People are okay if you are better than they are. But they don't forgive you if you are popular as well with the public.' The comparison with Messner was frequently made. 'Messner was good as a climber and he was good with money. This was just too much for many to accept.' Viki felt that one should concentrate on what was important – climbing. And in this regard, he felt that Tomaž's climbs stood alone. He pointed out that even when Tomaž didn't succeed on his climbs, they were so futuristic that they were still nominated for the prestigious Piolet d'Or prize. His opinion supported the theory that Tomaž was a true visionary, his ambition sometimes exceeding his grasp, but still in a way that dazzled.

Tomaž has a somewhat pragmatic opinion of his own abilities, stating frankly that he knows he is not as good a technical climber as many others. But he brings other elements to the table: research, medical work, mind work, astrology, strategy, soul. He insists that his approach is to create a high-performance survival machine built of blocks that comprise much more than just training. His survival 'pyramid' builds on all that he has absorbed from each climber – and each wise person – he has known. His approach to alpinism is holistic, futuristic and unquestionably unique.

Tomaž accepts the ongoing criticism from other climbers quite philosophically: 'The more high profile I am, the more enemies I have . . . more or less the same – climbers. This is quite normal. In any sport, there are rivals. Without this competition you sleep on your own medals and you believe your own lies. If a lie is repeated twelve times it becomes true. So it is good to have this self-reflection.' He recognises himself as a public personality and knows that along with the perks of fame come a few drawbacks. Close scrutiny of every word and every action is one of them.

One of the most persistent criticisms is his relationship to, and use of, the media. For many people, it appears that Tomaž has sold his soul. Tomaž firmly rejects this criticism: 'The one thing in my life is that I'm the switcher guy. Nobody ever mentions that. I decide if the media is here or not. I decide if I will take internet with me or not. It is my decision, not the decision of my sponsors or my public.' There appears to be some truth to his statement, for on Aconcagua, Shishapangma, Jannu and Baruntse, he went quietly and with absolutely no fanfare. In stark contrast, there was Dhaulagiri. His decision when to include the internet on an expedition is guided by pure instinct. His harshest critics insist that his use of the internet on *any* expedition tarnishes the entire sport.

When not being criticised about the media's interest in him, Tomaž is often challenged to defend his climbs on their level of difficulty and their originality. When pushed to defend his climb on Dhaulagiri, he categorizes it as 'a good climb that in 50 years will still be considered a good climb'. He scoffs at the criticism and downgrading that often follow one of his ascents, claiming: 'I know what is what. I know which climbs are really hard.' Although Ganesh V was one of the hardest climbs for Tomaž personally, since it was the first time he had climbed above 3,500 metres, he doesn't consider it to be a highlight of his career, nor in terms of Himalayan climbing history. He feels the same about Annapurna. Even Ama Dablam, which won him the Piolet d'Or, was not the most memorable. 'Ama Dablam's face was, in my opinion, at least 1,000 metres short,' he explains. Even though the difficulty and the style were top level, he feels it would have needed to be a longer route to be completely memorable. He has the same view of Bobaye: 'It was a very good climb, done in good style, but 1,000 metres too short.'

But Nuptse, he feels, was truly a world-class climb. It pushed him to his very limit and he thinks that future generations would agree with him. Silvo Karo is one who does, stating that Nuptse was Tomaž's very best climb. Perhaps somewhat surprisingly, Tomaž rates Reticent Wall highly as well, although this is more for personal reasons. In Tomaž's opinion, Dhaulagiri speaks for itself. He has great confidence in the staying power of this climb. Škarja thought that his Dhaulagiri climb was the point at which his career actually began to fail. 'Dhaulagiri was early in his career and it was impossible to repeat . . . You cannot surpass this accomplishment,' he said. Historian Elizabeth Hawley disagreed that Dhaulagiri came too early in his career, saying, 'He had, after all, climbed several other difficult faces in Nepal before he went to Dhaulagiri I.' But despite the notoriety of Dhaulagiri, the climb that Tomaž places above all his others, in terms of boldness and commitment, is Jannu. His most extreme experiences were on Jannu, and he compares the level of risk he had endured on Jannu as equal to some parts of Dhaulagiri.

Tomaž sees fundamental differences between climbing below and above 7,500 metres, stating that this elevation creates a kind of threshold above which sustained technical climbing is extremely difficult. Climbing an easy route above 7,500 metres is not so hard, but when one combines the extreme elevation with the effort of dry-tooling or struggling up a difficult pitch of loose rock, the strain is intense. With each subsequent climb he added to his experience: 'Every climb changed me a lot. It is a creative process, like building a house.' Hawley had watched his progress, too, stating her opinion: 'Tomaz is a warm-hearted, outgoing man who has boundless enthusiasm for the extreme climbing challenges he sets for himself.'

Despite his consistency in choosing difficult and high objectives, Tomaž is a study of contrasts in terms of his style: one climb broadcast on an almost daily basis, and the next almost completely unknown. Yet he thinks that the public makes a fundamental mistake in confusing his climbing style with his public face. He insists that his climbing style is pure.

Tomaž struggles to prevent the ongoing controversies from destroying him. He has witnessed the effect of long-term battles on people he considers much stronger than him – climbers like Walter Bonatti. Bonatti abandoned climbing altogether when he and the Italian Alpine Club could not agree on his role in the 1954 Italian expedition that made the first ascent of K2. Instead of accepting their decision, he left the climbing community altogether, became a journalist and eventually retreated into seclusion. He refused to discuss one of the most important climbing events of his life. Tomaž has a different strategy: 'I will not lose my energy to deal with the past. You cannot change the past, but you can change the future if you are willing to change, and if you have lessons from the past.' He goes further, taking even more responsibility for his future contentment: 'You cannot change others. You can only change yourself. That is why I go into the mountains. There, I can find myself and face myself and make the changes that I need to do.'

Most of Tomaž's local training is now done with a small group of young climbers with whom he works in rather unusual ways. Not only do they climb together; Tomaž instructs them on a reading list, advises them to have regular blood work done to monitor their physiological improvements, and of course gives them a punishing training schedule that imitates his own. The entire approach is researched, structured and strategic. Some appreciate his mentoring and others eventually lose interest in the non-physical elements.

Even more than before, Tomaž is now ostracised from some of the most active climbers in the country. But he is friendly with some of the younger ones, including his partner Aleš. 'If I had to teach myself everything that I learned from him,' says Aleš, 'it would have taken me a long time. He is generous with his knowledge, and also in a general sense he is generous.' But Aleš adds that his relationship with Tomaž has not been without cost. Some of the more established climbers refuse to associate with him or climb with him now, and he is also somewhat alienated from the Kamnik club to which he belongs. In fact, some climbers refer to him as 'Tomaž's handmaiden', an image that makes him laugh. 'I would like to climb with him again, but not in Nanga style,' Aleš quietly adds, referring to the media hype that surrounded it. Aleš is an intensely private person, but unlike some other climbers, he looks beyond philosophical differences and counts Tomaž as a friend. The Mexican alpinist Carlos Carsolio also regards him as 'a friend for life'. Tomaž takes friendships seriously, supporting his friends in times of need, whether it be in a practical or an emotional sense. When Stipe tragically lost his son in a motorcycle accident in 2007, both Tomaž and Viki were immediately at his side.

Although certainly not a friend, Tone Škarja always smiles when he speaks of Tomaž. He assumes Tomaž is as physically fit as ever, but he feels there is something missing – a mental edge. Even so, he is convinced that Tomaž will continue climbing at the highest level that he can. Škarja's concern is not with Tomaž, but with the attitude of young climbers in general, who are changing the face of Himalayan climbing.

'Life is more valuable now,' he says, adding that 'Young people think like old people. Their lives are too valuable to them.' He recalled going to the Himalayas for between five and seven weeks at a time. 'Now, after a few days of storm, they go home.' Viki agrees that things are changing in the world of Himalayan climbing. His greatest concern is that climbers are moving to the lower peaks – still on very difficult routes, but not on the 8,000-metre giants. He maintains that there is a fundamental and profound difference in the level of commitment, and that it is the highest peaks that presented the biggest challenges, logistically and financially, and of course the lowest chance of success. Anything over 7,500 metres pushes the difficulty level up exponentially; this is where Viki feels the great challenges still lie. House agrees on the fundamental differences between climbing technical routes at 7,000 and at 8,000 metres, and confirms that there are still a number of 'interesting' things to do on the 8,000-metre faces.

On this point, Tomaž clearly represents his generation, inextricably drawn to the 8,000-metre faces. Just a year after his basement accident, while appearing as a guest speaker at the Banff Mountain Film Festival in Canada, he was socialising with climbing friends Carlos Carsolio and Ed Webster. Webster was showing them a photo of the North Face of Lhotse, a 3,000-metre face that had never been tried. Tomaž was transfixed with the details on the photo and immediately began pointing out weaknesses on the wall and strategies for what time of day would be best for this or that part. He became convinced that this face could be climbed. Webster recalls watching in amazement this person who at the time could still barely walk without crutches, yet had the courage and the technical skills – and the vision – to imagine a climb like this. He describes the moment: 'That was when he looked over at me and gave me one of those piercing looks and said, "This is a one-way-ticket climb."'

These 'one-way-ticket' climbs are only attempted by top-level Himalayan alpinists – climbers who have to climb fast, light and at a very high technical level. Most alpinists agreed that Tomaž has the first two skills. The disagreement was with the third. As Moro said, 'For the future . . . he only has to take care of his technical abilities.' One indisputable fact is that with his improvisational skills, his charm, his theatrical powers of projection and persuasion and his enormous confidence, there is not an A-list climber on the planet who can electrify a room like Tomaž Humar.

To balance his high-octane life, Tomaž depends upon his 'nest'. Despite the fact that he almost lost his life building it, and the painful knowledge that it was conceived as a family home for a family that no longer exists, his home is his respite and the launching pad for his adventures, whether in the mountains or in his mind. Nestled next to the forest that he cherishes, it is comfortable and tasteful, filled with mementos from his world travels. The pulsating heart is his office, crammed with books and slides and undeveloped film, posters and maps, large-scale photos of unclimbed faces, and his computers. Never satisfied with one computer, Tomaž usually uses all three at the same time. He multi-tasks, checking his email on one, doing a bit of research on the second, and organising his slides or videos on the third. It is a strangely efficient system, once one gets past the intensity of it. Phones ring, the fax machine purrs, printers print and scanners scan. From his tiny corner at the foot of the Kamnik Alps, Tomaž monitors and connects with the world.

The walls of his house disappear beneath paintings. Spiritual tokens are everywhere, from a myriad of crystals to figurines of the Virgin Mary to a prized photo of the Indian guru Sai Baba. Bookshelves groan with the weight of climbing tomes and dictionaries. All the greats are represented here, but his favourites are *Veliki dnevi*, the autobiography of his mentor Šrauf, and a thin volume titled *Pot* (*The Way*) by Nejec Zaplotnik. For most contemporary Slovenian alpinists, this small book has provided them with the value system, the knowledge and the will to go into the mountains and climb. It has given them a reference point from which to develop their own styles.

One corner of his bookcase is reserved for his most precious treasures: his birth bracelet, given to him by his mother; a small gift from His Holiness the Dalai Lama; the gold watch given him by President Musharraf; his dog tags from his army days; and next to these, two filthy, tattered train tickets – the tickets that allowed him to escape the hell of Kosovo.

In his basement, Tomaž has armed himself with enough equipment to climb the fourteen 8,000-metre peaks, and more. Buried in ropes and boots, helmets, carabiners, ascenders, tents and sleeping bags, the rooms are chaotic, but he knows exactly where everything is, how old it is, how often it has been used, if it has held a fall, if it could be used for lead climbing or only belaying. It is a veritable warehouse of hardware. Next to this arsenal is his training room. Better equipped than most club gyms, his bouldering gym is a kaleidoscope of steep, overhanging walls, plastered with colourful ceramic holds of all shapes and sizes. And when he can no longer throw himself around the room, there is a weight-lifting mechanism where he fine-tunes his body even further.

Always a strong proponent of healthy and locally grown foods, he is an enthusiastic and talented chef. But his concern for health goes much further. Drawers are filled with health foods of all kinds, herbs and pills, special plants to cleanse him of toxins, others to build both his immunity and his muscles, still others to clear his mind. His home even boasts an InterX5000 machine, a bio-scanner originally developed for the Russian space programme, and to top it off, a magnetic field system that makes him feel 'alive'. This is a man clearly obsessed with his body.

And when the pace becomes too much; when he has prepared his best pasta yet, lifted the biggest barbell, managed the trickiest move in his gym, and closed down his computers for the night, he can step outside and be immediately transported into the world of the forest. Night noises intrigue and eyes flash in the dark, as foxes and cats compete for mice. He can see the sharp outline of the beech forest against the night sky, and can smell the mushrooms pushing up the dirt. Here is his spiritual centre – his forest – and just beyond, the Kamnik Alps. When he needs silence, it is here that he retrenches, alone in the forest.

Tomaž remains a committed and passionate father. His children are an area of intense vulnerability. There is nothing on earth that means as much to him: not his first love, Sergeja, not his parents, not even climbing. He would do anything to protect his children and to help them create a good life for themselves, one with fewer obstacles than his. He spends most weekends and holidays with them, searching for mushrooms with Tomi, one of their greatest common passions, or sometimes climbing together. It turns out that Tomi is a natural climber, as comfortable on a 7a as he is on a 5c. When Tomaž is even remotely distracted while belaying his son, talking with others at the base of a crag or rummaging through his pack, Tomi calls down: 'Dad, pay attention. You had your ten minutes, now it's my turn.' Tomaž immediately becomes quiet and obeys him. But much more than climbing, it is football that dominates Tomi. He is a talented athlete, obsessed with all aspects of the game, even securing a kind of professional status at the age of eight. Urša is not interested in climbing, but she enjoys bossing her father around the house; he enjoys it even more. In fact he dotes on her, worrying about her vulnerable teenage years, seeing to her religious instruction, arranging his climbing plans around important milestones in her life, taking her shopping in London. Their conversations are deep and intense, whether about fashion or spirituality, budgets or boys. Tomaž constantly encourages her to think for herself and develop her own identity, but always within the context of a strong spiritual base created by her religious upbringing.

In the summer of 2006, Tomaž was summoned by his father, Max, to go up Slovenia's highest mountain, Triglav. Although there are many routes on Triglav, Max wanted to take a relatively simply one. Like all Slovenian mountains, Triglav has an easy ascent route, harkening back to the socialist days when a government policy decreed that every Slovenian citizen should be able to go to the sea and to the mountains. Going to the sea was relatively straightforward, but the mountains were something else. Many are steep and jagged at the top, with severe drop-offs. Climbing was considered an elitist activity, and socialism did not support that approach. So an elaborate and extensive system of via ferratas – iron structures comprising ladders and cables – was erected, on which any normally fit citizen can reach the top of every Slovenian mountain. As a result, the mountains are crowded with families, young and old people, climbers and walkers, all ascending their beloved peaks.

Not content with the easy route, Tomaž wanted to take Tomi up a North Face route, so they came up with a plan that would satisfy all. Tomaž's brother Marjan took Max up the normal route, and Tomaž led Tomi up the North Face, all meeting at the top. It was a wonderful family moment, memorable also for everyone else who was on the top that day, for Tomaž remains an instantly recognisable icon. When the climbers and hikers realised who was amongst them, they celebrated with the three generations of Humars. Tomaž, the children and Max continued their adventures together later that year when they went trekking in Nepal.

It is said that time heals all wounds, and it appears that the jagged scar caused by the breakup with Sergeja is healing as well. Still wary around each other, they have both softened somewhat. Reflecting upon her life with Tomaž, Sergeja said rather poetically: 'My message is simple . . . my life with you was like the ocean . . . the sea was not only never-ending and huge, but also deep . . . there was no time or chance for luck and peace . . . but still, we have two wonderful small boats called Urša and Tomi, which we can happily watch from different seas.' She went on to quote from a poem that resonated for her at this time of her life, written by Dr Preseren, the undisputed national poet of the country, who died alone and bitter after years of failed romances and heavy drinking: 'With all that it was, that it is, and that it will be . . .'

Tomaž believes that each person is given a certain number of gifts; everything one has to work with. And with them comes responsibility: 'Don't mess with your gifts. They were not given you to just lie on the couch.' He is convinced that he returned from Nanga Parbat for a reason. That rescue was one of his gifts, and he is determined to fulfil his destiny.

Amidst the swirl of talk and allegation, accusation and denial, jealousy and admiration, somewhere lies the truth about this man. He is aware of his weaknesses and is determined to beat them, not be destroyed by them. He is aware of his explosive energy and vows to use it, not abuse it. He believes he knows what truth is, and he is committed to living it, not ignoring it. He knows that his words and actions sometimes hurt people, but he believes that goodness begins with thoughts, and it is his thoughts that he concentrates on first. He knows that people feel he is racing against other climbers – and time – but he insists he is racing only with himself. His goal is to enhance his own consciousness, and this he feels can come only through pain. 'From pain comes joy . . . I'm training to have joy in my climbing.' He climbs constantly and he has big plans – some that could be described as 'death climbs'.

But Tomaž has no intention of dying in the mountains. In fact, he intends to grow old. He is also determined to have joy in his life, and in that respect he seems to be doing well. As he states with a typical flourish of arms and toss of his head, 'I cannot be more rich; I have family, freedom and climbing and dreams.'

Tomaž's last few years have not been easy, but somehow he thrives. He lost his marriage, but he has found love again with Maja. His body was broken, but it has healed. He was facing financial ruin, but that memory too is fading. Death stared him squarely in the face on the Rupal Face, but he survived. This is the lesson that Nanga Parbat gave him that no other mountain did: 'I know how to survive.' The lines on his face are more pronounced now. His eyes are sunk more deeply and his smile lights up less often. He is thin. But his heart and soul and body are intact. More than intact, for he is not just a survivor. He is a visionary.

His vision is defined by the one constant in his life – the mountains that nourish his soul, that make him feel alive and that give him joy. He continues to climb, for it is through alpinism that Tomaž feels those rare moments of grace. Despite a life that could have shattered him, his courage remains unbroken. He is bruised, but not defeated, and sees new challenges. 'Nanga Parbat helped me, in that the purists are leaving me alone now.' Then, with a cinematic reference, he adds, 'Cinderella can rise.'

THE SHOW MUST GO ON

On 29 October 2007, the climbing world was stunned to learn that Tomaž Humar had reached the East Summit of Annapurna the previous day, after soloing the South Face. The report came from Ang Tshering Sherpa, president of the Nepal Mountaineering Association and founder of Asian Trekking, the agency that Tomaž had used for his climb. Ang Tshering had received a satellite call from Tomaž and had subsequently notified ExplorersWeb about the ascent: 'Asian Trekking is very pleased and proud to announce that our great friend and popular mountaineer Mr Tomaž Humar from Slovenia successfully made a Solo Summit on Mt. Annapurna I (8,091 metres) via South Face on 28 Oct 2007. The name of the expedition is Humar Solo Annapurna I Expedition 2007.'

Nobody knew he was there; no one knew of his plans; many were sceptical at the news; everyone wanted to know more. The days that followed were maddeningly silent. This, from an alpinist better known for his self-promotional skills and media savvy than for low-profile ascents. What would motivate him to ignore the climbing media in this way? Was it naiveté? Almost certainly not. Arrogance? Doubtful. Ambivalence? Perhaps.

Word of the climb spread quickly and journalists, climbers and historians scrambled for details. Strangely there were none. Curiosity grew and climbers in particular demanded more information. As the days passed, a number of reports were posted on various climbing websites. None contained much concrete information and some expressed frustration at Humar's refusal to communicate. This, from some of the same journalists who had condemned him for blathering on, publicly, about his previous expeditions. In the absence of real information, scenarios about his climb proliferated. After all, this was the legendary South Face of Annapurna and the possibility of firsts was mind-boggling: new route, solo, alpine style.

The South Face of Annapurna had been a testing ground for the most ambitious Himalayan climbers for over thirty years. It was first climbed by Dougal Haston and Don Whillans on an expedition led by Chris Bonington in 1970. Theirs was a siege effort with eight climbers supported by high-altitude Sherpas supplying six camps along a continuous line of fixed rope over a period of several weeks. It took eleven years for the South Face to be climbed again, this time by the Japanese, again with fixed ropes. There were a few other ascents of the South Face over the years, including a spectacular alpine-style climb by the two Catalans Nil Bohigas and Enric Lucas in 1984. In a six-day effort, they climbed a leftward-leaning ramp through difficult rock bands and on ice as steep as 80 degrees. Four years later the Polish climbers Artur Hajzer and Jerzy Kukuczka climbed a new line on the 1,500 metre-high far east rib of the South Face. The rib rears up from the upper northeast corner of the South Annapurna Glacier to meet the East Ridge of Annapurna I just west of a point known as Kangsar Kang or Roc Noir. They fixed some lines on the lower part of the Face before heading up onto the 60-degree ice pitches on the upper part of the mountain and they descended over Kangsar Kang and down the East Ridge.

There were also some notable tragedies on the Face, including the British alpinist Alex MacIntyre in 1982, French climber Pierre Béghin in 1992, the Russian superstar Anatoli Boukreev, who died while attempting a new route towards the Annapurna Fang in 1997, and Ramiro Navarette Carera in 2006. Then, in the spring of 2007, the Swiss alpinist Ueli Steck made a solo attempt on Annapurna's South Face. Three hundred metres up, rockfall tossed Steck from the wall. When he regained consciousness, he realized that he had survived a 330-metre fall down the Face and promptly retreated.

That September Tomaž arrived at the Face, intent on applying his own contemporary approach to one of the Himalaya's last great challenges. He headed directly to Pokhara and on to Annapurna Base Camp. He didn't come with a specific objective; his goal was simply to climb an 8,000-metre peak again. The entire month of September was extremely rainy and snowy with only a few short breaks in the monsoon, and the three-member team consisting of Dr Anda Perdan, Jagat Limbu and Tomaž began referring to themselves as the 'expedition of patience'. They were alone on the south side of Annapurna with only a Korean expedition climbing on the Fang section of the mountain. Tomaž watched the face intently. He finally discovered a route that attracted him, and then he waited for his chosen line to come into condition.

Meanwhile, he climbed a new route on Tharpu Chuli (5,690 metres) for acclimatization. But because of the persistently bad weather he also had ample time to think, to explore his inner feelings and motivations and to write, some of which he recorded in his journal:

> *Excitement is the consequence of vibrations,*
> *They generate a thought, and it develops into an idea,*
> *The idea lives as long as it's taken care of in one's heart,*
> *It depends upon truthfulness in us, watchfulness of our mind,*
> *   life itself.*
> *When we surrender to the idea, there are no barriers, there is*
> *   only a WAY.*
> *Belief, courage, comprehension help us to reach the altar of*
> *   sacrifice . . .*
> *All that remains is the voyage, the voyage to the other side,*
> *Where courage, belief, understanding are needed no more.*

After more than a month of waiting, the weather finally began to clear. He determined that one particular line (not his first choice) might be safe after all the bad weather, and so he began, claiming that he chose his route 'by instinct'. On 24 October, Tomaž headed out with Jagat Limbu, the two men crossing the glacier and weaving their way through mixed rock and ice pillars under the main wall. Some of the ice sections steepened to more than 80 degrees, and the rock sections were primarily grade IV in difficulty in the UIAA classification, with some sections as difficult as V-VI. They staged their first bivouac on a small platform called Rock Island at 5,800 metres, where they remained the following day due to extremely strong winds.

At 6.00 a.m. on 26 October Tomaž left the bivouac and began climbing solo, going as light as possible: he took no helmet, no rope, no harness – just bivouac gear, some food and gas. He left everything else with Jagat, who would be forced to descend alone if Tomaž did not return from the Face. The terrain was a mix of rock and ice at an angle of around 60 degrees. At 3.00 p.m. he stopped and excavated a hole in the ice at 7,200 metres for his second bivouac. Up till now the climbing had not been technically difficult and he felt it was probably one of the safer lines on Annapurna. He spent the entire next day inside the ice hole in order to better acclimatise. Alone on the Face, he wanted to eliminate the possibility of oedema. During that day the wind reached speeds of greater than 100 kilometres per hour. While in the hole, he had ample time to think about how he would manage the 14-hour journey to the East Summit and back, without another bivouac. He knew that a night out on the East Ridge with such strong wind and no bivouac equipment would almost certainly be fatal. His decision to go fast and light was the most important – and difficult – decision he would make.

After a sleepless night, he prepared to begin again at 6.00 a.m. on 28 October. The sky was clear. The wind was strong and cold. He climbed very light, carrying just two litres of juice, which froze within the first hour. After two hours of climbing he arrived at the East Ridge at 7,500 metres, the spot where the Swiss alpinists Erhard Loretan and Norbert Joos had passed in 1984 during their committing and elegant first ascent of the East Ridge of Annapurna I and traverse of the mountain. Despite the extremely strong wind, Tomaž continued towards the East Summit.

By 10.00 a.m., he had crossed most of the East Ridge and the summit appeared close at hand. But with each passing hour, and the higher he climbed, the wind grew stronger with gusts now reaching between 100 and 150 kilometres per hour. It was impossible for him not to recall 1997, when a similar wind had caused the death of his partner, Janež Jeglič, on the summit ridge of Nuptse. The final section of the ridge took almost five more hours because of the breakable crust and unstable snow. During particularly strong bursts of wind he lay flat on the ground, moving only when the wind decreased so as not to be blown off.

Just before 3 p.m. he arrived at the 8,047-metre East Summit. Now he had to decide: should he continue on to the main summit of Annapurna? In Tomaž's words: 'I trust God, I pray, I feel safe! Even if the weather is good I would never dare to continue to the main summit at 8,091 metres. God gave me the possibility to reach it already once in 1995.' His spirits were at their highest as he recalled the moments on the summit: 'Even if the weather was not perfect, I felt calm. I felt alive, very alive! Because you really feel alive only when you have no fear to live or to die.'

After a short time Tomaž began to descend. Just below the summit he called Jagat to tell him that he was on his way down. Jagat was relieved, for he had been praying for Tomaž for over five hours, ever since their last radio contact at 10.00 a.m. But now began the most difficult part of the climb; the going was slow, and as night closed in Tomaž had only reached the beginning of the East Ridge. By this time he was very fatigued, for it had been many hours since he had eaten or drank. He was no longer able to see his upward tracks and he soon became lost. At this point he drew upon his spirituality to provide strength: 'I am lost, but in my soul I know that God is with me.' Just as on his descent from Nuptse, his headlamp malfunctioned due to the extremely low temperatures. He stopped and waited for the moon to rise before continuing. He finally reached his bivouac at 7,200 metres at 8.25 p.m. Although he was totally exhausted he managed to send the following text message:

BLESSED, IN BIVOUAC. NEW ROUTE UP TO 7500M +, THEN THE LONGEST JOURNEY TO MYSELF. ANNAPURNA EAST 8000M + AND BACK AFTER 14 HOURS IN EARTH TIME. EVERYTHING WAS O.K. BUT IF THIS WIND IS 60 KM/H THEN I DRIVE MY CAR SLOVLY.

Having sent the message he meditated, prayed, prepared a cup of tea and waited for the dawn to arrive. At 8.00 a.m. Tomaž continued his descent towards his first bivouac, at 5,800 metres, where, after four hours, he met up with Jagat. He then called his doctor, Anda Perdan, who had been waiting at base camp, as well as his parents, Maja, his children and his trekking agency, reassuring them all that he had reached the summit and had safely descended. He and Jagat continued down-climbing and arrived at Base Camp at 8.30 p.m. The next morning they packed up and prepared to return home, but before leaving they helped organize the rescue of three members of a Korean expedition on the Annapurna Fang. Then they descended to Chumrung at 2,100 metres. They continued on to Kathmandu on 2 November and met with Himalayan historian Elizabeth Hawley and Richard Salisbury for four hours, providing them with pictures and an official report of the climb. Hawley confirmed that he had climbed a new route. By 7 November he was back in Slovenia.

But in those intervening nine days since the initial report of the climb, the climbing world tied itself in knots trying to figure out what had happened. Emails swirled back and forth amongst climbing journalists, often beginning with 'If it's true . . . unconfirmed reports . . . possible climb . . .' In the absence of any real facts, speculation grew. The first point of discussion was whether it could be classified a solo climb. Some journalists felt that since Jagat Limbu had accompanied Tomaž to 5,800 metres at the base of the Face in order to allow him to safely navigate the ice fall, this would discredit a true solo.

Then it was determined that his route was a repeat of the 1988 Polish climb that had included Hajzer and Kukuczka. The climbing reports concluded that Tomaž's climb 'appears to have followed the Polish line more or less exactly, albeit in alpine-style and completely solitary.' The more diligent historians checked in with Hajzer, and upon inspection of detailed route drawings it became clear that the two routes were independent, covering completely different terrain other than one point of intersection at 5,800 metres on the ice platform where Tomaž established his first bivouac. Tomaž commented, 'I climbed a new route in pure alpine style without knowing that a team climbed this wall in 1988 not far from my new route.' Still, it seemed somewhat unusual that Tomaž was unaware of the Polish climb, for it was a well documented ascent.

Further investigation revealed something even more intriguing: apparently three French climbers had climbed a route in this vicinity in 2000, but they had not officially reported their climb because they were climbing without a permit. Journalists next contacted the Frenchmen, Christian Trommsdorff, Yannick Graziani and Patrick Wagnon, who were initially confused that they, Tomaž and the Poles had all climbed the same route. But upon closer examination of the photographs, they finally confirmed that their route was different from that of the Poles but identical to Tomaž's, for they had indeed climbed the 1,500-metre South Face of Kangsar Kang, right of the Polish east rib, exiting on to the East Ridge of Annapurna below Kangsar Kang's summit. The French had then tried to reach the summit of Annapurna East, but due to a combination of violent wind and exhaustion, they had instead traversed to the North Ridge, where they bivouacked one more night and then descended the North Ridge of Annapurna East. 'We were really on the edge,' recalled Trommsdorff.

This brought up another point of discussion about whether a route could be claimed if the summit had not been reached. The more traditional types said no, claiming that if it wasn't a summit, it wasn't a route. But the Europeans posited a more contemporary approach, saying that a 'route' went only to its logical conclusion, or could even stop 'at the end of difficulties'. This approach was also controversial, for it was not unusual for subsequent climbers to discover considerable challenge above 'the end of difficulties'. According to John Harlin, Editor of the *American Alpine Journal*, he now added a tag line of 'to such and such a point' when he reported a route that ended below the summit. Harlin felt that the priority was to simply and honestly report what had been done: other climbers could then decide for themselves what they thought of it. Certainly the

French had not reached their summit so, at least from the *AAJ*'s perspective, it would have been called a first ascent of a new route, but only to the East Ridge. But of course it hadn't been called anything because it hadn't been reported.

The French ascent was equally unknown to Elizabeth Hawley and it was not registered in her official Himalayan Database. Nor was it known by Artur Hajzer or Ueli Steck. But it had been written up in some European climbing magazines, and regardless of whether it was a 'legitimate' or 'legal' ascent, it certainly seemed to exist. The French had done it and were now ready and willing to claim it as a first ascent. That classified Tomaž's climb as a second ascent. On the other hand, it could be argued that if Tomaž *thought* he was climbing a new route he was still entering that realm of the unknown.

Trommsdorff commented that, 'Clearly he [Tomaž] didn't climb a new route, although our ascent was "unofficial".' He summed up Tomaž's situation with, 'If you are a hi-fi climber like Humar and want to climb a new route, you first search for info . . . At the very least he should have known about the Polish route.' It's true that, although the French climb was obscure, the Polish ascent was not. But ironically, the French had not known about the Polish ascent either. Trommsdorff felt that Tomaž could probably legitimately claim the first *solo* ascent of Annapurna 1 East. For his part, Tomaž accepted the French ascent, saying, 'If somebody climbs something with or without a permit, nothing changes about the climb itself. It is there, it is climbed. Finish story.' But he pointed out the underlying message that climbing without a permit sent: 'You can do it, if nobody catches you! Such a message reminds me of the Wild West.' As for the perceived value of a first or a second ascent, Tomaž responded: 'There is no difference about that for me. The soul of the climb will remain the same. The only things that change are the statistics. What matters most is up to the individual.'

Then the debate began about whether Tomaž's climb was technically on the South Face of Annapurna, or on some slightly less impressive face. The debate is perhaps not as ridiculous as it sounds, for Annapurna's south side is huge and complex. The wall is hemmed in by two main ridges: one leading up to Annapurna South and another in the east heading south from Glacier Dome. The east side of Annapurna goes up to the sub-peak known as Kangsar Kang or Roc Noir, and some aficionados felt that anything climbed below Roc Noir should not be labelled the South Face. It seemed that the experts were concentrating more on what he *hadn't* done, rather than on what he *had* done. Tomaž wryly reflected on all the commotion: 'They seem to know more about my climb than I do,' adding, 'I carried out a climb for my soul.' Although it was obviously important to have the correct statistics about this climb – and any climb – it was also relevant to understand something about the climber's motivations. In this case, it appeared to be more about feeding his soul than setting a record.

As the month of November came to a close, ExplorersWeb began interviewing other Himalayan alpinists in order to get their opinions of the climb. Piotr Pustelnik, Ueli Steck and Artur Hajzer agreed on two things: Humar's climb was cool, and they too had known nothing about the Trommsdorff route. When asked about the level of difficulty on that part of the wall, Artur Hajzer said, 'To us the climb was difficult . . . to me, what Humar did was great.' Simone Moro, who had been climbing with Anatoli Boukreev when he was killed by an avalanche on Annapurna on Christmas Day 1997 wrote, 'I congratulate Humar; new route, variation or a repetition, he realized a great climb!' House also sent a congratulatory message.

Still, the experts debated just how 'easy' the route might have been and one can't help wonder why this climb was viewed with such intense scrutiny and scepticism. Perhaps it was due to his huge public profile. Strangely, climbers seemed to dislike Tomaž for playing to the cameras but they now seemed to dislike him equally for *not* playing to the cameras.

Yet when questioned about his previous extensive use of media in contrast to this relatively quiet ascent, Tomaž pointed out that he had used cameras on only three expeditions, adding that it had been *he* who had decided when and where: 'I decide, completely on my own . . . without any external pressure, any help. So I take full responsibility and advantage from this situation. We all have a possibility to choose. Live and let others live. Just as Buddhists like to say.' As for the ongoing criticism of his climbing style and behaviour, he responded: 'Talk on the flat is cheap . . . for me, alpinism means climbing – not polemics.'

Perhaps it wasn't his profile, but rather that he had strayed outside the close-knit, somewhat elitist, climbing fraternity. Just as in the world of contemporary classical music, there is a certain satisfaction from performing esoteric music to miniscule audiences of cognoscenti. When those audiences grow, and the mainstream seems to 'get it', some of that insider magic is lost. Tomaž wasn't the first climber to have been rebuffed by his peers when he turned his gaze sideways to see what else was out there: lectures, writing, prosperity, popularity, fame. Climbers like Reinhold Messner, Chris Bonington and Todd Skinner had had similar experiences. Perhaps there was a lack of tolerance for this broader approach to what was supposed to be an elite and little-understood activity.

Finally, Tomaž expressed his opinion about the purity of the climbing fraternity.

I've discovered that there are two extremes of alpinism. Purists present their style as if it is the only one. They judge every different step as a deviation. If you are one step behind them, they judge you as inferior or weak. If you dare to step further from this 'pure style' they judge you as being too ambitious, too populist, too spiritual or too irresponsible. I don't want to be misunderstood: there is nothing wrong with the purist style if they really follow their own rules. But I feel there is a problem when purists make use of commercial benefits, for at that moment their spirit dies and a compromise comes to life. The other side of purism is what I would define as 'raping style': they don't care too much about opinions, ethics or nature. They climb in order to reach a goal, the summit, success, and they use all means available. It resembles a military style more than what we used to call classic Himalayan style. If they can't climb the face with ten people they come with twenty, and if this is not enough they increase the numbers more. Not only climbers: they bring oxygen bottles, kilometres of ropes, heavy camps and tons and tons of equipment. What about the environment, ethics and respect towards Mother Nature? My view about these two extremes is that both styles are not in harmony with the times we are now living in. Still, it would probably be better for all of us if we paid more attention to our own climbs instead of continuously complaining about those of others. If these two styles continue to increase and compete, manipulating each other, we will soon have a situation that Tiziano Terzani quoted in his book *Letters Against the War*: 'The first casualty, when war comes, is truth!'

When Tomaž returned from Nanga Parbat in 2005, he was as well known in his country as he could possibly be. With that fame he could have done anything: gone into politics, become a television personality, started his own line of clothing. Instead he focused on getting his business back on track, growing a garden, spending time with his family and friends – and training. He trained in Slovenia, in the Alps and in Nepal, preparing himself mentally, spiritually and physically. And in October of 2007 he made use of that training to make the first solo ascent of Annapurna's South Face, climbing alone for the last 2,247 metres to the East Summit. He did it in alpine style during a season with absolutely atrocious weather. He did it with no advance publicity and little post-climb fanfare, to which Vince Anderson had this to say: 'As for the absence of media, I applaud him for resisting the temptation for this obvious opportunity for self promotion prior to the climb.' Anderson added the proviso: 'However, only time will tell if he continues to carry this humble attitude on with what must be incredible pressure for post-climb publicity.' When Tomaž was asked if he was trying to make a statement with this climb – that he 'was back' – he simply replied, 'I'm always here. I haven't gone anywhere.'

After a brief trip to Egypt for some warmth and a quick climb of Mt Sinai by night, Tomaž finally returned home: to rest, to fully recover from frostbite on three fingers and to reflect. 'I've learned that it isn't important how many times you fall but that you always stand up, continue and look forward into the future. Every climb is a story in itself. You come back changed from each one. Your consciousness grows; this is the most important thing. And if you enjoy each journey, then there is nothing more to say.'

TOMAŽ HUMAR

After a while you learn the difference between holding hands and clasping the soul. You learn that love does not mean opening up and that company does not mean safety. You begin to realize that kisses are not contracts and gifts not promises. You begin to admit your defeats with your head held high and your eyes wide open, standing tall like a man, not with dejection like a child. You learn to build all your roads for today, because the ground of tomorrow is too uncertain for planning. After a while you find out that even the sun will burn you if you expose yourself to it for too long.

So plant your garden for yourself and adorn your soul, instead of waiting for someone else to bring you flowers. And find out that you really can make it through . . . that you are really strong and really worthy.

A challenge is part of you, part of your story. Don't be scared of challenges, they have chosen you. The more precarious and mysterious the challenge, the worthier it is. What about doubts? If we allow ourselves to doubt, we erase our future and become prisoners of the past. And afterwards, when memories fade, we end up trapped in a vacuum where we cannot help ourselves. The only thing that can save us is purpose. If we are able to recognize this, it is our duty to embrace it – and once again we have joined the circle of creation.

You are only worth as much as you believe you are. Feeling superior is to no-one's benefit, since you cannot be above yourself, you can only grow and fight your own weaknesses. Self-proclaimed purists comment from their pulpits on others in order to hide their own mistakes. As the saying has it, 'When talking of others, you are describing yourself.' Those who have nothing to say about themselves, talk about others. The more energy you waste on changing everybody else, the less there is for you. A compassionate thought: change yourself and you will change the world.

Talents are a gift to life. Talents are priceless; they can't be bought, they can't be upgraded, they can't be lent and they can't be lost… talents are a value, given with purpose and worthy of respect. Whoever rejects his talents, in the end loses himself. The more you accept them, and appreciate and learn to live with them, the closer you are to the purpose of your existence. We have come to this world with a purpose; when we are able to recognize ourselves by clearing our mind, we recognize our purpose in life.

I think a lot. This is something a person should be prepared for: thinking should not be taken for granted, and thoughts are our special creation. I feel the highest possible responsibility towards them. My times of 'absence' – most people understand this as meditation – are the only ones when I am able to comprehend the wonderful fullness of life. Just as the loudest noise is silence and in silence lies the answer to all questions, so the greatest things are born spontaneously. Knowing this is essential to our freedom. But we are only really free when we don't care and when we are not attached to anything. It is similar with truth; we don't have to look for it, even less fight it… the truth just is. It is, or it is not. All we have to do is accept it… Simple as that!

The hardest and most important things in life are easy – or, to put it another way, the best things in life are forbidden and free to us at the same time. I discover how much I love life through every trial it sets in my way; and I live it, once I am not afraid to die in the course of it. Both options are inseparably linked in an eternal circle. Therefore I do not search for the truth of life in earthly rewards, which merely gather dust. My life's dream is an eternal struggle for inner peace and happiness, imbued with love, the creator of the world.

NOTES

Chapter One: Rupal Face

1 *Delo*, 6 August 2005, 'Modern Gladiator on his Way'.
2 Steve House, 'Pure Alpinism on the Rupal Face', *The Alpine Journal*, 2006, p. 77.
3 Ibid.

Chapter Two: Base Camp

1 Alexander Odintsov, 'The Walls, The Walls', *Alpinist* 19, p. 76.
2 Located between the Savinja and Sava rivers, the range is part of Slovenia's Southern Limestone Alps, the northern extension of which stretches to the Austrian border. The densely forested range boasts 28 peaks higher than 2,000 metres and many of these are steep limestone walls, the perfect training ground for an aspiring alpinist.

Chapter Three: Kosovo

1 Alan Little and Laura Silber, *Yugoslavia: Death of a Nation*, Penguin Books, New York, 1997, p. 29.

Chapter Five: Ganesh V

1 Tomaž Humar, *No Impossible Ways*, Mobitel d.d., Ljubljana, 2001.

Chapter Seven: Ama Dablam

1 Vanja Furlan, 'The Northwest Face of Ama Dablam', *American Alpine Journal*, 1997, p. 18.
2 Ibid., p. 16.
3 Christian Beckwith, *American Alpine Journal*, 1997, p. 13.

Chapter Nine: Nuptse

1 Tomaž Humar, *No Impossible Ways*, Mobitel d.d., Ljubljana, 2001.

Chapter Eleven: Dhaulagiri

1 Tomaž Humar, *No Impossible Ways*, Mobitel d.d., Ljubljana, 2001.

Chapter Thirteen: After the Fall

1 Their 2,500-metre route took them a total of five days and presented difficulties up to M6, and steepness of up to 90 degrees, and slightly more, on the ice sections.

2 Alexander Odintsov, 'The Walls, The Walls', *Alpinist* 19, p. 80.

Chapter Fourteen: Rescue

1 Dan Duane, 'Tomaž Humar: Incredible Rescue, Angry Backlash on Pakistan's Nanga Parbat', *National Geographic Adventure Magazine*, November 2005.

Chapter Fifteen: Cinderella Rises

1 Ian Parnell, 'Victors of the Unwinnable', *Alpinist* 16, p. 60.

SOURCES

Huber, Alexander, and Zak, Heinz, *Yosemite: Half a Century of Dynamic Rock Climbing*, Bâton Wicks, London, 2003

Piana, Paul, *Big Walls: Breakthroughs on the Free-Climbing Frontier*, Sierra Club Books, San Francisco, 1997

Škarja, Tone, *Slovenci v Himalaji*, Planinska zveza Sloveniji, Ljubljana, 2004

Websites

HimalayaNet, Newsletter 76
http://forums.climbing.com/forum/

Magazines

Alpinist 16, 'Victors of the Unwinnable', Ian Parnell
Alpinist 7, 'Aconcagua, Mobitel Swallow – Johan's Route, New Route',
    Aleš Koželj
American Alpine Journal, 1997
National Geographic Adventure Magazine, October/November 2005

Newspapers

The Observer, 'Home on the Range', Sunday 3 October 2004

ACKNOWLEDGEMENTS

It was while climbing in Paklenica a few years ago that I first began encouraging Tomaž Humar to write his story. Listening to him recount his experiences was fascinating, and I was sure others would feel the same. Despite repeated urgings, he wasn't interested. More likely, he didn't have the time, for his priority was climbing – not writing. Finally, he threw it back to me, challenging me to write it and promising full cooperation. And so began this adventure.

The British writer and climber Andy Cave suggested that I speak to Tony Whittome at Random House, for it was Tony who had edited Andy's award-winning book, *Learning to Breathe*. I followed up on his suggestion. Thank you, Andy. And thank you, Tony, for your enthusiastic reception.

What followed was a lot of time spent commuting back and forth between my home in Banff and Slovenia, as well as hundreds of hours attempting to keep up with Tomaž and other Slovenian alpinists, all of whom move faster than me. But what fun it was, racing around the Slovenian Alps with tape recorder in hand, trying to keep the interviews focused and my hyperventilation under control.

I owe a great deal of thanks to those who spent time with me, answering dozens of questions and explaining things as I struggled to understand the labyrinthine, high-powered, over-achieving Slovenian climbing community. Thank you to Viki Grošelj for his detailed accounting of events. Dr Anda Perdan went to a great deal of trouble, not only recalling the details of Tomaž's recovery but giving me a complete medical history in writing. Stipe Božić was similarly helpful, and I thank him for that effort. Tone Škarja and Bojan Pollak helped enormously in educating me on the history and politics of the Slovenian Mountaineering Association, a part of this story that I had not anticipated would be so interesting and complex. Slovenian climbers Silvo Karo,

Marko Prezelj, Maria Štremfelj and Aleš Koželj were all generous with their time and their insights.

And back in North America I was fortunate to speak with many others who knew Tomaž or knew of him, and whose opinions I valued: Valery Babanov, Mark Twight, Vince Anderson, Steve House, Barry Blanchard, Christian Beckwith, Dougald MacDonald and John Harlin.

There were many long-distance phone calls and extended email conversations with climbers around the world. I sincerely thank those who were so forthcoming: Simone Moro, Carlos Carsolio, Alex Huber, Christian Trommsdorff, Nazir Sabir, Reinhold Messner, Lindsay Griffin and Ed Douglas. A special thank you is due to Reinhold Messner for his generous offer to write the Foreword.

Elizabeth Hawley and Richard Salisbury were extremely helpful with both facts and opinions.

I was privileged to learn from Gerold Biner about the complexities of helicopter rescue, and my ongoing correspondence with Rashid Ullah Baig remains a gift from the process of writing this book.

There was one evening in May of 2007 when Chris Bonington dined with Tomaž and me in Trento, Italy that will remain a turning point in the project. His advice made all the difference and calmed our rattled nerves. Thank you, Chris.

I am grateful to those who reviewed the sections of the manuscript that pertained to their own areas of expertise: Jeff Boyd on the medical aspects and Ann Krcik and Francesca McCartney on the alternative medical material. Thanks as well to Marc Ledwidge for examining the helicopter chapters with such precision.

Working with my editor, Tony Whittome, has been a joy. His experience, tact, gentle prodding and genuine encouragement have provided the fuel to keep me going. I am equally grateful to his team at Random House, especially James Nightingale. As well, I was expertly guided by Leslie Miller, who read and helped structure an early version of the manuscript. Thanks to Janez Aleš for his extremely informed and accurate translations.

As in the past, I received a lot of support from my community of friends, family and fellow writers. Maria Coffey, Tom Hornbein, Charlie Houston, Christian Beckwith, Bill Buxton, my former Banff Mountain Culture team, writers at the 2007 Banff Mountain Writing Program, Marni Jackson, and Julie Summers were always interested and supportive. And of course from my husband, Alan, who read early drafts, listened endlessly as I recounted the adventure of writing this book, and without whose support I could not have done it.

Those individuals closest to Tomaž were amazingly open to my enquiries. Rosalija and Max Humar welcomed me warmly; Sergeja was thoughtful in her responses; Tomi seemed to enjoy the intrusions and Urša tolerated me with patience and amusement. I'm not sure how I can adequately thank Maja, who shared her thoughts, her emotions and her substantial written materials on the Nanga Parbat expedition, and who provided such an important perspective to the book.

And then there was Tomaž. I still can't believe that he remained still long enough to give me what I needed for this book: not only his stories, but access to his photographs, video material and personal mementos and his own written record in his book, *No Impossible Ways*. He has been unstinting in his support, but this is a biography, not an autobiography, and I take full responsibility for any mistakes.

I won't forget the first time that Tomaž, Tony Whittome and I met in the rather formal dining room at the Tate Gallery in London. Surrounded by lunching professionals, Tomaž came close to decapitating a dozen waiters as he enthusiastically regaled us with his stories. Or the time that I returned to my room after a day of chasing Tomaž around the mountains, intent now on listening to and transcribing the several hours of tape I had recorded. Imagine my horror when the only audible sound was my own rasping breath as I tried to keep up to his blistering pace. Throughout the two years of writing, Tomaž may have worn me out in the mountains, but he also opened his heart and soul and shared his dreams and his disappointments. I only hope that his passion for life is adequately represented in this volume.

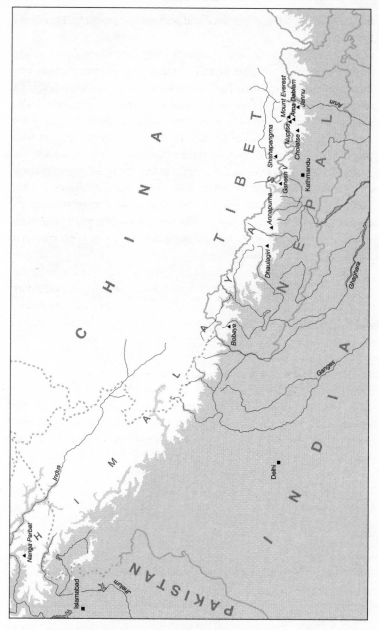

The Himalayas

Ama Dablam, showing Humar's and Furlan's new route up its
North-West Face, climbed in 1996.

Nuptse, showing the new route climbed by Humar and
Jeglič in 1997.

Bobaye, showing Humar's route, which he climbed solo in 1996.
Solid line is ascent and dotted line is descent.

Dhaulagiri, South Face, showing four routes: from left to right, Messner attempt, the Polish route, Humar solo climb, Slovenian route.

Annapurna, South Face, showing Polish route on left and Humar's route, climbed solo in 2007, on right.

INDEX